HELLENISM IN ANCIENT INDIA

HELLENISM
IN
ANCIENT INDIA

BY

GAURANGA NATH BANERJEE,
M.A., Ph.D., F.R.S.A.

SECOND EDITION,
THOROUGHLY REVISED AND ENLARGED

GYAN

Published by

GYAN

Gyan Publishing House
5, Ansari Road
Daryaganj, New Delhi-110002
Phone: 011-47034999, 9811692060
E-mail: books@gyanbooks.com

Distribution Network
gyanbooks.com
India, USA, Canada, UK, Australia, France

ISBN : 978-81-212-29852 (PB)
First Published, 1920

2nd Impression 2021

Printed at: Gyan Press, Delhi.

Hellenism in Ancient India
Author: Gauranga Nath Banerjee

HELLENISM

IN

ANCIENT INDIA.

BY

GAURANGA NATH BANERJEE, M.A., PH.D., F.R.S.A.

LECTURER ON EGYPTOLOGY AND ORIENTAL HISTORY AND SECRETARY TO THE COUNCIL OF POST-GRADUATE TEACHING IN ARTS, THE UNIVERSITY OF CALCUTTA ; PREMCHAND ROYCHAND SCHOLAR ; MEMBER OF THE CENTRAL ASIAN SOCIETY, LONDON.

SECOND EDITION,
THOROUGHLY REVISED AND ENLARGED.

BUTTERWORTH & Co. (INDIA), LTD., 6, HASTINGS ST.
CALCUTTA :

WINNIPEG :	SYDNEY :
BUTTERWORTH & Co. (Canada), Ltd.	BUTTERWORTH & Co. (Australia), Ltd.

LONDON :
BUTTERWORTH & Co., BELL YARD, TEMPLE BAR.

Legal Publishers.

1920

BODHISATTWA STATUES FROM GANDHARA.

(Indian Museum, Calcutta.)

यत्पादाम्बुजरेणुरीश्वरपदादप्यर्चणीयो हि मे
प्राप्तं यस्य कृपाकणेन जगतां जीवेषु मानुष्यकम् ।
तस्यैवाङ्घ्रियुगे चिरं प्रणयिना भक्त्या नवोपायनं
चित्तोद्यानभवं प्रयत्ननिचितं पुष्पं मया दीयते ॥

CONTENTS

BOOK I.

BOOK II.

THE HELLENISTIC INFLUENCE ON THE ART OF INDIA.

CHAPTER I.

ARCHITECTURE.

CHAPTER II.

SCULPTURE.

CHAPTER III.

PAINTING.

CHAPTER IV.

COINAGE.

BOOK III.

THE EVOLUTION OF SCIENTIFIC AND LITERARY CULTURE IN INDIA AND HELLENISM.

CONTENTS

CHAPTER V.

ASTRONOMY.

CHAPTER VI.

MATHEMATICS.

CHAPTER VII.

MEDICINE.

CHAPTER VIII.

ART OF WRITING.

CHAPTER IX.

LITERATURE.

CHAPTER X.

DRAMA.

BOOK IV.

INDEPENDENT EVOLUTION OF RELIGION, PHILOSOPHY, MYTHOLOGY AND FABLES IN INDIA AND IN GREECE.

CHAPTER XI.

RELIGION.

CONTENTS

CHAPTER XII.

PHILOSOPHY.

CHAPTER XIII.

MYTHOLOGY.

CHAPTER XIV.

FABLES AND FOLKLORE.

BOOK ONE

INTRODUCTION

On the dismemberment of the conquests of Alexander the Great, Græco-Bactrian and Indo-Grecian kingdoms were called into existence, by which the plastic and the intelligent genius of the Greeks had been united to that of the imaginative and pious, or according to the view of others, superstitious Orientals and by the amalgamation of the West with the East, produced a new formation of historical relations, viz. Hellenism. Hellenism was first restrained from spreading to the East, and India proved here triumphant against the Greeks and for a longer period Greek influence continued to prevail in the Empire of Arsacids, the friends of the Greeks, who did not wage war against Greek civilisation. Ultimately, Hellenism revived in a narrower sphere, in the domain of arts and sciences and continued its activity with greater success.—Christian Lassen, "Beitrag zur Geschichte der griechischen und indoskythischen Könige in Baktrien, Kabul und Indien."

HELLENISM IN ANCIENT INDIA.

INTRODUCTION

I

LESS remote than China, bathed by an ocean which bore the fleets of Egypt, Chaldæa, Persia, Greece and Rome, India was never beyond the reach of the Western Nations. The Assyrians, the Persians, and the Greeks carried their arms into the basin of the Indus, some portions of which were annexed for a time to those Empires which had their centre in the valley of the Euphrates and stretched westwards as far as the Mediterranean. There was a continuous coming and going of the caravans across the plateau of Iran and the deserts which lie between it and the oases of Bactriana, Aria and Arachosia and through the passes which lead down to what is now called the Punjab ; between the ports of the Arabian and Persian Gulfs and those of the Lower Indus and the Malabar Coast, continual commercial movement went on, which though fluctuating with time, was never entirely interrupted. "Nous savons," writes M. Gustave le Bon, in his celebrated work "Les Monuments de l'Inde", "que des une antiquité fort reculée, l'Inde communiquait directement avec les empires de l'ancien Orient, la Chaldée, la Babylonìe, et l'Assyrie. Les relations se faisaient à la fois par mer et par terre. Par mer des communications règuliéres ètaient établies entre ports de l'Inde et ceux de Golfe Persique. Par terre, plusieurs routes reliaient les grands centres de l'Orient avec le nord-ouest de l'Inde. Plusieurs provinces de l'Inde furent soumises à l'empire des Perses dont elle formirent une satrapie." From the Malabar Coast, Western Asia drew her supplies of aromatic spices, of metals, of precious woods, of jewels and other treasures—all of which came mainly by the sea-route (vide "Periplus of the Erythrean Sea").

All this, however, was but the supply of raw-materials for the Egyptian, Assyrian and Phœnician industries. There is no tangible evidence that up to the very last days of antique civilisation, the inhabitants of Hindusthan with all their depth and originality of thought ever exercised such influence upon their neighbours as could have made itself felt as far as Greece. The grand lyric poetry of the Vedas, the Epics and Dramas of the following epoch, the religious and philosophical speculations, those learned grammatical analyses of Panini and Patañjali (which have evoked such unstinted praise from the eminent philologists as Bopp, Klaproth, Goldstücker and Kielhorn), all the rich and brilliant intellectual development of a race akin to the Greeks, and in many ways no less richly endowed, remained shut up in that basin of the Ganges into which no stranger penetrated until the time of the Muhammedan Conquest. Neither did the Assyrians, Arabs nor Phœnicians reach the true centres of Hindu civilisation. They merely touched the fringe of Indian culture by frequenting those sea-board towns, where the mixed population was more occupied with commerce than with intellectual pursuits. The conquerors, previous to Alexander the Great, did no more than reach the gates of India and reconnoitre its approaches, while Alexander himself failed to penetrate beyond its vestibule.

When the weary veterans of the Great Emathian conqueror laden with plunder and sated with conquest refused to cross the Hyphasis and to try the fortunes of war in the valley of the Ganges, the exclusive, conservative East, won a victory over the intruding, progressive West, which to the actors on the scene must have appeared final and decisive. But it was neither final, nor decisive. For though the obstacles thrown by hostile man and nature could stop the onward march of the Macedonian phalanx, nothing could arrest the sure and world-wide progress of ideas and culture, which constituted the real strength of Hellas and were but rudely expressed by the disciplined array of Alexander's armies.

India has not willingly sought the treasures of foreign wisdom and guarded by encircling seas and the loftiest mountain-ranges in the world, she had tried throughout the long course of ages, to work out her own salvation. Again and again, both before and after Alexander, the barriers have been broken through and her children, who would fain believe that all light comes from the East, have been compelled to admit the rays of the Western Sun.

"In the twilight of pre-historic times," asserts Dr. Hommel, "we discern faint indications that India in common with all regions of Asiatic and European civilisation drew supplies from those stores of Egyptian, Babylonian and Assyrian antique-lore, which were so far as we know, the ultimate sources of the knowledge which distinguished civilised man from savage." (vide Fritz Hommel, "Grundriss der Geographie und Geschichte des Alten Indiens"). But it is only fair to say that the history of those long past times is lost, and save perhaps in some faintly sketched and dubious outlines, cannot be recovered. The Indian expedition of Alexander the Great was the first occasion of the close, conscious contact between the East and the West. The arms of the conqueror, it is true, subdued no more than a mere corner of India and that only for a time, but that Hellenic culture to the diffusion of which Alexander devoted attention as great as that bestowed by him on his material conquests, long survived his transitory empire in Asia and even, in India, made its presence felt in many and different directions.

The invasion of India by Alexander is placed at 327-6 B. C. After having achieved the conquest of Persia, the Macedonian hero decided to undertake the conquest of India, so that he might attain to the sovereignty of Asia. To look from the standpoint of a world-conquest, the effects of the invasion of Alexander bore perfectly nothing, inasmuch as a few years after his departure, there was not left a single Greek garrison in India. But that expedition which brought India for the first time in contact with Europe, had produced consequences of the utmost importance. In the following pages, we have not attempted to lift the veil which enshrouded the relation between India and the Western world in the ages before Alexander, but have considered the kind of post-Alexandrian influence on the civilisation of ancient India.

We know that Northern India at the time of the expansion of Greater Greece, that is to say, when Alexander entered the vestibule of the gates of India, had attained to a high degree of civilisation, which must have been the product of evolution continued through many centuries. Unfortunately no monuments have yet been discovered which can be referred to the period anterior to Chandragupta with absolute certainty and the archæologists are unable to bring forward tangible evidence afforded by excavations, to support the statement of the Greek observers. The earliest known example of Indian art and architecture, with one or two exceptions, still date from the reign of Asoka the Great. But if the explorations of the sites of Nalanda, Vaisali, Taxila and other cities of high antiquity are undertaken seriously and on an adequate scale, it is possible that the remains of the early Maurya period, as well as those of previous ages, may be recovered, and which may throw new light on the plastic arts of ancient India. But it should be borne in mind that the larger edifices of ancient India, like those of modern Burma, were constructed of timber for the most part, brick or stone being used mostly for foundations and plinths (vide Dr. Spooner's statement in *re.* Excavations at Pataliputra). No Indian specimen in stone either of architecture or sculpture earlier than the 4th century B. C. has yet been discovered and the well-known theory of Dr. Fergusson, that the sudden introduction of the use of stone, instead of wood, for the purposes of architecture and sculpture was the result of communication between the empires of Alexander and the Seleucids and that of the Maurya Dynasty, is to some extent infallible.

With the descent of Alexander the Great upon the Punjab a new period indeed had commenced, for India entered into far more intimate relations with the foreign countries than had hitherto been the case. Not the least important part of Western India was for more than 250 years under the government of the Greek kings and when Grecian influence was broken off on this side, in no less a significant manner did it strike upon a new path, namely that of the sea-borne commerce from Alexandria, by which it continued in full swing till A. D. 400. The Hellenic influence, working by this means, has been much more important than for a long time it has been believed. Not only a few motifs of Hindu architecture and sculpture, coining and such like arts, adhered closely at their commencement to the Grecian models, but Astronomy too—at least its scientific phase—was based somewhat on Grecian works, by which a great number of Greek expressions have found their way into Indian Astronomy. For, Indian art was just blossoming at the time of Alexander, while the artists of Greece were in full possession of all their powers; they had produced inimitable masterpieces in each of the great divisions of art, and yet their creative force was far from being exhausted. It was the age of Lysippus and Apelles, of those great architects, who in the temples of Asia Minor, renewed the youth of the Ionic Order by their bold and ingenious innovations. Under such conditions, what would the effect have been, had those two forms of civilisation entered into close contact with each other?

In all probability the result would have been similar to that which ensued, when the ancestors of the Greeks began to deal with the more civilised Phœnicians and the peoples of Asia Minor. But in the case of the Hindus, the disciples had a less instead of a greater aptitude for imitating the plastic arts than their teachers, the Greeks (it is asserted that Parthenon itself was built after the plan of the Hypostyle Halls at Luxor!) and moreover the contact between the two was never complete nor was it of long duration. The only frontier where the interchange of ideas was frequent and continuous was the north-west, which divided India from that Bactrian kingdom of which we know not a little more than the mere names of its princes and the date of its fall. Before the end of the first century B.C. this outpost of Hellenism had even fallen before the attacks of those semi-barbarous hordes, known as the Sakas or the Scythians. In such an isolated position, it could not long hope to maintain itself, especially after the rise of the Parthian monarchy. Its existence must always have been precarious, but the mere fact that it did not succumb until the first century B. C., is enough to prove that several of its sovereigns must have been remarkable men.

Through the obscurity in which the details are enveloped, we can yet perceive that those princes were men of taste. They were, as was natural, attached to literature and the arts, which reminded them of that distant fatherland with which year after year it became more difficult to communicate. Although they were obliged in order to defend themselves against their many enemies, to employ those mercenary soldiers, Athenians, Thebans, Spartans and Cretans, who then overran Asia and to pay them dearly for the services, yet they called skilful artists to their court and kept them there at great expense; the beautiful coins—which have preserved their images down to our day, are evidence of this fact—the decoration of their cities, of their temples and of their palaces must have been in keeping with them; everywhere, there were no doubt Corinthian and Ionic buildings, statues of the Greek gods and goddesses and heroes and heroines, mixed up with those portraits and historic groups which had been multiplied by the scholars of Lysippus and Apelles, wall-paintings and perhaps some of their easel pictures signed by famous masters, for which the heirs of Alexander were such keen competitors. Artisans, who had followed the Greek armies in their march towards the East, with the object of supplying the wants of any colonies which might be established in those distant regions, reproduced upon their vases and their terra-cotta figures with motives of the painting, the sculpture and the architecture which they left behind, and goldsmiths, jewellers and armourers, cut, chased and stamped them in metal. And it was not the Greek colonists alone who employed their skill. Like the Scythian tribes among whom the Greek cities of the Euxine were planted, the nations to the north of India were astonished and delighted by the elegance of their ornament and the variety of its forms. They imported from Bactriana those products of an art which were wanting among them, and soon set themselves, with the help perhaps of the foreign artists settled amongst them, to imitate Grecian design in the courts of the Indian kings and potentates.

That such was the fact, is proved by those coins which bear on their reverse such Hindu symbols as Siva with his bull and on their obverse Greek inscriptions ; and by the remains of what is now called Græco-Buddhist art,—an art which seems to have flourished most in the upper valley of the Indus in the 3rd. and 2nd. centuries B. C. [These remains were studied and described originally by Sir Alexander Cunningham (vide Archæological Survey of India, 3vols. 1871-3) ; Drs. Curtius and Grünwedel have described and published reproductions of the most curious among them (vide Archæologische Zeitung) ; Dr. Grünwedel's "Buddhistische Kunst in Indien" and Dr. Curtius' "Die Griechische Kunst in Indien" are authoritative treatises on the subject ; while M. Foucher has treated them in a masterly way in his celebrated works, "L'Art Gréco-Bouddhique du Gandhara" and "The Beginnings of Buddhist Art"]. They are mostly found in the north of the Punjab upon a few ancient sites, where excavations have recently been made by Sir Marc Aurel Stein, Mons. A. Foucher and others. Some of them have been transported to Europe in the collection of Dr. Leitner, while others remain in the Museums of Peshawar, Lahore and Calcutta. (The Louvre has only lately acquired some curious examples of this art). In those sacred buildings, which have been examined, the plan of the Greek temple has not been adopted *in toto*, but the isolated members of the Greek architecture and the most characteristic details of its ornament are everywhere made use of. It is the same with sculpture, in the selection of types, in the arrangement of drapery, in the artistic design there is the same mixture of Greek taste with that of India, of elements borrowed from the foreign with those drawn from the national beliefs : helmeted Athené and Helios in his quadriga figure, by the side of Buddha.

Traces of the same influence are to be found in a less marked degree in some other parts of India. Near the mouth of the Indus and the Malabar Coast, the native sculptors and architects were able to obtain more than one useful suggestion, more than one precious hint as to their technique from the works of art brought in the ships of the maritime traders. It is even possible that Greek workmen may thus have been introduced in seaport towns and there employed in the decoration of palaces and temples. However this may be, it is incontestable that all the important sacred edifices of the Gandhara region, whether stone-built or carved in the living rock, date from a period more recent than that of Alexander and that most of them show details which imply acquaintance with Greek architectural forms and their Asiatic imitations. The fact is, the Greeks excelled all other nations of antiquity in the width and depth of their æsthetic sentiments ; their architects, their sculptors, and their painters were superior both to their masters and their pupils, to the Egyptians, Assyrians and Babylonians on the one hand, and to the Etruscans and Latins on the other. We need feel no surprise, therefore, at their central dominating position in the history of antique art. We are thus inevitably forced to this conclusion, that in the domain of plastic arts, Greece owed nothing to India with which she made acquaintance very late and that Indian arts on the contrary were only partially developed at the time of the early relations with Greece and it would seem that her first great stimulus was derived from the models which Greece put within her reach.

II.

Now about the term Hellenism. The word Hellenism is derived from Greek *Hellenizein i. e.* to imitate the Greeks, who were known as *Hellenes*, the sons of Ducalion. But the

2

term is ambiguous. It may be used to denote ancient Greek culture in all its phases, and even those elements in modern civilisation which are Greek in origin or in spirit; Matthew Arnold made the term popular in the latter connexion, as an antethesis of "Hebraism." The word Hellenism is again used by the immortal Grote, for the high culture of Athens and as substantive corresponding to the adjective "Hellenic." On the other hand, in the great work of Droysen (perhaps the greatest historian of the modern times), the "History of Hellenism," the term excludes the purest Greek culture and corresponds to the adjective "Hellenistic." The German historian introduced the fashion in 1826 of using it to describe particularly the later phases of Greek culture, from the conquests of Alexander to the end of the ancient world, when those over whom the culture extended were not largely Greek in blood *i.e.* Hellenes, but perhaps the peoples who had accepted Greek speech and ways of life, Hellenistai. Dr. Mahaffy in his "Progress of Hellenism in Alexander's Empire," meant by the word "Hellenism," the "silver age" of Greek art and literature, when they became cosmopolitan and not parochial; and by Hellenistic, not only what was Greek, but what was assumed to be Greek and derived therefrom, the highest and noblest imitation down to the poorest travesty. Greek culture had however both in Hellenic and Hellenistic times, a common essence, just as light is light, whether in an original luminous body or in a reflection, and to describe this, the term Hellenism seems most natural. It is customary to date the origin of Hellenism from the reign of Alexander whose arms carried it into the Far East. Had Alexander been killed in the first mêlèe at Granikos, when the Persian nobles fought so valiantly with him, the whole history of Hellenism would have been different (vide Lamartine, "Vie d' Alexander").

"But the story of Alexander," says Ida Wheeler in "Alexander the Great," "has become a story of his death. He died himself before his time. With his life, he brought the old Greece to its end, with his death, the state he had founded. But they all three, Alexander, Greece, the Grand Empire, each after its sort set forth, as history judges men and things, the inner value of the saying, 'Except a grain of wheat fall into the earth and die ; it abideth alone.' "

In the centuries following Alexander, the urban life based on the Greek culture gradually sought its centres outside the old limits of Greece, in the domain of a greater world. Alexandria, Rhodes, Pergamon, Antioch, Byzantium instead of Athens, became its representatives. The forms of Greek culture, which was transmitted direct to the after-world through Rome, were those who lived there—in greater Greece. Until modern scholarship tunnelled a route back to the old Greece, it was the taste and intellectual interests of Alexandria, rather than those of Athens that passed current as Greek. In the new Greece, the culture of the old assumed a world-form and prepared itself for universal extension. The dialects of cantons shrank back before a universal type of standard Greek, the *lingua franca* of Greater Greece. Local citizenship slowly yielded to a citizenship of the world and cosmopolitanism was thus born. The worship of the old city-gods based on community of blood gave place to a yearning for something that symbolised the higher unity of human life. The old cities had passed over into the life of a greater whole, but this was as yet without a body and except for the vision and type of a deified Alexander, without expression or symbol. It remained for Rome to satisfy the instincts of the times. Its deified Emperors replaced the Alexander type and with the acceptance of Christianity a Holy Roman Empire, joined of body and soul, arose to claim the larger allegiance of men—

prototype of which had been the old allegiance to the Greek cities, now melted and dissolved into the fluid of the state.

In the Hellenistic age, the Greek art followed the conquests of Alexander to new centres in the East; it is no longer to Athens or Argos or Sicyon, but to Alexandria and Antioch and Pergamon that we look for its most characteristic products. The beginning of the Hellenistic age is dominated by the personality of Alexander. He had changed the relations of the East and West and Greek civilisation was henceforth the prevalent influence in Western Asia. His career which might well seem, more than human, induced the Greeks to accept the oriental custom of deification of kings, and his features came to be repeated even in the types of the Gods. His head too was placed upon coins, an honour hitherto reserved for the Gods alone; although his successors with a less justifiable arrogance claimed even higher privileges.

Now, in India including the valleys of the Kabul and its northern tributaries, then inhabited by an Indian, and not as now by an Iranian population, Alexander planted a number of Greek towns. The most important of these, Alexander "under the Caucasus" commanded the road from Bactria over the Hindukush; it lay somewhere among the hills in the north of Kabul, perhaps at Opian, near Charikar (see McCrindle, "Ancient India" p. 87; Cunningham, "Ancient Geography of India" *loc. cit.*): but that it is the city meant "by Alasada, the capital of the Yona (Greek) country," in the Buddhist Mahawansô, as is generally affirmed, seems doubtful. But soon after 324 B.C., Macedonian supremacy beyond the Indus collapsed before the advance of the Maurya Dynasty. Moreover large districts, west of the Indus, were ceded by Seleucus Nicator. The chapter of Greek rule was however not closed thereby. The Maurya Empire broke up about 180 B.C. and at the same time the Greek rulers of Bactria began to lead expeditions across the Hindukush. The Scythian people from Central Asia, the Sakas and Yue-chis, having conquered Bactria, gradually squeezed within ever narrowing limits the Greek power in India. The last Greek King Hermœus seems to have succumbed about 30 B.C. It was about this time that the Græco-Roman power of the West was consolidated as the Roman Empire and although the Greek rule in India had disappeared, active commercial intercourse went on between India and the Hellenistic lands.

The Greek influence then seems to have reached further eastwards. The Bactrian province of Ferghana (in Chinese, Ta Yüan) was occupied by the Chinese general Li Kuang Li in Chinese 101 B.C. We find here the bridge connecting the Greek and civilisations over which came the movement which revolutionised Chinese Art under the Emperor Wu Ti (140-87 B.C.). It had long been clear that the Chinese at this time and from this district imported the noble Turcoman blood-horses and the vine, it is also more than mere conjecture that Chinese Art, which had stood still since the second millennium B.C., owed its sudden renaissance to the Gréco-Bactrian influence and the naturalism of Greek Art. The excavations of Sir M. A. Stein in Chinese Turkestan, specially in Khotan, have brought to light fresh evidence of the expansion of Greek culture, as well as a further station on the road, by which the peoples of the West migrated towards Eastern Asia. A Pallas Athené, represented on a seal in archaic style, a seal with a sitting Greek figure, probably Eros, and above all, a seal with a portrait-head after a classical model, but with thoroughly Chinese features show that here, half-way between West Iran and Pekin, Greek culture had established a firm footing. The types of the coins from Transoxania or Western Turkestan originated in the Greek centres of civilisation in Bactria, so that the silver tetradrachms found in

Samarkand and Tashkent must have been struck after the pattern of coins of Heliocles and Euthydemus and similarly the path of Greek influences must have led thence through Ferghana, past the Greek city of Alexandria Eschate and Kashgar and Yarkand to Khotan. And while thus in the remotest east of the countries, which were included in the habitable world, on the fringe of the East Asiatic world, the Greek spirit, wantonly prodigal of its forces, was tearing itself to pieces, but nevertheless was able to influence Coinage, Arts, and Sciences as far as India and East Asia.

III

But what precise influence did Hellenism during the centuries in which it was in contact with India exert upon the native mind? Only qualified answers can be given to the question. Capital data are possibly waiting there underground—the Kabul valley, for instance, is almost a virgin soil for archæologists and any conclusion we can arrive at is more or less defective. If certain statements of classical authors were true, Hellenism in India flourished exceedingly. But the phil-Hellenic Brahmans in Philostratus' "Life of Apollonius" had no existence outside the domain of fiction, and the statement of Dio Chrysostom that the Indians were familiar with Homer in their own tongue (Or. liii, 6), is a traveller's yarn. Similar statements of no greater value are also found in Plutarch and Ælian. Plutarch says that through Alexander Asia was civilised and Homer was known there : while Ælian asserts that the Indians and the Persians have translated the poems of Homer.

The vexed question of Greek influence on India has received a good deal of attention in recent years. The extravagant views of Weber, Windisch and Niese have provoked not an unnatural reaction. The paradox of Niese to the effect that the whole subsequent development of India was dependent upon Alexander's institutions is only true in a qualified sense. His words are : "Man kann daher mit Recht behaupten, dass von den Einrichtungen Alexanders die ganze weitere Entwickelung Indiens abhangig gewesen ist" (vide Geschichte der griechischen und makedonischen staaten seit der Schlacht lui Chæronea I Teil, p. 508, Gotha, 1893). Undoubtedly the general tendency of the European scholars has been to exaggerate the Hellenistic effects of Alexander's invasion and of the Indo-Greek rule on the north-western frontier. The most extreme "Hellenist" view is that quoted above of Herr Niese. Such notions are plainly opposed to the evidence that might be supposed to need no refutation ; but they have been accepted to a certain extent by Indianists of repute, who are inclined naturally to believe that India, like Europe and a large part of Asia, must have yielded to the subtle action of Hellenic ideas.

Of late years, on the contrary, it has been the fashion to minimise the influence of Greek art on India. Messrs. Havell and Coomarswamy have vindicated the independence of Indian artistic tradition. It has been attempted to trace the origin of the Gandhara sculptures to the Indo-Scythian source rather to Bactria. Mr. Vincent A. Smith even goes so far as to say that "Niese's astounding paradox is not supported by a single fact." From the purely Indian point of view Mr. Havell in his "Indian Sculpture and Painting," and Dr. A. K. Coomarswamy in his "Mediaeval Singhalese Art" repudiate with vigour the suggestion that Indian Art owes anything to the West. They contend that the occupation of India by the Greeks, who followed Eukratides and Menander, was purely a military and commercial matter ; and the invaders were swept away, just as the relics of the invasion of Alexander had been swept away, without leaving any permanent trace behind them. India, these sceptics observe, has yielded no Greek inscription except "the coarse coins of the Greek Kings and their Scythian rivals and successors." They base their arguments on the strength of the fact that "no inscriptions in Greek have yet been discovered and the single Greek name Theodore met with in a native record comes from the Swat Valley and is of late date perhaps 56 A.D." (vide Journal of the Indian Art, Jan. 1900, p. 89 ; Journal of the Royal Asiatic Society, 1903, p. 14). They say, "To what extent can it be inferred from legends on coins that Greek was a living speech in India? Perhaps to no large extent outside the Greek courts." The fact however, that the Greek character was still used on coins for two centuries after the last Greek dynasty had come to an end, itself shows that the language had a prestige in India, which any theory to be plausible, must account for. The latter class of writers argue that it is not likely, that rough and illiterate Macedonian soldiers and their descendants would have any great knowledge of Greek literature much less imbue their neighbours with a taste for it. Their main line of attack, as has already been pointed out, is that not a single Greek inscription belonging to the Bactrian period has yet been unearthed in India and so they at once come to the conclusion that palpable evidence of active Hellenism have not been found in the East.

"The history of these Greek dynasties," says this class of writers, "is for us almost a blank and for estimating the amount and quality of Hellenism in Bactria, we are reduced to building up hypotheses upon the scantiest data." This is undeniably to a certain extent true ; the thick mists of obscurity, which unhappily hang like a pall upon the early history of India, at least over some of its periods, make anything approaching to certainty, impossible. But this very fact makes it almost as rash to deny Greek influence *in toto*, as to make too much of it ; and a few considerations make it appear highly probable that the Greek settlers in India were not altogether " the illiterate military colonists " that the anti-Hellenists would have us suppose them to have been. First and foremost, the splendid coins which distinguished the Bactrian Empire can only have been the work of an extremely cultivated race. The traditions of Menander and his capital at Sagala, as preserved in the Milinda Pañha, appear to indicate that the Bactrian Greeks were a cultured nation at the time of their greatest prosperity. The description of the Greek monarch's court seems to show that he was not a mere semi-barbarous conqueror, but a ruler, who if he did not seek to rival the great pomp and splendour of the Ptolemies or the Seleucids, at any rate upheld the traditions of Hellenic civilisation in a not unworthy manner. The paucity of Greek inscriptions is due to the fact, archæology in India is still in its infancy—the Kabul valley is practically untouched, yet the last four years have brought to light many valuable materials which should modify considerably the views of the anti-Hellenists upon the Græco-Indian Art. The famous Gandhara sculptures belong of course, not to the period of the Greek occupation but to the more settled and prosperous rule of powerful Indo-Scythian monarchs who succeeded them. It does not appear to be likely that the imported artists were employed in great numbers to execute the numberless friezes, statues and bas-reliefs which have been discovered in the Gandhara region. But an inscription discovered by Sir John Marshall, the present Director-General of Archæology in India, at Besnagar in Malwa in 1909, (J. R. A. S. 1909, pp. 1053-56) shows very clearly that during the rule of the Bactrian Kings, Bactro-Greek workmen were employed in India on account of their technical proficiency. This inscription which is of utmost importance in the study of the Greek influence on Indian Art was found on a pillar, surmounted by an image of Garuḍ. The inscription records that Greek workmen *did* work in India at the time of the Bactrian Greeks and might therefore have influenced the native craftsmen very considerably. The inscription is unique, because it is one of the few contemporary Indian records of the Bactrian Kings. It runs thus : "For the sake of Kâsiputra, Bhagabhadra the saviour, the King of Sankâssya ; King Chandadâsa caused the Garuda pillar of Vâsudeva, God of Gods to be made here by Heliodorus, son of Dion, a votary of Bhagavat, a Yona data (dûta ?) [an emissary from the Greeks] of Takshashila who came from the Mahârâja Antalkidas." This inscription is of supreme importance as throwing much light upon the dark pages of Indian history when the Greeks and the Indians were in close contact with one another. The inscription is in Kharosthi. Again, speaking of the Gandhara statues of Buddha, the celebrated French savant M. A. Foucher remarks, "Les sculpteurs qui pour le bénéfice des pieux donateurs du Gandhara adapterent le type d'Apollon à la représentation des divinités bouddhiques semblant bien les petits-cousins de ceux que vers le même époque coiffaient le Mithra persan au bonnet phrygien de Ganymede......et donnaient au Jesus de catacombs les traits d'Orphie ou du bon Pasteur" (L' Art Gréco-bouddhique du Gandhara.)

A further proof is found in the likeness between most of the Gandhara works and the coins of the later Bactrian Kings. A Triton group with serpent legs—["evidently a reminiscence of the Pergamene sculptures," says Rawlinson] —in the Lahore Museum, resembled very remarkably with a similar design on the coins of Hippostratus (vide Gardner, "Catalogue of Coins of Greek and Scythic Kings," Plate xiv, 6). Marine subjects, Tritons fighting with Gods and so forth, are commonly used for decorative purposes, just as Poseidon and other maritime subjects appear on Bactrian coins. Antimachus, it will be remembered, struck coins bearing the figures of Poseidon. A peculiarly beautiful example of Græco-Indian workmanship was the priceless reliquary discovered by Dr. D. B. Spooner in the remains of the great Stupa of Kanishka, near Peshawar in 1909. This again was the work of a Greek artist, for it bears an inscription to the effect that it was made by "Agasilaos, overseer at Kanishka's Vihar in the Sangharâme of Mahâsena." (vide J. R. A. S., 1909, p. 1058).

Similarly, in a Buddhist Chapel, on the west of the main building of the Dharmarajika Stupa, Sir John Marshall has only recently discovered a steatite vessel, containing a vase of silver. Inside this vase, was a small relic casket of gold together with a silver scroll, the inscription on which reads as follows :

L. 1. Sa 100, 20, 10, 4, 1, 1. Ayasa Ashadasa masasȧ divase 10, 4, 1 isa divase pradistavita Bhagavato dhatuo Urasa—

L. 2. kena Lotaphria-putrana Bahaliena Noachæ nagare vastavena tena ime pradi-stavita Bhagavato dhatuo dhamana

L. 3. ie Tachhasie Tanuvæ Bodhisatvagahami maharajasa rajatiraja devaputrasa Kushanasa arogadachhinae.

In the year 136 of Azes on the 15th day of the month of Asārh—on this day, relics of the Holy One (Buddha) were enshrined by Urasakes, son of Lotaphria, a Bactrian resident at the town of Noacha. By him these relics of the Holy One were enshrined in the Bodhisattwa Chapel at the Dharmarajika Stupa in the Tanuva district of Takshashila for the bestowal of perfect health upon the great king, king of kings, the divine Kushana.

It is interesting to notice in this connexion, that in the various Buddhist caves in the Bombay Presidency, the names of the Yavana donors of sculpture, cisterns, pillars etc. frequently occur. The earliest mention of Yavana workmanship appears to be in the Girnar inscription in Kathiawad, which records that the Girnar Lake was "furnished with conduits by the Yavana Raja Tushâshpa for Asoka." Tushâshpa appears by his name to have been a Persian. In the case of the Karli caves, some of these inscriptions date from the second century A. D. and point to the continuance of Græco-Buddhist settlements at quite a late date. Inscriptions nos. 7 to 10 (Bombay Gazetteer Vol, xviii), refer to pillars, the gift of Siladhyay and Dhama, Yavanas from Dhanakakata (Benkataka in the Nasik District) [see Rapson, Andhra Catalogue, xxix and xlvii]. Perhaps those Yavanas took Buddhist names on their conversion. So the Yavanas in Milinda Pañha have apparently Indian names or perhaps they retained very little of their Greek origin, except a tradition of their birth. In Nasik cave, we find one *lena* owned by "Indrâgnidatta, son of Dhammadeva, a Yonaka from the north, from Dattamitra." Here both father and son appear to have Hindu names ; residence Dattamitra in Sind is thought to have been founded by Demetrius. [Lassen in his "Indische Alterthumskunde," has already established that the word Dattamitra corresponds to Demetrius, as Yavanas to the Greeks (Ionians.)] In the Junnar caves we have three inscriptions referring to the Greeks, one of them is named "Irila" (vide, Archæological Survey of Western India vol. iv, no. 5, p. 92), which sounds suspiciously like a Greek name, perhaps Euryalus or something of that kind (see Indian Antiquary, 1911 (Jan.) pp. 11-14).

There is no positive proof that Buddhism became the religion of the Bactrian Kings of Sagala. There is however nothing against such a supposition, the probabilities indeed are in its favour. That converts were made even to the more conservative Hinduism among the Greeks, have been proved by the inscriptions quoted above. Asoka was anxious to make Greek converts and in later days, there were colonies of "Yavana" Buddhists—as the Karli cave-inscriptions show. Agathocles is the first prince to mint coins with Buddhist symbols. Menander curiously enough, besides the epithet *Dhramikasa* (Dikaíon), has nothing very definitely Buddhistic on his coinage ; but the evidence of his conversion seems definitely established. Firstly, there is the tradition embodied in the Milinda Pañha, which is certainly not a mere romance of the type of Xenophon's Cryopædia. Secondly, there is the story of his funeral in Plutarch's tract Republicæ Gerendæ Præcepta, p. 821, where occurs the following passage : "A certain Menander ruled with equity among the Bactrians and died in the field during a campaign. The states in other respects joined together in celebrating his obsequies, but over his relics a dispute arose among them which was after some difficulties settled upon the following terms : each was to take back an equal share of his ashes, that memorials (mnemeía = stupas) might be set up among them all." Now this precisely is the kind of funeral which was accorded to Gautama Buddha, as described in Mahāparinibbāna Sutta (see Sacred Books of the East, vol. xi. p. 131). This practice is peculiar to Buddhism and confirms the Siamese tradition of Menander's conversion and even his attainment to Arhatship (vide von Gutschmid). It may be taken for granted that Buddhism made converts pretty freely among the various foreign tribes of North-western frontier. It finally became the religion of the Kushanas and under

Kanishka and his successors, Buddhism reached its apogée.

Thus occasionally, the West Indian cave-inscriptions give us the names of certain private Yavana individuals, who made gifts to the Buddhist Chaityas or monasteries and consequently were unquestionably Buddhists and not only did they embrace Buddhism, but all except one, borrowed Indian names : "in short," says an eminent Indianist, "if the word Yàvana had not been mentioned in these inscriptions, their foreign extraction would have remained undetected." But it must be carefully noticed that the term Yavana in these inscriptions, was indiscriminately used, during this period not only to denote the Ionians or the Greeks but also the Parthians, Arabs and Persians. (For a further treatment of the subject, vide Chapter IX—Literature).

It is difficult to estimate from the evidence we have, the precise nature of the debt which Indian art owes to Greece. It is true that we have few artistic remains in India, which belong positively to the pre-Alexandrian period. The truth is that before the time of Asoka stone was very little used for sculpture ; in the Bhilsa carvings and other early Buddhist works, we can still plainly trace the influence of wood-carving in the treatment of the stone. The Buddhist rail-pattern, for instance, is an imitation in stone of actual wooden-railing used in earlier times for fencing in the stupa. On the other hand, it would be impossible to say, that the Greeks taught India, the art of carving in stone, as the earliest stone monuments, the Bhilsa carvings and the Asoka pillar at Sarnath, show no signs whatever of Grecian influence. The same remark applies to the Indian Architecture to a modified extent ; the earliest structures, like the Karli caves, show no traces of Greek influence. The Indo-Greek school of the Kushana period with its Corinthian and Ionic pillars and stucco ornaments is undoubtedly of later growth. The practice of using regular coins, properly stamped and shaped, in the place of the rude, punch-marked ingots, must have been introduced by the Greeks; the Indians however never excelled in the art of coining and their best coins were only clumsy imitations of Greek models. It is important in this connection to remember, that contact with the West imparted an impetus to the indigenous arts of India, it was like an electric shock, waking the land to a new life after the lethargy of countless years of undisturbed peace. The vigorous rule of the Maurya monarchs, which saw the beginning of a great Indian renaissance, was indirectly the result of Alexander's invasion. But the Gandhara or the Indo-Greek school of architecture and sculpture, which is almost entirely foreign, influenced India only to a limited extent. It was partly the work of the foreign artists, patronised by foreign kings and was swept away entirely by the Brahminical revival of the 4th century A.D. The Gandhara sculptures moreover are not always very artistic, either from the Greek or the Indian point of view, though they are of immense interest to the student of Buddhism, recording as they do, the legends and episodes of the life of Gautama in a unique manner.

IV.

Three centuries however had scarcely rolled away, after the Macedonian legionaries first struck terror in the hearts of the Aryans of the Punjab, since the last traces of the Greek rule in India disappeared from the pages of history. No written record preserves for us the melancholy story of the gradual dwindling and final extinction of the miserable remnants of the once irresistible phalanx of the great Macedonian conqueror. Incessant fighting was partly the cause. "The viciously valiant Yavanas," to use the contemptuous phrase of the great Sanskrit grammarian, were for ever at war with their neighbours, when not engaged in the equally absorbing pastime of internecine struggle. The inherent vice of the successors of Alexander's vast empire caused its disintegration everywhere. The great conqueror's premature death had prevented him from adopting any kind of constructive policy and his possessions fell into the clutches of men, whose trade was war, whether serving as mercenaries to the Egyptian Pharaohs in the days of Egypt's decline or waging war for plunder and rapine with the imbecile successors of a Cambyses or a Crœsus and consequently who cared little for or did not understand any other pursuits. The Greeks had been forced to abandon their territories north of the Hindukush, because they had been "drained dry of blood" by incessant wars and the same process was repeated in India. They suffered the same fate which had overtaken Sparta some four centuries earlier. Another equally powerful factor in obliterating Greek rule in India was the gradual process of absorption to which the coins bear such vivid witness. From Eukratides to Hermæus we perceive a steady decline of Greek element in these records of artistic and national feeling. Greek weights and standards gave place to Indian systems ; Indian inscriptions became more usual, while the Greek equivalents began to show signs of corruption ; the figures betrayed with interesting frequency, the handiwork of native craftsmen. It is tolerably easy to conjecture what was happening ; the Greek, cut off from his home and all chance of intercourse with his countrymen, was intermarrying with his neighbours with the usual effect. (Alexander, it will be remembered, himself took an Oriental Princess for his wife and encouraged intermarriage with the Asiatics among his Greek soldiers). The very fact that Kadphises shared the throne with Hermæus, seems to indicate that Scythian and

Greek amalgamated readily. The cosmopolitan descendants of Alexander's colonists, had of course none of the Hellenic exclusiveness which formerly dubbed all non-Greeks as "barbarians" and shunned any kind of social intercourse with them. Moreover, the barbarism of the invaders from Central Asia and the consequent isolation of the Greek colonists were the other potent factors in the extinction of Hellenism in the East. Euthydemus had warned Antiochus III that this would be the result, if the Greek kingdom of Bactria were destroyed. In this case, said Euthydemus "neither of them would be safe, seeing that the great hordes of nomads were close at hand, who were a danger to both; and that if they admitted them into the country.................it would be certainly barbarised" (Polyb. xi, c. 35.)

But although the Parthians and the Scythians overthrew the rule of the Seleucids and the Græco-Bactrians, the end was long delayed. As long as the Greek cities of Babylonia and Mesopotamia were free, as long as the Greek princes ruled in Kabul, Hellenism survived although moribund. But its communications with the West were impaired and immigration had almost entirely ceased. The Arsacids, when at the height of their power, were phil-Hellenes; Greek was understood at their courts and Orodes (57-37 B.C.) for one, patronised the Greek theatre, while Greek was apparently allowed a secondary place in public use alongside the Persian language (vide Mommsen, "Provinces of the Roman Empire," ii. p. 12). But throughout the first century A. D., the Parthians were distracted by internal dissensions and in a state not far removed from anarchy. At the end of the century, the rule of the Greek princes of the Kabul valley was finally extinguished. The degradation of the legends on the coins and the degeneracy of the artistic products, reveal the growing barbarism of the time. The Greeks then as a political factor disappeared completely from the Indian soil at the end of the first century or the beginning of the second century A.D. It is a curious fact besides, that few races have disappeared so utterly in India as the Greek. But though the Greek rule in India disappeared, active commercial intercourse continued in full swing between India and the Hellenistic lands till about 400 A. D.

Resumé:—Greece has played a part, but by no means a predominant part, in the civilisation of ancient India. The evolution of Philosophy, Religion, and Mythology has gone along parallel, but independent paths. India owes to Greece, an improvement in Coinage and Astronomy, but it had begun both ; and in Lyric and Epic poetry, in Grammar, the Art of Writing, the Drama and Mathematics, it had no need to wait for the intervention or the initiative of Hellenism. Notably perhaps in the plastic arts and especially in the details of some of the Architectural forms, classical culture had acted as a ferment to revive the native qualities of the Indian artists, without robbing them of their originality and subtlety. But in any case, the fascinating story of the Greeks in India is not only full of suggestion, but is also a most interesting chapter in the history of the development of ideas. The question does not interest itself solely to the Indianists and the Hellenists, but likewise to all those who occupy themselves in tracing the evolution of general history and to those who above all love to follow even in their more remote expansion, the antecedents of our modern culture and civilisation, the different phases of our national development and progress.

BIBLIOGRAPHY

1. Weber, A. ... ... "Die Griechen in Indien" in Transactions of the Royal Prussian Academy.
2. Lévi, Sylvain ... "Quid de Græcis veterum Indorum Monumenta tradiderint."
3. Prilaux ... ... "Apollonius of Tyana."
4. Perrot and Chipiez ... "History of Ancient Egyptian Art."
5. " ... "History of Art in Persia."
6. Smith, W. ... "Dictionary of Greek and Roman Antiquities."
7. Lévi, Sylvain ... "La Gréce et l'Inde" (in Revue des Études Grécques).
8. Bevan, E. R. ... "The House of Seleucus."
9. Wheeler, B. Ida ... "Alexander the Great."
10. Mc Crindle ... "Invasion of India by Alexander."
11. " ... "Ancient India as described by Classical Authors."
12. Okakura, K. ... "The Ideals of the East."
13. Harrison, J. E. ... "Prolegomena to the Study of Greek Religion."
14. Wheeler, Talboys, ... "History of India."
15. Lamartine ... "Vie d' Alexandre."
16. Tarn, W. W. ... "Hellenism" in the Journal of the Hellenic Society.
17. Pococke ... ... "India in Greece."
18. Ragozine, Z. ... "Vedic India" in the Story of the Nations.
19. Rhys-Davids, T. W. ... "Buddhist India" in the Story of the Nations.
20. Smith, Vincent A. ... "Early History of India."
21. Droysen, J. G. ... "Grundriss der Historik."
22. Gottheil, R. ... "Hellenism" in the Jewish Encyclopædia.
23. Mahaffy, J. P. ... "Progress of Hellenism in Alexander's Empire."
24. Lassen, Christian ... "Beitrag zur Geschichte der Griechischen Könige in Bactrien, Kabul und Indien."
25. Fritz Hommel. ... "Grundriss der Geographie und Geschichte der Alten Indiens."

26. Goblet D' Alviella, Count ... "Ce que l'Inde doit à la Grèce."
27. „ ... "Les Grecs dans l'Inde."
28. „ ... "Des influences classiques dans la culture Scientifique et Litteraire de l'Inde", in vols. xxiii and xxiv of Bulletin de l' Academie Royale de Belgique.
29. Spence Hardy ... "Eastern Monachism."
30. Turnour ... ... "Mahawanso."
31. Niese ... ... "Geschichte der griechischen und makedonischen staaten seit der Schlacht die Chaeronea."
32. Weber, A ... ... "The History of Sanskrit Literature."
33. Macdonell, A. ... "Sanskrit Literature."
34. Duncker, Max ... "Ancient History of India."
35. Rawlinson, H. G. ... "Bactria."
36. Droysen, J. G. ... "History of Hellenism."
37. Burnouf, J. ... "Vie et Voyages de Hiouen Tsang."
38. Journals of the Royal Asiatic Society, 1909—1919.
39. Zeitschrift der Deutschen Morgenlandischen Gesellschaft, 1893—1913.
40. Indian Antiquary, Vols xvii—xxii.
41. Encylopædia Britannica, Art. "Hellenism."
42. Journal of the Asiatic Society of Bengal, 1889, 1892.
43. Journal Asiatique, 1896 (Jul.—Dec.)
44. Cunningham, A. ... "Ancient Geography of India."
45. Mommsen, Th. ... "Provinces of the Roman Empire."

BOOK TWO

THE HELLENISTIC INFLUENCE ON THE ART OF INDIA

CHAPTER I

ARCHITECTURE

SECTION I

Land and People : Indian Architecture: the theory of its probable native origin : the discovery of Græco-Buddhist Architecture in the Peshawar Valley.

FROM the Himalaya, the highest mountain range, covering with its vast glaciers an extent of territory equal to the length of Scandinavia, there slopes down in grand terraces a land which projecting southwards in a compact mass, stretched its tapering point far into the Indian Ocean. The great peninsula, which from its northern boundary to its most southern headland, Cape Comorin, occupies an extent as great as that from the shores of the Baltic to the most southern Cape of Greece, was predestined by its natural position for an exclusive civilisation, separated from the northern countries by the rocky walls of the Himalaya and enclosed towards West and East by the mighty streams of the Indus and the Brahmaputra. This immense territory of Hither India is compressed in a continental mass, only divided by a rich net-work of rivers. Among these is the most important stream of the Ganges, which with its tributary, the Jamuna, rushes down from the ice-fields of the Himalaya and flowing in one united stream from the Prayaga (Allahabad), empties its waters by hundred mouths into the Bay of Bengal. As everywhere else in the earliest history of mankind, so also in India a higher development of civilisation followed the course of mighty streams. The ancient glory of the Hindu Empire first flourished in the land enclosed by the two sacred rivers, the Ganges and the Jamuna. Here stood the magnificent capitals of the Hindu rulers, Hastinapur, Indraprastha and Mathura and further down the Ganges, Palibothra—great cities, whose size, wealth and magnificence were extolled in the old Indian epics. Nor ought this to excite our wonder; since the earliest ages, the nature of the land produced a civilisation of rare abundance and splendour. No country in the world displays such luxuriant productiveness, combining in the north, in Hindusthan proper, the natural phenomena of all the zones from the eternal ice and scanty vegetation of the glacier world, to the exuberant undergrowth and majestic palms of the tropics. Under the glaring tropical sun, the moist soil becomes fertile beyond imagination, producing for man, in lavish abundance, all that he needs for life. But it also subdues the mind with the overwhelming force of its fecundity. It could not have been otherwise than that the exuberance of tropical nature should have captivated the mind of man, stirring up his imagination, filling it with brilliant pictures and fostering in him a love of contemplation and luxurious ease. With this were blended in the Indian character, a deep delight in the contemplation of the secrets of nature and enthusiastic devotion to the native soil and a leaning towards subtle speculation. The old poems of the people with their poetic charm exhibit the first of these traits; indeed the tender enthusiasm for nature exhibited in Kalidasa's Sakuntala betrays a deep sympathy rarely known to the other nations of antiquity. The Hindus however afford another illustration of the general truth that the original character of a people acquires fixed traits in consequence of the peculiarities of climate and the unceasing correlation between nature and the mind. Instead of an impulse to a practical activity, there early appears a powerful bent towards the investigation of the spiritual life, in thought as well as in action. It is owing to this reason, that the ancient Indians did not turn their attention to the development of merely material things, in the earlier stages of their history.

" With the victorious advancement of Buddhism ", writes Professor Lübke in his "Geschichte der Plastik", "monumental art-creations seem to have begun in India." So far as enquiry has yet ascertained, there is nothing to confirm the belief that so long prevailed, as to the extreme antiquity of the existing Indian monuments. The splendid descriptions of palaces and temples in the old epics, the Ramayana and the Mahabharata, which are cited in proof of the great antiquity of Indian Architecture, may be considered as interpolations at a much later period of culture; but when they are considered as real they point to slight and temporary structures, gorgeous with colour and polished metal and adorned with stuffs (cf. the description of the palace of King Asoka at Pataliputra by the Greek writers). Indian architectural art seems, therefore, to have really begun with the rise of Buddhism, and from the very first to have displayed a type of its own, in its magnificent monuments. This style was subsequently adopted by Brahminism and aided by more luxurious wealth and brilliant imagination, produced wonderful results. Even when India owing to its political weakness, submitted to the powerful inroads of the Muhammedans, when the old Brahminical cities vanished to make room for the new capitals of the conquerors, the Hindu people retained with their ancient religion, their native style of architecture, and later, in modern times, this architecture underwent a revival, which was in no wise behind that of the earlier ages.

It is true that the Hindus were in possession of numerous

treatises on Architecture, Sculpture etc., which were collectively called Silpa-Sāstra, but unfortunately few traces of them now remain. There appear to have been according to some, 32 and according to others, 64 standard treatises on the above mentioned arts; but of these, except some scattered fragments, which are occasionally to be met with among the artists themselves, nothing but the titles of the works are now generally known to the learned. Some fragmentary remains of the treatises, entitled Mânasâra, Mâyâmata, Câsyapa, Vâyghanasa, Sacalâdhikâra, Sanatkumâra, Pancharâtram and others are still occasionally, though rarely to be met with in Southern India. Mutilated as they invariably are in many important portions, almost every line of them is not only disfigured by gross errors but the technical terms and memorial verses are little understood either by the artists or the scholars of the present day.

Now, the monuments of India may be divided into two classes, excavated and constructed; the former being that wherein a building has been hollowed, or as it were, quarried out of the rock; the latter, that built of different and separate sorts of materials, upon a regular plan, as may be seen in the buildings improperly called pagodas, which ornament the enclosures of sacred edifices of which they are component parts. Of the first sort are the caves of Elephanta and Ellora, which are hollowed out of hard and compact granite. Again, as Daniell observes: Painting and Sculpture are not only intimately connected with Architecture on account of the embellishments they are capable of affording it, but are handmaids at her service in that it depends upon them for taste, the principles of beauty, the laws of proportion, the preservation of character and various other respects. Nature in one sense is the model upon which architecture is founded; not as subject of imitation but as presenting for imitation, principles of harmony, proportion, effect and beauty, for which the arts are generally indebted to nature. We think it was Madame du Stäel who said that Architecture was frozen music. Now in Architecture, as in other arts, there is a sensible imitation of nature, and by a study of her mode of operating, it may be tempered and modified, so as to give it the power of language and the sublimity of poetry. In respect of the connection of this art with Sculpture little need be said ; in a material light, an Architecture is but a sculptured production, and its beauty in every country is in exact ratio with the skill which is exhibited in the use of the chisel. Facts also prove that as is the state of Architecture in a country, so is that of the other Arts.

Man is naturally prone to imitate and is mainly stimulated to exertion by his capacities for this purpose. The desire of imitation is the exciting cause which directly contributed to the invention of each of the arts. Nature, in some shape or other, forms the object of imitation. Imitation, however, is merely the source of art ; it is not to be regarded as the end, much less the only end of art. In the invention of each art, two things are required : an accident or necessity to produce or call forth the invention of the art or the practical pursuit on which it is grafted, and a capacity of mind to take advantage of the circumstances. But utility ordinarily precedes ornament in all inventions ; it is the parent, and Nature, the refiner and perfecter of the discovery. Thus in the case of Architecture in India, the different orders are said to have been invented from the imitation of natural structures. The Hindu orders consisted mainly, of four principal parts viz. the *upapitha* or pedestal, the *atisthána* or base, the *stambha* or pillar and the *prastara* or entablature. These several members of the order have also been subdivided into various inferior parts which are curiously compared to the several parts of the human body, and in all of which, a striking similarity may be perceived between the Indian and Greek systems. Let us consider only the several mouldings which enter into the composition of pedestal bases. They are : *(a) Upána (b) Campa (c) Galá, cantha, griva* or *candhara (d) Uttara (e) Vajina (f) Prativajina (g) Pattica (h) Alinga (i) Antarita (j) Cumuda (k) Padma (l) Capota* etc. The moulding called *Padma* (lit. lotus) is supposed to resemble a petal of that flower. [This moulding forms the principal ornament of Indian Architecture]. In some specimens, this moulding is placed at the bottom or base of the column and looks very much like *apophyge* or ogre of the Ionic or Corinthian orders. Sometimes it is made exactly like an ovolo of the Western architects. A *capota* is a section of the moulding made in the form of a pigeon's head from which it takes its name. The beak of the bird is so placed as to serve the purpose of a spout to throw off the water (vide Mânasâra, Chapters xiii and xiv). In this respect it resembles in some measure, the Corona of the Grecian order. In the same way, Vetruvius supposed that the Greeks invented the various orders of architecture to typify the different sexes and ages of mankind ; that the Ionic volutes were in imitation of female curls and that the bases of pillars represented the modes of shoeing, peculiar to those times. In a corresponding manner, on some of the Egyptian columns may be seen represented the whole plant of lotus, palm or papyrus, whose calyx flower or tuft of leaves bound together at the pinnacle, form the capital. Nearly all the flowers and leaves, peculiar to Egypt, will be found copied here, frequently exhibiting all the most delicate and minute parts, such as petals, capsules, pistils and seeds ; not only the shape but the colour of these leaves and flowers has been faithfully portrayed (vide Perrot and Chipiez, "History of Ancient Egyptian Art"). Belzoni moreover conjectures that the shape of the rocks in the plains near the Pyramids, which resemble so many Pyramids of various sizes, first suggested to the Egyptians, the form of Pyramids themselves. The state of flame, spiral and pointing upwards, is also supposed by some Egyptologists to have constituted the model of the Pyramids.

Again, in the remains of Indian temples and stupas, we at once see the original invention of the art from an imitation of natural caves and the trees of the forest; these temples not only resemble but are mainly constructed out of the former, and closely imitate the latter in their carvings and pillars. According to Hesiod, Greek temples were also first carved out of the hollow trunks of large trees in which rude images were placed. Works of art should therefore follow Nature in combining in the same object both the useful and the ornamental; in the case of trees and animals, they please us as much with their beauty as they are valued for their utility, and their strict adaptation to their appointed ends.

Thus in India, the plastic arts most probably have been invented by the Indians themselves, without any foreign suggestion. The style of architecture, which had been invented and adopted, seems to bear to a certain degree resemblance to the foliage and structure of the trees which are grown there, as also to the style of the mountains and rocks, which give a peculiar character to the country, and which must have had a powerful influence in directing the taste of the people, even supposing they did not supply the original patterns for their artistic designs.

But when it was discovered that there existed in the old architecture and sculpture of the Indus valley, details which must have been derived from a classical source, it was natural to suppose that the Greeks, who had followed Alexander, had been the agents of their introduction. The theory presented itself, that the Greek architects and sculptors had come to

Bactria during the period when the Satraps, after Alexander, ruled at Balkh. It has been suggested that these architects worked in that region until the Greek form was more or less established; that it had afterwards crossed the Hindukush and filtered slowly down to the Indus. In doing this, it became mixed up with native features of construction and thus produced that peculiar jumble of forms, with which we are now familiar. Sir Alexander Cunningham at first called it "Arian," but at a later date he classed it as Indo-Grecian; and as a form of the Corinthian capital is principally found in the remains, he called it "Indo-Corinthian". It had also received the name of "Indo-Bactrian". In 1864, General Cunningham found at Mâliarka-Hora, near Shah-Dehri, the ancient Taxila, the base of a column formed of sandstone. This is now preserved in the Lahore Museum. No one with the slightest knowledge of the "Three Orders", could after seeing this fragment doubt the existence of a classic influence of some kind, in that part of the world. Cunningham said respecting it, that "it is of very great interest as it is the first specimen of pure Greek architecture that has yet been discovered in the Punjab" (vide Arch. Sur. of India, Vol. ii. p. 129). It may have been about 1870, that Dr. Leitner made excavations in the Peshawar valley, which resulted in the discovery of a considerable number of sculptures. They are now kept in the Museum of the Oriental Institute at Woking. As almost all the remains, in which the classical influence is found, are Buddhistic, Dr. Leitner gave it the title of Græco-Buddhist,—the title by which the style is now generally known among the Orientalists. Græco-Buddhist art is so called because it adopted classical forms to express Buddhist motives. It treated only Buddhist subjects, which sometimes demanded modifications even of form if they were to be in accord with the rules of the religion. Unlike what is to be seen in ancient Indian art, the Græco-

Buddhist art introduces the representation of Buddha in human shape, his prototype being Apollo and the sole addition, being a nimbus. As for the state of Bodhisattwa, it is represented by the figure of an Indian prince in all the splendour of his ornaments. It is also in the bas-reliefs of Gandhara that the figures of Buddha and the saints appear seated on a reversed lotus-bloom, the base of whose bell-shaped calyx serves for a throne. The favourite subjects, unlike those of the older Indian art, are rarely scenes from the Jatakas, but principally from the life of Buddha, and are of an edifying character.

The best specimens of the Græco-Buddhist art are preserved in the Museums of Calcutta, Lahore and Peshawar, and also in the British Museum, and the Museum für Volkerkunde at Berlin.

SECTION II.

The Geographical distribution of the Græco-Buddhist Art. The Gandhara region. Sir M. Stein's Discoveries in Chinese Turkestan.

The geographical tract, containing the remains which bear evidence of the classical influence, ought to be defined. A very few are in the Punjab and they are situated between the Indus and the Jhelum (the Hydaspes of the Greeks). Taxila, the city which Alexander first reached after crossing the Indus and which was probably visited by Apollonius of Tyana, is within this area, being represented by extensive mounds. The Manikyala Tope is about 40 miles to the south-east of Shah-Dehri ; the Balar-Tope, which is similar in architecture, is only about four miles in the north. There are also some remains in the Salt Range. The Temples in Kashmir are almost all Brahminical, but in these, Greek influences can be traced in many of the details. But the locality, which has produced most of the Græco-Buddhist sculptures is the Peshawar valley, the ancient Gandhara—now called the Yusufzai country. The finding of the remains here has been due to the excavations, which have been carried out systematically, since 1864. But the Buddhist remains have in most cases become shapeless mounds and the spade only can reveal what is in them. From this it will be understood that there may be much yet concealed and new data may in future be discovered. The influence also exists in the Buddhist remains of Afghanistan. A form of the Corinthian order is found in almost all the Buddhist remains of the Indus valley and Afghanistan. In saying that it is Corinthian, however, it must not be supposed that it is an exact imitation of that order. The remains only show a rude copy, which has been recognised as Corinthian, and it is now accepted that they were derived from Greek models of some kind. In combining it with other forms, fragments of the order only have been introduced. Pilasters are found at times in which the mouldings of the base are classic ; in some cases the capital is added, but over this there is often placed a dwarf-pillar with the Persepolitan bell-capital. In some the friezes may be recognised as classic, while in others there is no frieze. Moreover, the Indo-Corinthian capitals used here are generally short and stumpy. (For illustrations, see V. A. Smith, "A History of Fine Art in India and Ceylon.")

One building, supposed to be a monastery, has been found at Shah-Dehri in the Peshawar valley with pillars, the capitals of which appear to have been derived from the Ionic. In all the topes, where any fragments of the capitals remained, they were quasi-Corinthian. In the Kashmir and the Salt Range in the Punjab, there still remain a few temples, with columns, which have been described as Doric. The column and capital of this order are the only features which have yet been found in the very few examples that are known. The absence of the friezes in the architecture peculiar to the Doric order, may be accounted for by the fragmentary manner in which the orders have been copied. The most famous building of this order is the Temple of Marttanda in Kashmir.

At the time when Greek Kings, were ruling in the North-west and when Taxila was the foremost among the cities of that region, the plateau of Central India, north of the Vindhya range was dominated by the powerful city of Vidiça, now a mere waste of desolated mounds, near the modern Bhilsa. The sole monument now standing in the ruins of Vidiça is a stone Garuḍa Pillar, set up in honour of Vasudeva by a Greek named Heliodorus, son of Dion, who came from Taxila as an Ambassador of King Antialkidas to the Court of Bhagabhadra, King of Vidiça. The inscription on the Pillar, which relates these facts was first copied by Sir John Marshall in 1909 and published during the same year in the pages of the Royal Asiatic Society's Journal. It is the first record found in India in which mention is made of a Greek King of the Punjab. In view of its unique interest and historical value, its site has been scientifically explored by Prof. D. R. Bhandarkar at the instance of His Highness the Maharaja of Gwalior. This column of Heliodorus which plainly shows traces of Greek influence is locally called Kham Baba.

Excavations have also been carefully carried out in recent years under the guidance of Sir John Marshall in the Gandhara region, where the Græco-Buddhist School flourished most.

Taxila—The remains of Taxila are situated about 20 miles north-west of Rawalpindi, in a particularly pleasant and well-watered valley, with the snow ranges of Kashmir to the north and east, and the lower hills including the Margala range, completing the circle on the south and west. This position on the great trade-route, which used to connect Hindusthan with central and western India, coupled with the strength of its natural defences and constant supply of water sufficiently explains the growth of the city in early times. The foundation of Taxila indeed goes back to a very remote age, but of the epoch before Alexander the Great we know practically nothing, beyond the fact that it was probably included in the Achæmenian Empire of Persia and that it enjoyed a great reputation as a University town, famous for the Arts and Sciences of the day. The site, according to Sir John Marshall, embraces three separate cities namely, the Bir Mound to the south, which was in occupation from the earliest times say 1,500 B.C., until the close of the Maurya dominion about 180 B.C.; secondly, the city known as Sir Kap, further north, which is believed to have been founded by the Greek invaders in the first half of the second century B.C., and to have been occupied by the Greeks and their successors, the Scythians, Parthians and Kushanas, until about 70 A. D.; and thirdly, the city of Sir Sukh, still further north, to which there is reason to believe that the capital was transferred from Sir Kap by the Kushanas. Thus within four centuries, Taxila became subject to five different empires—the Macedonian, the Mauryan, the Bactrian, the Parthian and the Kushana and from these widely different civilisations, extending from Greece to western China and from the steppes of Russia to the Bay of Bengal, it must have inherited much of the culture and of the arts peculiar to each. With the decline of the Kushana power and the rise of the Imperial Guptas in the 4th century A. D., the history of Taxila comes to an end. Its power and importance gradually waned and when the Chinese pilgrim, Hiuen Tsang visited the city in the 7th century, he found the state had become a dependency of Kashmir and the monuments of its former greatness were in ruins. Besides the three cities, there are scattered over the face of the country a vast number of other ancient mounds and ruins. One of the most important of these is the Chir Tope on the south-side of the Hathial ridge and another is a lofty mound at Jhandial, in which are the remains of a most interesting temple. The Gandhara sculptures carved at the Chir Tope, were executed mainly in the second century, during the reigns of Kanishka and his successors. These sculptures are all of good style, equal to that of any specimens which we possess in Sir Kap; the most prominent building is an apsidal temple—the largest of its kind in India—surrounded by a spacious compound and rows of chambers for the monks. The temple was erected in the early Kushana period, probably during the reign of Kujula Kadphises (in the first century A.D.) There are some small finds of importance made in this temple and its neighbourhood, which deserve to be noticed. One of these is a beautiful bronze statuette of a child, of pure Hellenistic workmanship. An earthen jar closed at the top with a silver disc and containing a large quantity of gold jewellery, a head of the Greek God Dionysius of silver repoussé has also been found. Among the jewellery were several finger-rings—one with lapis lazuli entaglio, representing a Greek warrior and engraved with an early Brahmi legend. The bronze statuette is assigned by Sir John Marshall to the middle of the first century B. C., and the lapis lazuli ring, and the head of Dionysius which is the finest example of Greek work ever discovered in India, to a century earlier. Another earthen jar, which is proved to contain a small figure of winged Aphrodité executed in gold repoussé, a gold medallion, bearing the figure of a cupid and a number of jacinths cut *en cabuchon* and engraved with figures of

Artemis, Cupid etc., has been recovered from the same site (vide plates xvi, b, c, e ; xvii, b in the Annual Report of the Archæological Survey of India, 1913-14]. At Bir Mound, Sir John has recovered a number of monuments of Parthian and Kushana epochs, and by fixing their relative dates has established a series of much-needed landmarks in the history of architectural development in India. The prevailing spirit of the Parthian architecture has been found to be Hellenistic, the Indian elements being subsidiary and this architecture leaves no room for doubt, that the Parthians played a prominent part in the diffusion of classical ideas in India.

The complete excavation of the temple of Jhandial in recent years (vide Annual Report of the Archæological Survey of India, 1913-14) has proved quite satisfactorily, that it is unlike any temple yet known in India and its resemblance to a Greek temple is remarkable. The ordinary Greek peripteral temple is surrounded on all sides by a peristyle of columns, and contains a pronaos or front porch, a naos or sanctuary and at the rear an opisthodomos or back porch, known to the Romans as posticum. In some temples, such as the Parthenon at Athens or the temple of Artemis at Ephesus, there is an extra chamber between the Sanctuary and the back porch, which in the case of the Parthenon itself was called "Parthenon" or the chamber of Athené. Now the plan of this temple at Taxila is almost practically the same. Sir John Marshall is of opinion that the details of the superstructure, including the architrave, frieze etc. were of the Ionic order and in harmony with the Ionic style of the columns, pilasters and bold mouldings round the base of the walls. Thus the Taxilian temples with Ionic pillars were like all the known examples of Indo-Hellenic architecture, dedicated to the service of the Buddhist religion.

In the interior of India, the most conspicuous remains of

the Indo-Hellenic art but mainly sculptural, are those which have been found at Mathura (vide Chapter II.—Sculpture, sect. III.) Again, Monsieur Foucher is right when he discerns in the Sanchi sculptures more subtle indications of Hellenistic influence in certain examples of bold fore-shortening, in the clever presentations of three-quarters of face-figure and in harmonious balancing of groups. It is indeed inconceivable that the Indian sculptors of Asoka's time should have failed to learn something from the Greek art, which was so readily accessible to them. But whatever they borrowed, they made their own, so that their work as a whole is unmistakably Indian in character and original in substance. It should also be noted that such foreign elements as are distinguishable in Sanchi and Bharut reliefs, are readily accounted for without assuming intentional imitation. The mature art in every country is bound to assimilate to itself motifs and ideas from the foreign schools, with which directly or indirectly it comes in contact and Indian art is no exception to the rule. The columns of Asoka might have been the works of Asiatic Greeks, because Greek or semi-Greek artists were often employed in Northern India to execute such commissions ; but the sculptured columns of Asoka are widely different in style from the reliefs of Bharut and Sanchi. Whatever exotic elements there may be in Bharut and Sanchi sculptures, these do not detract from their value as manifestations of true Indian genius. "We are no more justified", asserts Sir John Marshall, "in calling these compositions as a whole, Hellenistic or Persian or Assyrian than we should be in calling the Palace of Knossos, Egyptian or the Palace of Mandalay, Chinese." No trace of the existence of 'pure' Greek architecture however, in either India proper or on the borderland, has ever been discovered ; that is to say, no building yet examined, was designed upon a *purely* Greek plan, or with an elevation exhibiting one or the other of the Greek orders, Doric, Ionic and Corinthian. But the Indo-Hellenic architects freely used certain Greek architectural forms, columns, pilasters and capitals for decorative purposes. The Doric column is found in the late Kashmir style. The Ionic column has been found in two temples on the site of Taxila, associated in one case with the coins of Azes I, who is supposed to have reigned between 90 and 40 B.C. Growse also noted the occurrence of a "niche supported by columns with Ionic capitals" on a fragment of sculpture at Mathura, and Simpson found the plaster fragments of a capital with corner volutes of the Romano-Ionic kind in the Ahinposh Stupa, near Jelalabad, in the valley of the Kabul river (see Proc. J.A.S.B., 1879, p. 279). More recently, two quasi-Ionic capitals have been discovered, one at Patna and the other at Sarnath, both of Asokan age and are said to resemble the capitals of the temple of Apollo Didymæus at Miletus. The abundance of modified Corinthian columns, pilasters and capitals in the art of Gandhara, contrasts strongly with the total lack of Doric and the extreme rarity of Ionic forms.

The classic elements in the art of India have been carefully noted by M. A. Foucher in his celebrated work on "L'Art Gréco-Bouddhique du Gandhara." "Le terrain," the learned writer goes on, "se trouve ainsi déblayé d'un grand nombre d'éléments importants et qu'on ne saurait omettre de mentionner, mais dont l'attribution à l'école gréco-bouddhique serait au moins contestable. Nous n'en apercevons que mieux à présent ceux qui peuvent être considérés d'emblée comme lui appartenent en propre et constituant l'apport nouveau qu'elle a introduit dans la répertoire artistique de l'Inde. Sa part d'originalité reste encore assez belle et ne fait que gagner à une aussi stricte délimitation. Bein entendu, il s'agit d'une originalité toute relative et locale ; et, quand nous parlons de certains motifs comme etant la propriété exclusive de l'art du Gandhâra, c'est toujours au point de vue indigène que nous nous plaçons. En réalité ce ne sont que des reproductions plus au moins fidèles d'œuvres classiques, et nous ne songeons pas le moins du monde à diminuer l'importance d'un fait auquel nos sculptures doivent le plus clair de l'intérêt qu'elles ont excité en Europe : mais le trait qui nous touche le plus pour l'instant est que ces rééditions étaient jusqu'alors inédites dans l'Inde. Aussi bien, dans cet art indien dont les plus anciens monuments ne remontent pas pour nous plus haut que le IIIe siècle avant notre ère et sont déjà si fortement empreints d'influences occidentales, on peut encore soulever des questions de priorité entre les diverses écoles : mais que oserait prononcer à leur propos, et en donnant sa pleine valeur à ce terme, le mot "d'originalité" ?... Nous en étions restés aux piliers indo-persans ; aux autres modèles qui s'en recontrent, Cunningham propose encore, et avec non moins de raison, d'appliquer l'épithète "d'indo-Grecs." L'idée lui etait chère qui les trois ordres helléniques avaient pénétré dans le nord-ouest de l'Inde avec les Grecs euxmêmes. Si l'on entendait par là que des temples doriques, ioniques au corinthiens ont été construits dans le Penjab, la thèse serait plus que risquée et tout ce que nous avons vu plus haut de l'architecture du pays la réduirait à néant ; mais si l'on veut seulement dire que des pilastres ou des colonnes plus au moins conformes á ces trois styles y ont été employés dans la décoration des édifices, l'assertion n'a plus rien que des très vraisemblable. A la vérité nous ne possédons au Gandhara même de preuves abondantes que pour l'usage de l'acanthe corinthienne ; mais à Taksaçila Cunningham, à Hidda W. Simpson ont trouvé des débris d'ordre vaguement ionique ; et quant aux colonnes pseudo-doriques du Kaçmir, nous n'imaginons pas par quel autre chemin elles lui seraient venues".

Thus in Gandhara as far north in Khotan, and in Mathura in the interior of India, the art of Greece makes its power felt. We know how immense that power has been as a living influence through centuries of European art, and we may be tempted to ascribe to it a governing influence in Asia. Yet in truth these traces that we have noticed marked the ebb of a receding tide. In 323 B.C., Alexander died in Babylon. He had carried the arts and civilisation of Hellas far into the East. The will of one man, whose magnificent ambition was to conquer the whole world for the mind even more than to possess its riches and dominions, had hurried with him a home-sick army, thousands of miles from its base, over deserts of burning sand, over mountains of perpetual snow into the fertile plains of India and to the beautiful shores of the Indus. But Alexander died not forty years old, and after his death the two continents shrank apart. Even his own exploits relapsed into fable. He became a hero of Romance. Even now in common opinion, he is conceived as a dazzling figure of knight-errantry in the mists of history, too remote to be more than half-believed by the ordinary people. His empire was split up into fragments, one of these fragments was Bactria ; and there it has been supposed, a School of Architects and Sculptors maintained some tradition of the art of Greece, as corroborated by the traces of the Greek style still visible in the statues of Gandhara and its vicinity. But the most unexpected influence of Græco-Buddhist art, and one which was only discovered a few years ago, is that which it exercised on Central Asia, and probably through that region, on China and Japan. Excavations carried out in recent years by learned expeditions from France, Germany, England and Sweden have thrown a vivid light upon Buddhistic art in Chinese Turkestan and the territories immediately adjacent to the Chinese provinces of Kan-su. In the south of this country also, the art of Gandhara and subsequently that of mediæval India, were transported, to be modified only by the exigencies of the plastic medium, namely clay, which the artists were obliged to employ, for quarry-stone does not exist in this region. From Khotan Buddhist art penetrated farther to the north-west towards the oasis of Kashgar and beyond to Tamchuk (to the north-east of Maralbashi), where have been discovered sculptures of the pure Indian type. More to the north, near the town of Kucha, numerous frescoes have been found in underground buildings, the subjects and execution of which are Indian with traces of Iranian and Chinese influences. To the east of Kucha, in the marshy regions of Lake Lob-Nor, other frescoes have been noted by the learned traveller, Sir Aurel Stein—very remarkable and closely akin in style to the works of Hellenistic art. Finally, outside Turkestan, but quite near to it's frontier at Tun-huang, the "Grotto of the Thousand Buddhas," visited by Sir Marc A. Stein and M. Pelliot, has supplied us with several specimens of Buddhist art dating from the sixth to the tenth centuries, which present a very remarkable mixture of Indian, Chinese, Persian and Tibetan styles.

SECTION III.

The Age of the Græco-Buddhistic School. Is the Influence traceable to Indian Art, Greek or Roman?

Regarding the age of the Græco-Buddhistic School, Sir Alexander Cunningham said, "As to those specimens of the Indo-Grecian Architecture and Sculpture, my belief is that the great mass of them belong to the most flourishing period of the Indo-Scythian rule under Kanishka and his immediate successors or about 80 B.C. to 100 A. D." (vide Archæological Survey, Vol. V, p vi). In the same volume, he remarked, "As the different styles of Greek Architecture must certainly have been introduced into the Kabul valley and the district lying along the Indus as early as B.C. 200, it is a source of much disappointment to me that no specimen of Indo-Grecian architecture has yet been discovered to which I can assign an earlier date than about 80 B.C." (Ibid, p. 189). To this he added that "this style so far as I can judge must belong to the most flourishing centuries of Indo-Scythian rule from B.C. 50 to A.D. 150." Sir Alexander was led to these conclusions partly by inscriptions and partly by coins, for he asserted in the case of the sculptures, "That they are not of later date than 150 A.D. I infer from the use of Arian letter only as mason's marks, as it would appear from the testimony of both coins and inscriptions that the Arian alphabet fell into disuse shortly after A. D. 100, when it was supplanted by the Indian alphabet." (Ibid, pp. 187-188). Dr. Fergusson was inclined to believe that the style continued to a much later date. He said, "the erection of the topes in Gandhara was spread pretty evenly over the whole time that elapsed from the Christian era till Buddhism ceased to be the religion of the country in the 7th or 8th century A. D., and that the most flourishing period was about the year A. D. 400, when Fa Hian visited the country" (see Indian and Eastern Architecture, p. 181). We need not be astonished if there is a wide divergence of opinion, regarding the extreme limits of the age in which the Gandhara School flourished. Appended is the table, which clearly illustrates the differences of opinion among the various scholars :—

	Extreme Duration.	Flourishing Period.
M. E. Sénart ...	1 B.C. to 200 A.D.	100 to 150 A.D.
Sir. George Birdwood	200 „ to 700 „	... ...
Sir. Alexander Cunningham	80 „ to 500 „	50 to 150 „
Mr. W. Simpson ...	... ...	100 to 273 „
Mr. Vincent A. Smith.	1 „ to 600 „	200 to 350 „
Dr. James Fergusson	100 „ to 800 „	300 to 550 „
M. J. Deniker	100 A. D. to 500 A. D. ...	... „

The inevitable conclusion, which may be derived from all these opinions, is that in the north-west of India, the local art received the classical influence in the first century B. C. The most ancient coinage, to which the Greek influence may be ascribed, dates also from the reign of King Azes whom we know to have ruled in the last decade of the first century B. C., and it is to be observed that the coins of that prince have been found in ruins near Taxila, where there are also vestiges of more ancient Buddhistic architecture.

The influence of Greek art, as it existed in the Yusufzai country, was very marked from the first and second centuries B. C. to about the second and third centuries A. D. Though various writers have propounded diverse theoretical dates, yet it is undeniable that the classical influence generally manifested itself between the second century B. C. and the third century, A. D. and that the most flourishing period preceded the reigns of the great Kushana rulers, Kanishka and his successors. [Here we wish briefly to note the special interest which attaches to the Besnagar pillar. It was set up, as may be remembered, by one Heliodorus who calls himself a Greek ambassador from King "Antialkidas to King Bhagabhadra." It clearly shows in what manner, about the middle of the second century B. C. Greek influence could penetrate from the Græco-Bactrian kingdom in the north-west to the Hindu states of Central India. It is the earliest known architectural monument, in the interior of India, of the contact between the two great civilisations of Asia and Europe.]

But whatever influence, Hellenism had exercised on Indian Art, was practically exhausted by 400 A. D. After that date the traces of Hellenistic ideas are too trifling to be worth mentioning. The mediæval Brahminical and Buddhistic Schools have nothing in common with Greek art, and the strange artistic forms introduced by the Muhammedan Conquerors at the beginning of the thirteenth century A. D. were equally alien to Hellenic feeling. From the fifth century, the Art of India, stood or fell on its own merits without reference to Hellenic standards. The mediæval Hindu revival and the advance of Islam in a large part synchronise; both involved a revolt against Hellenic ideas and a reversion to ancient Asiatic models—a "renaissance aux depens des influences héllenique."

The theory, held up to the present, has been that the influence originated from Bactria, where a Greek government was established on the conquest of Seleucus Nikator, with Balkh as its capital. A large and important city, which was the seat of the government, no doubt would attract artists who would remain permanently in such a place. So far we have evidence the Greek artists, or at least artists familiar with Greek art, did exist in Bactria, for the coins of early rulers afford evidence of this. The coins struck by Euthydemus, Demetrius and Eukratides may be taken as examples (vide Gardner, "Catalogue of Coins of Greek and Scythic Kings"). The art upon these is not only after the Greek manner, but they have also Greek inscriptions and Greek deities represented upon them. The theory suggests itself that if the Greeks came to that region capable of producing coins, there might also have been others who were architects or builders as well as sculptors. This Bactrian Dynasty is supposed to have continued for a century and a half, when it was swept away by a Scythian or a Mongol horde, known as the Yue-chi ; but a hundred and fifty years would be quite sufficient for the introduction of new forms, in architecture and sculpture, as well as for establishing them as a permanent style. Being once established, the supposition is, that the style in course of time found its way into Afghanistan. We have authentic evidence of the celebrity in which Bactrian architecture had been held at an early period from the Chinese pilgrim, Hiouen Tsang, when in the south of India, at a place supposed to be Amarâvati, he describes a monastery as follows : "un ancien roi de ce royaume l'avait construit en l'honneur du Buddha et y avait déployé toute la magnificence des palais de Ta-hia (de la Bactriane)" (Vie et Voyages de Hiouen Thsang par Julien Burnouf). Although the passage does not indicate in the slightest, what the style was, yet it is clear that the architecture of Bactria was known as far as South India for its "magnificence."

In these views on the subject, the Greek origin is assumed, but later on doubts arose and for sometime past the question had been : Is the influence Greek or Roman ? Dr. Fergusson said, "Among Indian antiquaries, there are two different views as to the age of sculptures found in or near the valleys of the

Indus, regarding either of which a great deal may be urged with a considerable degree of plausibility. The first is, that the Bactrian Greeks carried with them into Asia, the principles of Grecian sculpture and the forms of Grecian architecture and either during their supremacy or after their expulsion from Bactria, established a school of classical culture in the Peshawar valley. It further assumes that when Buddhism was established there under Kanishka and his successors, it bloomed into that rich and varied development we find exhibited in the Gandhara Sculptures and Monasteries." This is also the view adopted by Dr. Grünwedel in his "Buddhistische Kunst in Indien" and by General Cunningham ; the latter however admits that, as all the sculptures are Buddhist, the earliest must be limited to the age of Kanishka, which he assumes to be between 80 B. C. and A. D. 100 or thereabouts. The other theory equally admits the presence of classical element, derived from the previous existence of the Bactrian Greeks, but spreads the development of the classical feeling through the Buddhist art over the whole period, during which it existed in the valley, or from the first to the seventh or eighth century of the Christian era and ascribes its peculiar forms as much, if not more, to a constant communication with the West from the age of Augustus to the age of Justinian, rather than to the original seed planted by the Bactrians (vide "Indian and Eastern Architecture," p. 177). But this question has been set at rest by the weighty opinions of Dr. James Burgess, sometime Director-General of Archæology in India. He says, "whether the influence traceable in the remains in the north-west of India, is strictly to be called Greek or Roman, is a matter chiefly dependant upon the source to which we directly trace the influence and the period at which it was felt. Roman, it must be remembered, is only a later form of Greek art." It is a noteworthy fact that Hellenism had towards the middle of the 1st century B. C., founded for itself in the West, a province of Hellenic manners and customs and had completely enslaved it. This was the Roman Empire, now coming to the fore, which offered the Greek intellect a new home with a new angle of vision. The renaissance of the 2nd century A. D. roused a widespread enthusiasm for the old culture of Greece. The imperial throne of Rome was occupied by no more a splendid representative of this movement than Hadrian. He tangibly showed his love and reverence for Hellas by completing ancient edifices and by erecting new temples. And after Caracalla had conferred the citizenship upon every subject of the Roman Empire, Hellenism again became supreme in the East. But old Greece was dead, vices and superstitions had slowly filtered into Greek life. A nation of lazzaroni physically effete, self-indulgent, without loyalty and religion, having no confidence in themselves or hope for the future—as the Arcadian historian Polybius sorrowfully describes them—were hardly able to infuse new ideas into the art-creations of the distant oriental world. The age of the widespread realism of the Rhodian school, with its Laocoon group, of the noble products of the Attic school, as for instance, the Hera of the Ludovisi and the Venus of Milo and of the great creations of Lysippus and Apelles had passed away, never to return. Greece proper now had no large share in the production of masterpieces and the centres of intellectual activity shifted elsewhere.

But it should be noted also that from "the strange jumble" of architectural forms in the remains of the Gandhara region, it is evident that no conscious effort was made to mould the forms after strict classical patterns. We find Persian, Hindu and classical details all mixed up, as if (assuming the style had not been formed previously) the directing workman had taken his hints from his varied acquaintance, here a capital from Persepolis, there a base from Western India, and from a Yavana artist, a spirited sketch of the acanthus foliage on the Corinthian capital and of decorative dentils and mutules, all of which he had utilised in his own way. To break the plain surface of a pilaster, a small panel was inserted, or often human figures in relievo were carved on it. In one of the Jamalgarhi sculptures (vide Report on Amaravati Stupa etc. p. 180), we have Persepolitan capitals on shafts, with the true Hindu water-pot base, as if copied from Nasik or Karli and supporting two arched passages, the roofs of which are panelled in a way that deserves attention as a feature of classical origin. A frieze of the "Buddhist rail-pattern" type rests on the extended abaci of two of the pillars and above all is the garlanded torus-moulding. The sculptures on this slab are strongly marked by classic freedom and indicate classic influences. In India proper, pillars either have no bases or one of the forms of water-jar as at Kanheri, Karli and Nasik, of the second century; and when it was tried to improve on this, as in the striking examples at Junagadh (Rep. Arch. Sur. West. Ind. vol ii, Plate xxiv), we feel that it is only hidden by ornament, akin to the Corinthian capitals of the north. Among other Gandhara sculptures we have distinct imitations of favorite Greek subjects, as for example, in one from Sangas, which reproduces with but little variation, Leochares's Rape of Ganymede, and the Pallas Athené in Lahore Museum (vide Grünwedel, "Buddhistische Kunst in Indien").

SECTION IV.

The supposed Persepolitan influence : The Indianisation of the Classical motive. True extent of the Hellenistic influence.

Before entering into the subject of the Indianisation of the classical motive, we wish to dispose of the question of the so-called Persepolitan influence upon the evolution of plastic arts in India. "The style of Architecture appropriately named Indo-Persian by Sir Alexander Cunningham" says Mr. Smith, "and obviously derived from that employed in the Achæmenian palaces of Susa and Persepolis was extensively used throughout northern and western India for several centuries before and after the Christian era." Cunningham remarked long ago that "the pillars are characterised by a bell-shaped lower capital, surmounted by an upper member formed of recumbent animals back to back. The series of examples in Northern India of pillars, more or less corresponding to this definition, begins with the monoliths of Asoka and ends with the pillar of Buddha Gupta at Eran in the Sagar District of Central Provinces which bears an inscription dated 485 A. D." (vide Cunningham, Archæological Reports). The latest adherent to this theory of an Indo-Persian school flourishing in the valley of the Ganges, is Dr. D. B. Spooner of the Archæological Department.

The great "Hall of Columns" in the Asokan Palace at the Kumrahar site, which judging from the scanty remains as still survive, appears to Dr. D. B. Spooner, the explorer of Pataliputra, to exhibit a close resemblance with the famous Hall of a Hundred Pillars at Persepolis. This outward resemblance, the learned archæologist traces still further in other features and notably in the spacing of the columns, which like the columns of Persepolis are set at a distance of 10 cubits apart. But Dr. Spooner goes still further than this; from the presence of a number of circular shafts and from the discovery too of the head of a statue in one of these shafts, he conjectures that numerous statues once stood in the hall and that the hall itself was in fact nothing more or less than a Persian *talar* divided into three stories, in each of which stood Atlant statues upholding tier upon tier, the royal throne above their heads and thus typifying the subject-people of the monarch. Such a *talar* is portrayed on the sculptured façade of the tomb of Darius at Persepolis and another on the portal of the "Hall of a Hundred Pillars" at Persepolis. Dr. Spooner's view regarding the design and purpose of the Hall at Pataliputra, finds some confirmation in a clay seal recovered on the site, which depicts just such a three-storied hall as he predicates (vide his article, "The Zoroastrian Period in Indian History," in J. R. A. S., 1915). Brilliant and attractive as these theories are, it must be borne in mind that the evidences on which they are based, are very slender and more or less untrustworthy. Acting on this vague supposition, he has, by a careful measurement, instituted a comparison between the Kumrahar site and the platform of Persepolis and has sought to prove that the general configuration of the two is surprisingly similar: for not only in its colour does the Kumrahar site resemble the platform of Persepolis but the positions occupied by the House of Xerxes and the Palace of Darius at Persepolis, are at Kumrahar marked out by conspicuous mounds which may be presumed to conceal the ruins of ancient edifices. Indeed Dr. Spooner, carried away by enthusiasm, "to prove the palace of Chandragupta to be a base imitation of the Hall of a Hundred Pillars," finds the likeness of the two so striking, that he is inclined to believe that the palace at Pataliputra was a direct replica of that at Persepolis and that the small rocky hill with a terrace and cave, which Hiouen Tsang tells us once existed south-west of the old palace, was artificially constructed by the Maurya Emperor Asoka, in imitation of the hill containing the royal tombs at Persepolis. Here again, however, it must not be forgotten that the remains of the Mauryan age are buried some 20 feet below the ground-level and that undue importance must not be attached to superficial indications of the surface, which have resulted from deposits made by floods during the last 2000 years or by débris piled up by the ruins of mediæval structures. In short, Dr. Spooner's bold theory of Persepolitan origin of the Asokan palace is quite untenable. Now let us see whether the monoliths of Asoka were really imitated from the Persian, as Dr. Spooner and Mr. V. A. Smith suppose them to have been. We are inclined in unison with Mr. Arun Sen of the Calcutta University, to reject their theory for the following reasons :

(*a*) Material : Asokan columns are invariably made of monolithic grey sand-stones. In Persia, on the other hand, various materials are used—a limestone of good quality, artificial stone, burnt brick, crude brick, also a kind of plaster, white and as hard as stone (vide Perrot and Chipiez, History of Art in Persia etc. pp. 47-48).

(*b*) Base : The Maurya columns have no base ; in Persia, they invariably have that appendage, owing to the fact that the Persian structures were built from wooden models—and some stone was necessary to prevent the access of damp to the wooden columns (Perrot and Chipiez, ibid, p. 91).

(*c*) Shaft : In India it is plain, round and highly polished, while in Persia there is no mention of any polish. That would not be necessary because of the coating of paint, plaster, or metal, which would be invariably added. Secondly, it is invariably fluted there.

(*d*) Abacus : The lower elements of all abaci in India

are lotus, represented with extraordinary realism. Nothing like it is found in Persia.

(*e*) Entablature: The Asokan entablature is almost always, Zoophorous : in Sarnath, four lions are placed in close juxtaposition. Regarding the capital from the front, we see only two lions with the backs to each other, exactly contrary to the Persian design. If the Persian artist had executed Asokan sculpture he would have carved an essentially Persian thing or at least would have betrayed his nationality by the representation of some feature characteristically Persian.

The Persian influence may however be traced only in one particular class of buildings and in one particular locality, namely the Buddhist Vihara Caves of Western India.

We have already seen that the Greek architectural and sculptural forms are mainly confined to the site of the ancient city of Gandhara. The boundaries of the kingdom of Gandhara, as it existed in ancient times, are known with approximate accuracy. Hiouen Tsang, the great Chinese pilgrim, who had visited India between 629-645 A. D. describes the kingdom, as extending 1000 li (about 166 miles) from east to west, and 800 li (about 133 miles) from north to south, with the Indus as its boundary on the east. The great city of Purushapura, now Peshawar, was its capital (vide S. Beal, "Buddhist Records of the Ancient World"). At 400 A. D. the earlier Chinese traveller, Fa Hian assigns the same position to the kingdom of Gandhara (see Legge's Fa-Hian). The region, referred to by both Chinese pilgrims, corresponds to the tract known to the Greeks as Peukalaotis (Sans. Pushkalâvati), the capital of which occupied the site of modern Hashtnagar, $\frac{1}{8}$ miles north of Peshawar (vide Cunningham's Ancient Geography of India). The Gandhara territory, the situation of which has been thus defined, was the principal seat of Hellenic culture in India and from one or other part of it, nearly all the examples of Indo-Hellenic art in its most characteristic forms have radiated. Traces of the Greek teaching may however be detected in the remains at some particular localities in the northern and western India. "At Bharut, Sanchi, Buddha-Gaya, Ajanta and Amaravati," says Mr. Smith, "proofs may be given that the local style of art was modified by contact with that of the western world, but the evidence does not lie upon the surface."

The Gandhara and Mathura sculpture and architecture exhibit the strongest classical influence. The Greek influence at Sanchi and Bharut is much less evident. It is however true to say that the early schools are compounded of Assyrian, Persian, Hellenistic and Indian elements. Mr. Vincent Smith remarks, "The way in which Indian sculptors of the Kushana period adopted Græco-Roman fashions and mixed them up with the familiar Persian forms may be compared with the modern practice of mingling European and Asiatic designs without much regard to congruity. The fact that the Indo-Corinthian pillars and pilasters were used much in the same way as they are in many modern European buildings for decorative purposes and applied to buildings of Indian design and not as members of an order in the technical sense is clearly proved by the manner in which the Indo-Persian and Indo-Corinthian forms are employed together. In comparing the dimensions of the pillars in the famous choragic monument of Lysicrates at Athens (B. C. 334) with the structural pillar found in the Gandhara buildings, Cunningham had come to the conclusion that the Indian examples differed from the Greek standard "solely in giving an inward slope to the perpendicular narrow fillet which separates the scotia and the torus." The remains of structural Indo-Corinthian capitals found chiefly at Jamalgarhi and Takhti-Bahi are numerous." (History of Fine Art in India and Ceylon).

We shall now see how Greek "motives" were Indianised. The earliest Indian example of "motive" is the Bharut draped figure of the Yakshi Chanda. That may be dated about 300 B. C. (vide Grünwedel, The Stupa of Bharut in Bud. Kunst). The lady also appears on the Sanchi gateways and in Gandharan art, over and over again, with many variations. Slightly modified, she becomes Maya, the mother of Buddha, in the nativity scene. In Greek art, the motive occurs in the fourth century B. C., a century or two before its first appearance in India at Bharut, and so the pro-Hellenists ascribe an intentional borrowing of the motive from the West. According to them the Hellenistic artists transported the motive to Egypt where by reason of contact with the native Egyptian sensual notions, its treatment acquired a lascivious tinge, agreeing strangely with the Mathura presentation, the nude figure however, in Egypt being often male instead of female (vide V. A. Smith, Ibid, p. 382). For though it is true, that in the existing treatises on Hindu architecture, *e. g.* Mânasâra, Cásyapa, Pancharátram, Vayghánasa etc, no mention is made of anything like a substitution of human figures for columns to support the entablature, yet these direct that the shafts should be adorned with the figures of demons and animals, and various examples are to be met with, in which human figures as well as representations of animals are employed in bold relief in the size of pillars, temples and porticoes but by no means like those found in Grecian architecture. The antiquity of its invention in India is not yet determined (in spite of the positive assertions of a Greek origin by Mr. Smith on the contrary !), but the Grecian architects refer the origin of their Caryatides to the commemoration of their captivity of Carian women, while others assert that they were derived from the Egyptian source.

Monsieur Strzygowski of the Imperial University of Vienna

gives the name of Copto-Alexandrian to the mixed and mongrel art produced by the intermingling of Coptic and Hellenic ideas. The most striking illustration of the close resemblance between the Mathura representation of the Woman and Tree motive and the Copto-Alexandrian form, is found in a most unexpected place—the Cathedral of Aachen or Aix-la-Chapelle in Rhenish Prussia. Six remarkable ivory panels on the sides of the Cathedral pulpit have been examined in a special disquisition by M. Strzygowski, who has proved that the Aachen ivories are of Egyptian origin and should be considered as examples of the Copto-Alexandrian School. They may have reached their resting-place by way of either Ravenna, or Milan, or Marseilles (vide J. Strzygowski, "Hellenistische und Koptische Kunst in Alexandria"). "The resemblance between Mathura and Aachen figures," again says M. Strzygowski, "is so close that it cannot be accidental : but must have a common origin, which should be sought in Syria or Asia Minor from which Egyptian Hellenistic art drew its inspiration." The motive was variously treated in Egypt. "There is no difficulty," points out Mr. Smith, "in believing the transference of Alexandrian ideas to India either before or after the Christian era. In Asoka's time, for several centuries, intercourse between the ports of the Indian and Western world was continuous. The cupids, the birds and the beasts interspersed in the foliage of the Aachen ivory are also often found in India (cp. for instance, the Garhwa Pillar and various other Mathura sculptures)."

Again, at Amarâvati and Gandhara a favourite subject is the departure of Gautama Buddha as Prince Sidhartha from Kapilavastu on horseback. Generally, the horse is shown in profile, but occasionally is represented as emerging from a gateway and facing the spectator fore-shortened. This latter form of design specially seems to be connected with the Redir motive as seen in Barberini ivory dipytch in the Louvre, of the fourth century A. D., and in one of the Aachen panels, the origin of both being traced back by M. Strzygowski to the Egyptian representations of Horus, triumphing over the powers of evil represented by crocodile (vide Breasted's History of Egypt and Maspero's The Dawn of Civilisation). The Indian sculptures usually show earth-spirits as Yakshas, male or female, holding up the horses' hoofs. As Grünwedel and Strzygowski point out, the sculpture indicated the Buddhist legend that the earth goddess displayed half her form, while she spoke to the departing hero and also was a reminiscence or translation of the Greek motive of Ge (Gaia) rising from the ground, familiar to Hellenic art from the fourth century B. C. Similar earth-spirits are seen in the Barberini dipytch. "But later forms of motive" emphatically declares Mr. Smith, "are clearly of foreign origin, being based on the garland carried by amorini, Erotes, or Cupids which were constantly used in later Hellenistic and Græco-Roman art. In Gandhara, an intricate roll, quite in the Græco-Roman fashion, carried by boys, equivalent to Cupids or Erotes, is substituted for the Indian lotus-stem. The hippocamps, the tritons, centaurs and other weird creatures, which certainly were borrowed from Western Art, occur at Gaya and other places, in the sculptures of the early period. Forms more or less similar occur at Mathura and Amarâvati and in Gandhara. The strongly marked muscles of some of the Gandhara figures and the snake-tailed monsters suggest the notion, that the sculptors of the North-west felt the influence of the vigorous Pergamene School. The Atlantes of Jamalgarhi, specially seem to be a reminiscent of Pergamum ; from the Buddhist point of view, they may by regarded as Yakshas." (V. A. Smith, "A History of Fine Art in India and Ceylon").

In examining the above statements, we wish to reproduce the following weighty criticism of the most distinguished archæologist of India. The key-note of Mr. Smith's criticism appears to be that the Indian art, throughout the ages draws its inspiration mainly from foreign sources. This note is first sounded in connection with the sculptures of Bharut and Sanchi. Mr. Smith tells us that "the composition and style of the composition are so much remote from the Persian and so akin to the Alexandrian that it is impossible to doubt that the Indian artists imitated European rather than Indian models." The key-note of foreign influence is again struck when he comes to deal with the Amarâvati School. Perhaps he has recognised the close relationship between the style of Sanchi and that of Amarâvati, and having attributed the former to Alexandria, has found himself compelled to seek a somewhat similar explanation for the latter. However this may be, he defines the general style of these reliefs as an "Indianised adaptation of an Antonine development of Alexandrian art." In challenging this proposition, let us first quote what Mr. Smith and Dr. Burgess have to say respectively about the date of the Amarâvati sculptures. Mr. Smith writes, "it is safe to say that the outer railing may be referred to the second half of the second century A. D. and must be contemporary with Huvishka, the Kushana king of Northern India . . . . . The inner rail might be slightly later in date." Dr. Burgess on the other hand says, "its rail (sc. outer one) at least must have been reconstructed before our era or shortly after the sculpture representing the veneration of relics etc. but no representation of Buddha ; and then about the middle of the second century A. D., a great "restoration" had been effected." If Dr. Burgess is correct in his chronology, then it follows that, so far as the sculptures on the outer-rail are concerned Mr. Smith's proposition falls to the ground. Apart however from chronological considerations, the question may be asked what is this "Antonine development of Alexandrian art" to which Mr. Smith alludes, and on what extant works of art, does he base his theory? Until we know something precise about the particular Roman sculptures of which he traces the connection with Alexandria on the one hand and Amarâvati on the other, it would be premature to attempt to analyse his proposition in detail, but in the meantime, we venture to point out that none of the characteristic traits of Antonine art, such as distinguish, for instance, the reliefs or the columns of Antoninus Pius or Marcus Aurelius from Trajanic or Hadrianic work are to be found at Amarâvati. "The reliefs of Amarâvati," says Sir John Marshall, "indeed appear to be as truly Indian in style as those of Bharut and Ellora. They follow as a natural sequence on Mauryan art, when that art was finding expression in more conventionalised forms. They have inherited certain motifs and types which filtered in from the North-west, but these elements have been completely absorbed and assimilated without materially influencing the indigenous character of these sculptures."

Again, in support of his contention Mr. V. A. Smith goes on to quote a passage from Prof. Ernest Gardner's "Handbook of Greek Sculpture," in which that writer describes very briefly the typical genre series of Alexandrian bas-reliefs. Mr. Smith's theory strikes so deep at the root of Indian Art, that it is worth while repeating the passage in full :

"There is usually a group of figures in the foreground (and in these figures the analogy in subject to pastoral poetry is striking. Sometimes the scene is mythological, but usually representing such mythical personages as we read of in Alexandrian poems—Satyrs and Nymphs, the Cyclops of Polyphemus, Adonis and Paris and Oenone). Often the scene is from actual country life—(a herdsman minding his cattle or milking, a peasant on his way to market, or drawing a thorn from companion's foot, or even a group of animals, a sheep and lamb, a lioness and cub. Sometimes too, we find scenes from comedy, or a poet in meditation over his works). The background which is the most characteristic part of these reliefs, varies so as to be appropriate to the subject. Sometimes it is purely architectural, sometimes it represents nothing but rocks and trees treated with a strange combination of naturalism and conventionality. More often it consists of a mixture of the two—a country-scene with peasants' huts and rustic shrines scattered over the landscape or a group of buildings with trees and bushes lending variety to their stiffer outlines. (And there is a beauty and refinement of detail throughout, which reminds us of the minute finish given by Theocritus to his pictures of rustic life). The flowers on the rocks, the leaves of the trees, are often carved not only with utmost care, but with botanical accuracy. The country is seldom left untenanted by man or his imaginings, small shrines or altars, thyrsi or masks or their symbols are scattered freely over the scene. (Similar subjects treated in a similar style are also found in other works of minor arts, such as bronze or silver vessels and even gems); and they are interesting (not only from the way in which they illustrate the literary tendencies of the Hellenistic age and the social conditions they reflect, but also) because they show us an undoubted example of influence of painting on sculpture."

The above description, Mr. Smith tells us, applies *mutatis mutandis* to our Indian motifs and reliefs of Bharut, Sanchi etc., and he adduces this as an argument for a close kinship between the latter and Alexandrian work. But a similar argument may be applied to half the genre series of the world's art. Let the reader, for example, compare Prof.

Gardner's description, as quoted by Mr. Smith, with the genre scenes depicted by Chinese or Japanese artists. He will find that *mutatis mutandis*, it applies no less to them than to the Indian motifs and reliefs, but he will not be justified in assuming a near kinship between the art of Pekin or Tokio and that of ancient Alexandria. The fact is that such a description contains nothing that can be made the basis of a critical and trustworthy comparison; nor is it conceivable that any description in words could be accurate enough for such a purpose. If it could be shown that the Bharut and Sanchi motifs and reliefs possess distinctive features which are common to them and Alexandrian school alone, the evidence would go far to strengthen Mr. Smith's case: but at present no such analogies have been established; and in any case, it would not follow from them that the Indian motifs and reliefs are mere imitations of European models.

Let it not be understood however, that we wish to deny the debt which the early school of Indian Architecture and Sculpture owes to Hellenistic Art. That debt is admitted on all hands. What we do venture to maintain is that we are not at present justified in attributing Hellenistic influence in any special degree to Alexandria or in laying stress upon it as Professor Stryzgowski and Mr. Smith do. The internal evidence of the Indian motifs and reliefs seems to us directly opposed to their views. Dr. Fergusson was undoubtedly nearert he truth when he insisted that the art which they display is purely indigenous. We have now more knowledge of Asiatic art than when Dr. Fergusson wrote and some motive may now be traced to Persian, some to Mesopotamian and some to Hellenistic sources; but it still remains true that the *conception that gave birth to the architecture and sculpture and the spirit that animates them are essentially Indian.* Mr. Smith tells us that the composition and style of Indian and

Alexandrian reliefs are the same, we must confess, however, that they are radically different. All that is best in the Indian reliefs—the wonderfully skilful and accurate modelling of animals and plants for instance—are admittedly Indian. Yet are we to believe that the artists capable of these efforts had to go to Alexandrian models to learn how to compose their figures, and that having done so, every artist should have signally failed to grasp the real essential qualities of Alexandrian art? Or are we to believe that while they took their inspiration from Alexandrian proto-types, they transmuted those prototypes so effectively that no unmeaning or insincere features betray themselves in any part of their work?

The exotic elements as are noticeable in Indian Architecture have been very lucidly and authoritatively explained away by the eminent archaeologist, Sir. John Marshall, and we are in one accord with his learned and authoritative opinions. He says, "so far as the Hellenistic influence is concerned, it is precisely such as the cosmopolitan art of the great Empires of Western Asia might have been expected to exert, but it seems to me impossible, in our present state of knowledge, to refer this influence with certainty to this or that particular centre of Hellenistic culture. The streams that fed the great Western Asiatic art are many and various and though they may be distinguishable near the sources they quickly lose their identity as the flood moves eastward. Alexandria, no doubt like Rhodes, Pergamum, Antioch, Seleucia and many other cities contributed her quota to the development of Hellenistic art in general, and through this medium exerted an indirect influence on India; but more than this, it is impossible to my mind to concede. Her influence from her geographical position is probably less than that of Seleucia or Antioch, and none of these cities can be proved to have materially inspired the art of India."

The truth cannot be more forcibly and plainly expressed and we accept it unreservedly as the key-note of our criticism on Indo-Hellenistic Art in general—

"L'art dans l'Inde sera Indien, ou il ne sera pas."

BIBLIOGRAPHY

1. Burgess, J. ... Archæological Survey of Western India No. 9.
2. Fergusson ... "The Cave-temples of India".
3. " ... "Tree and Serpent Worship."
4. " ... "History of Indian and Eastern Architecture".
5. Cole ... "Preservation of National Monuments in India".
6. Fleet, J. F. ... "Corpus Inscriptionem Indicarum." Vol. III.
7. Cunningham, A. ... "Reports of Archæological Survey of India." Vol. II.
8. Anderson ... "Catalogue and Handbook of the Archæological Collections in the Indian Museum".
9. Grünwedel ... "Buddhistische Kunst in Indien"
10. Lübke, Wilhelm ... "Geschichte der Plastik."
11. Perrot and Chipiez ... "History of Art in Persia".
12. " ... "History of Ancient Egyptian Art".
13. Gwilt ... "Encyclopædia of Architecture".
14. Schliemann ... "Mycenae : a narrative of researches and discoveries at Mycenae and Tiryns".
15. Cunningham ... "On the Aryan Order of Architecture as exhibited in the temples of Kashmir".
16. Langles, L. ... "Monuments anciens et modernes de l'Hindustan".

17. Gustave le Bon ... "Les Monuments de l'Inde".
18. Foucher, A. ... "L'Art Gréco-Bouddhique du Gandhara".
19. Curtius ... "Die Griechische Kunst in Indien".
20. Cunningham ... "The Bhilsa Topes"
21. " ... "The Stupa of Bharut".
22. Minayeff, P. ... "Recherches sur la Bouddhisme" (Ann. du Musée. (Musée) Guimet), Paris.
23. Maisey "Sanchi and its remains".
24. Simpson, W. and Phené Spiers ... "The Classical Influence in the Indus region and Afghanistan" in the Journal of the Royal Institute of British Architects, 1894.
25. Griffin, L. ... "The Famous Monuments of Central India".
26. Stein, M. A. ... "The Sand-buried Ruins of Khotan".
27. " ... "The Ruins of Desert Cathay."
28. Smith, V. A. ... "A History of Fine Art in India and Ceylon."
29. Strzygowski, J. ... "Hellenische und Koptische Kunst in Alexandria".
30. Mosso, Angelo ... "The Palaces of Crete".
31. Coomarswamy, A. K ... "Medieval Singhalese Art".
32. " ... "Viswakarma".
" "The Aims of Indian Art."
33. Gayet ... "L'art Persan".
34. Maindron, Maurice ... "L'art Indien".
35. Rosenmüller ... "The Biblical Geography of Asia Minor, Phœnicia and Arabia".
36. Lassen, Christian ... "Indische Alterthumskunde".
37. Archæological Survey of India, 3 Vols. 1871-3 ; 1904-19.
38. Journal of the Royal Asiatic Society, 1898, 1899, 1911, 1912.
39. Indian Antiquary, 1908, Vol. xi, p. 128.
40. Le Grande Encyclopedie, arts. "Inde", "Art".
41. Choisy ... "Histoire de l'Architecture".
42. Cole ... "Illustrations of Ancient Buildings in Muttra and Agra".

43. Annual Reports of Arch. Sur. of India, 1909-17.
44. Banister Fletcher and
Banister F. Fletcher ... "A History of Architecture."
45. G. Jouveau-Dubreuil ... "Archèologie du Sud de l'Inde". (Annales du Musée Guimet). 1914.
46. The Punjab Historical Society's Journal, 1914 (Archæological Discoveries at Taxila by Sir John Marshall).
47. Marshall, Sir John, ... "A Guide to Taxila" (1918).
48. " ... "A Guide to Sanchi" (1918).
49. Foucher, A. ... "The Beginnings of Buddhist Art".
50. Epigraphia Indica, Vol. viii, pp. 36 et seq, p. 50; Vol. iv, p. 246.
51. Gazetteer of the Bombay Presidency Vol. i, p. 160.
52. Ram Raz ... "Essay on the Architecture of the Hindus".
53. Mânasâra (a treatise on Hindu Architecture).
54. Gardner, E. ... "Handbook of Greek Sculpture".
55. Harris, George ... "The Theory of Arts".
56. Okakura, Kakasu ... "The Ideals of the East with special reference to the Art of Japan."
57. Hamilton, A. D. F. ... "Origins of Indian Architecture" in the Dictionary of Architecture and Building.
58. Simpson, F. M. ... "A History of Architectural Development"
59. Havell, E. B. ... "History of the Aryan Rule in India." (1918).
60. Evans and Fyfe ... "The Minoan Palace of Knossos, Crete."
61. Deniker, J. ... "The Gods of Northern Buddhism".

CHAPTER II

SCULPTURE

SECTION I

Post-Buddhist and Pre-Gandhara Sculptures. The Græco-Buddhist Sculptures of Gandhara: the "Ekaçringa" Statue, and the Bacchic Episodes.

SCULPTURE in India followed faithfully the destinies of Architecture; the Hindus have always treated it as an auxiliary art, made for contribution to the decoration of an edifice. Sculpture appears to be of an ancient date in India, the rituals and the epic legends allude to its gradual development. But its *history* did commence only with Buddhism. If the piety of the first followers of the Buddhist faith refused to carve the image of the Master with symbols, it contented itself to indicate clearly his personality by representing either the two feet ornamented with conventional marks, or by an elephant as on the rock of Khalsi at the top of the inscription of Asoka. The Mahabharata and the Ramayana contain frequent references to "storeyed towers, galleries of pictures and castes of painters," not to speak of the golden statue of Sita and the magnificence of personal adornment. "Indeed," asserts Dr. Okakura, "it is difficult to imagine that those centuries in which the wandering ministrels sang the ballads, that were later to become the epics, were devoid of image worship, for descriptive literature, concerning the forms of the gods means correlative attempt at plastic actualisation." This idea finds corroboration later on in the sculpture on Asoka's rails, where we find images of Indras and Devas worshipping the Bo-Tree. "Among the monuments of Asoka", says Sir John Marshall in his "Guide to Sanchi" (1918), "there are some of the most perfect and highly developed specimens of Sculpture in India." In the time of Asoka however, indigenous art was still in a rudimentary state, when the sculptor could not grasp more than one aspect of the subject at a time, when the law of "frontality" was still binding upon him, and when 'the memory picture' had not yet given place to direct observations of nature. But the bas-reliefs of the ancient balustrades at Bharut or Bodh-Gaya upon which are depicted the famous episodes of the career of Buddha in the series of his former existences or Jatakas, are the result of an original art 'ripe, perfectly sure and master of itself'. If perspective is wanting there, the idealisation of the pieces are exquisite, the animals and the trees which figure there, are drawn with surprising accuracy. Gazelles, elephants, apes and human figures are perfect copies of real life, the personages are so truly and faithfully depicted in their various attitudes and expressions that they afford a very pleasing sight to the eye. There are also literary evidences of images in post-Buddhist and pre-Gandhara times. Thus the Mahawanso informs us that in the relic chamber of Ruvanveli Dagoba, King Duttha Gamini (161-137 B. C.) placed a resplendent golden image of Buddha in the attitude in which he attained Buddhahood.

The invasion of Hellenic art introduced by way of Bactria diverted that indigenous development in another channel. The reliefs of the Sunga Period at Sanchi, as well as at Bharut and Bodh Gaya reveal the influence, which the foreign and especially Hellenistic ideas were exerting on India, through the medium of the contemporary Greek colonies in the Punjab ; but the art of these reliefs is essentially indigenous in character and though stimulated and inspired by extraneous influence and teaching is in no sense mimetic. Its national and independent character is attested not merely by its methodical evolution on Indian soil, but by the wonderful sense of decorative beauty which pervaded it and which from the first to the last has been the heritage of Indian soil. But there preceded another inspiration before the Hellenic one and under its influence the sculptor paid no heed to the expression, for it did not correspond either with the physiognomy or the character ; he fashioned the arms, the legs, the heads, and the body to suit the materials upon which he worked, and multiplied these limbs in some cases, to indicate the divine or super-natural, but in most others followed his unbridled fantasy. However, experience thus solidly acquired by working upon hard materials coupled with natural æsthetic taste, preserved the sculpture from its decadence : elephants, lions and gazelles were displayed in picturesque friezes of the temples ; and the combats of the Ramayana inspired on more than one occasion, the genius of the native artists, even before the introduction of the Hellenic element. Thus we may conclude that before the intrusion of Hellenic art, India possessed a national art, whose exuberance, power and sensualism were the dominant qualities. It is these which gave her sculptures that distinctly Oriental character which might be taken as a connecting link between the art-creations of India and those of Babylon and Assyria.

Therefore, the School of Art which arose and flourished in Gandhara, was not the first School to arise on Indian soil. Long before the Gandhara School, we have the art of the Mauryan Empire, and the more realistic art of the Sungas, and even this is not primitive, a fact which everyone will recognise who sees it. It was only at a later date that the peculiar form of art found in Gandhara came into favour, and this appears to have arisen through the influence of those later Greek princes of Bactria who came in touch with Buddhism. The art represented by the Gandhara sculptures is the result of the union of the older Indian art and Hellenistic art as it was known in Bactria. It was thus not a new departure, but merely a new development. Many of the old motifs were retained practically unchanged ; others were modified, others almost transformed. While in addition to all these, many entirely new ideas were introduced by the Græco-Bactrian artists. Of all the new additions to Indian art, which resulted from this union of the Hellenistic genius with Buddhist piety, by far the most important was the figure of Buddha himself. As has already been observed, the older Indian monuments never show any representation of the master, his presence in any given composition being indicated by some sacred symbol. It is as though the figure of Buddha himself had been deemed too holy for representation until the Hellenistic artists of Gandhara familiar with the comprehensive pantheon of Greek art, came to the assistance of the Indian Buddhist and tutored his first attempts at portraying the divine. That the ideals thus inculcated failed ultimately to satisfy the Indian heart, there can be no wonder, but that is no reason why full credit for the first attempt should not be given to these Græco-Buddhist artists. For, whatever we may think of the later development of the Buddha figure in India proper, there is no doubt that it originated here in the Peshawar valley, and that the Buddha figures of Gandhara are not only the oldest in the world, but also the direct source from which the artists of Central Asia and the Farther East, drew their inspirations. All this no doubt invests them with very great historical interest and importance.

We may notice in this connection that the sculpture of India proper—the India of the Gangetic valley is mainly indigenous. But the sculpture here is generally in bas-relief : and this forms its chief characteristic and its main distinction from the Hellenised sculpture of the Gandhara region, which consisted of sculpture in the round. It is true that the sculpture in the round was not unknown in India, but it was as little practised there as at Persepolis or at Nineveh. The Indian sculpture is lavished chiefly on the vestibules and the doors, and the most important single figures guard the entrance to the gateways of palaces after the Persian fashion ; the sculptured risers of the Jamalgarhi monasteries recall the inclined ascents to the palaces of Darius and Xerxes. Of the decorations of the earlier Buddhist monasteries we know practically nothing ; but the decoration of the later Vihara caves of Nālanda and the Sangharams of Gandhara is considered by some orientalists to be "Persian and that not so much after the fashion of the Sassanides as of the Achæmenides. There is the same lavish employment of colours, the use of enamelled and metallic tiles upon the roof, the gilded rafters and the elaborately painted ceilings, the rich capitals of the pillars, the application of inlaying. The two schemes of decorations are almost the same." But to the general question, concerning the direct influence of Babylon on Indian Sculpture we must answer in the negative. [The Babylonian influence may however, be traced in one particular locality, namely the Buddhist Vihara Caves of Western India. These caves differ in many of the leading features from what we meet elsewhere. The four or five storied Viharas of Western India are tower-like buildings each stage set upon the lower one. They undoubtedly recall the impression of a Babylonian Ziggurat (vide Fergusson's Cave Temples of India).] India, till the 3rd century B.C., did construct her buildings not of stone, but of wood, in most cases therefore, nothing is left of these edifices, palaces and temples, they being so liable to destruction. (One or two stray cases of structure in stone are found in some Viharas of Central India, which can be placed before the 3rd century B.C.) The first constructions in stone most probably date from the reign of Asoka. The religious zeal of the Buddhist Emperor was responsible for the edifices in stone and legend attributed to him the erection of 84,000 Stupas in a single day.

The Hellenistic sculptures of the region of the North-western frontier, anciently known as Gandhara, have received their full share of attention in Europe and have been the subject of voluminous discussion. The existence of an Indo-Hellenic School of Sculpture was not recognised generally, until 1870, when the late Dr. Leitner brought to England a considerable collection of specimens to which he gave the name of Græco-Buddhist. But so far back as 1833, Dr. Gerrard had disinterred the first known example of a circular relief of Buddha from the chamber of a ruined Stupa near Kabul. In 1836, James Prinsep published his account of the so-called Silenus, discovered by Colonel Stacey at Mathura. During the last forty years, thousands of Indo-Hellenic sculptures have come to light while considerable numbers including most of the choicest specimens, have been catalogued, described and photographed.. A few of the figures mark the gradual disappearance of the Hellenic tradition and the progressive Indianisation of the treatment.

The country from which comes this wonderful wealth of semi-foreign sculptures, as has already been described in general terms, is the North-western frontier. It includes the modern district of Peshawar, the valley of the Kabul river, Swat, Buner, and other tribal territories, as well as the western portion of the Punjab between the Indus and the Jhelum. The kingdom, of which Peshawar was the capital, having been known in ancient times as Gandhara, the sculptures are most conveniently described by that territorial name. The richest sites as yet explored are those crowded together in the Yusufzai country, comprising Jamalgarhi, Sahri-Balol, Takti-Bahi and many more which it would be tedious to enumerate. (vide supra Architecture, *Section II.*) The Sculptures which are found here, in Gandhara, bear strong evidence of classic influence. The formal conventionalism which is such a marked feature of Indian sculpture, has in this case almost disappeared. In figures of Buddha, rigid lines of drapery were superseded by more picturesque folds, even the round knobs by which the hair of the head was represented by Indian artists had given place to more naturalistic treatment. The Punjab as well as Afghanisthan adorned their monasteries and their palaces with classical pasticcio : Buddha was cast in the type of Apollo. "L' inspiration," says the great French Orientalist, M. Sylvain Lévi, "et le sentiment hindous, caulis dans ces formes hétéroclités allontit parfois, à des œuvres hybrides d'une singulière et puissant effet : tel le Buddha, ascèté de Sikri, où le canon de Praxitèle est reduit an squelette émacié ; décharnée d' un yogi, avec la tête entourèe d'un nimbe" ('Inde' dans "La Grand Encyclopédie"). [This emaciated figure, together with the image of the Ascetic Gautama in the Peshawar Museum, is meant to recall the six years of fasting and austerities which Gautama under-went as a Hindu ascetic in the period of his life just subse-quent to the Great Renunciation, and prior to the attainment of Buddhahood.]

The Museums of London, Berlin, Vienna and Lahore are rich in specimens of that art which is termed Indo-Greek. The Gandhara sculptures mark the highest pitch attained by the indigenous combined with the occidental art. "Another example," says Sir Marc Aurel Stein in his recent book, "The Ruins of Desert Cathay," "showing how the forms derived from the late classical, that is, Hellenistic Art were adapted to the representations of subjects from Indian Buddhism. Here, seated on a low throne, we see the figure of a teacher meant in all probability for Gautama. But just as Græco-Buddhist sculptures, where similar representations of Buddha in the attitude of teaching are frequent, the drapery is treated in a fashion that is unmistakably classical." The classical influence on the Gandhara Sculpture in fact, is quite as marked as on the Architecture of North-West India.

The recent excavations around the village of Sahri-Balol, some 8 miles to the west of Hoti Mardan in the Peshawar district, have yielded apart from valuable information on various topics of general archæological interest, a great quantity of Sculpture in the Græco-Buddhist style of Gandhara, representative of its successive phases and often of considerable iconographic interest. In point of novelty, the first place belongs undoubtedly among these finds to one of the statues which have been found here. This mutilated statue has been recognised by Sir M.A. Stein with the Risi Ekaçringa or Unicorn Hermit, figured as carrying to town the courtesan who beguiled him. This frivolous legend is related in one of the most popular Jatakas and has found its way also in mediæval folklore. Hiouen Tsang relates it in connexion with a convent which he places about a 100 li to the north-west of Po-lu-sha or Shabaz-garhi and to the south of a great mountain (see Watters, Yuang Chang, vol. I, pp. 218 et seq). Following up a hint supplied by Col. Sir Harold Deane, Dr. Stein was able to locate the remains of the ruined monastery at the site of Butan at the southern foot of the Shahkote Pass. M. Foucher with true iconographic intuition had already expressed himself confident, that a legend so popular, once localised in Gandhara, could not have remained there altogether without sculptural representation. "Les ruines voisines de Palai," asserts the eminent savant, "nous doivent toujours la mise en scène de l'histoire du risi Unicorne (Ekaçringa), que Hiuan-Tsang y a trouvée localisée ; si profane, que fût ce conte, primière version de notre 'lai d'Aristote' et des fables qui débitent sur la licorne les Bestiaires du moyen âge, il n' était pas pour faire reculer les sculpteurs à qui nous devons les scènes de bacchanales figurées plus haut" (see Foucher, L'Art Gréco-Bouddhique du Gandhara, i. p. 270). Regrettable as its mutilated condition is, enough remains of the saint's figure to show the remarkable realistic skill with which it has been modelled. Once again we have a proof, how cleverly the Græco-Buddhist sculptors of Gandhara could fix their attention upon the most characteristic "act" of a story and thus produce a significant representation of the Indian legend with classical restraint in the setting.

The only definite examples of the Indianisation of classical subjects again are those, which are distinct imitations of Greek types, found mainly in the Gandhara region and in the ancient city of Mathura. We regard specially the Bacchanal scenes as having been derived from the classical source. Their magnificent decorations are not so much in question here, as those reliefs which intersperse between the giant wrestlers and grape-gatherers and the goat of Dionysius hidden among the vine-branches; and thus we have a veritable continuation of Bacchic episodes, which are so common in the ancient sculptures of Europe. In a fragment in the Louvre, for example, (Fig. 128, in Foucher's L'Art Gréco-bouddhique du Gandhara) we see a young faun draped in tunic, open at the thigh, offering drink to a female Bacchante with his arms amorously twined round her neck. The chignon in the fashion of the Greeks of this latter and of her neighbour, is particularly striking.

In another group, a hairy man dressed as Pan is running towards the left, turning sideways to a female cymbal-player (whose back is only visible), who follows him while dancing. Then in another group, we find two Menades, of whom one is holding a pitcher, while the other raising her veil with her two hands stands in front of a corpulent Silenus leaning on his elbow. On a bas-relief at Lahore (Fig. 129, Ibid), we find a fat person, riding astride not on an ass but on a lion ; a Menade with flowing drapery, which bears a strong resemblance to the representations on the coins of Maues and Azes, stands in the midst of the vine-branches, leading the animal ; to her right, wine is gushing forth from a wine-press, and to the left, after a group of Bacchantes, two young fauns are attempting to make a panther or a lion drink out of a cup ; the vine-grove overhangs these diverse scenes, which are separated by vine-stalks. We recognise in this panel, most of the figures, found habitually in the trains of Bacchus—whom he seems to have forgotten on his return from India, in that distant valley, where tradition places the celebrated Nysa, famous still to-day for its magnificent vine-groves. M. Foucher describes another scene which also plainly betokens that it has been borrowed from Bacchanal representation. "D'un côté" he continues, "une jeune femme souriante évente de la main gauche avec un écran un homme à la barbe fleurie, qui semble l'inviter à partager sa large coupe ; de l'autre, sa compagne est assise, sur le genou d'une jeune homme imberbe qui achève d'écarter ses voiles. A toutes deux, d'ailleurs, leur draperie a glissé jusqu'au-dessous des reins, exactement comme à ces Néréides également vues de dos, mais la tête tournée de profil et parfois, aussi le bras allongé, vers l'épaule de leur amant, que les Tritons emportent, sur leur croupe. Ici encore on se sent tout près du modèle antique ;

surtout l'occasion est bonne pour constater la remarquable chasteté de l'école gréco-bouddhique". "C'est le dernier éloge," says the learned writer, "qui l'on songerait à faire non seulement de l'art grec de la décadence mais de l'art bouddhique postérieur. Si l'on reprend une à une les compositions dont l'origine hellénistique nous a semblé le plus évidente, on aperçoit çà et là quelques petits détails qui ne sont pas inutiles pour nous empêcher d'oublier que ces sculptures n'ont pas été trouvées à Alexandrie ou à Pergame, non pas même à Palmyre ou à Séleucie, mais dans un Orient, encore plus lointain, sur les bords de l'Indus ou du "fabuleux Hydaspe." C'est ainsi que les Amours qui se mêlent aux guirlandes portent des bracelets aux chevilles et jouent d'instruments de musique indigénes, notamment de certains tambours à deux mains." This leads up to the Nagas and their persecutors the Suparnas or Garuḍas. The Nagas have their origin doubtless in some indigenous race, but this cannot be said of their enemies. Garuḍas, as M. Foucher notes in his Vol. II. of L'Art Gréco-Bouddhique du Gandhara (1918), never assumed a human aspect in Gandhara art ; it was reserved for a more modern period, when he became a carrier of Vishnu, to give him a human semblance, only slightly suggesting his origin by a beak-like nose. We may note here however, that the scene of the carrying off of a Nagini by Garuḍa is represented in almost purely Greek Style in an intaglio recently discovered, which strongly suggests the Rape of Ganymede as its origin.

Remarkable abundance of delicately carved heads, busts or torsos, have also come to light from the débris of certain cellars in the ruined Buddhist shrine at Ming-oi site in the prefect of Kara Shahr. Some of the heads are as classical in their modelling and expression as any to be found among the Græco-Buddhist Sculptures of Gandhara. The bearded heads are unmistakably derived from the representations of Satyrs in Hellenistic Art.

SECTION II

The Relic-casket of Kanishka: the Hellenistic influence, it exhibits. Professor Bhandarkar's Besnagar Find.

By no means secondary in antiquarian interest is the now famous Buddhist relic-casket exhumed from the ruins of the great Stupa of Kanishka near Peshawar. The discovery of this monument—the clue to which was given by M. Alfred Foucher in his brilliant study of the ancient Geography of Gandhara—has shown how much can be achieved by patient and systematic research. The excavations carried out by Dr. Spooner in that site in 1907-08 had not yielded any certain results. They were resumed in the following year and led to the discovery not only of Kanishka's monument, the largest Stupa of Northern India, but also of the relics which it contained. The relics, according to the testimony of Hiouen Tsang, were believed to be the corporeal remains of Gautama Buddha and therefore have been made over to the Buddhist community of Burma, to be worthily enshrined in a new pagoda at Mandalay.

The relic-casket of Kanishka exhibits the Hellenistic influence on Indian Art in the final stage of its remarkable action. It seems that the Kharosthi inscriptions mention a Greek artist, at least one bearing a Greek name Agisâla. The decoration on the casket shows a curious blending of classical and Indian element familiar to us from Gandhara Sculpture. It points to a time when the graceful plant of Greek art transplanted on Indian soil had become choked by the luxuriant growth of indigenous culture. It appears from the inscription that this period of artistic design, was synchronous with the reign of the great Kanishka whose effigy figures prominently on the casket. [It is interesting to compare in this connection the gold relic-casket from a Stupa at Bimaran near Jelalabad, now preserved in the British Museum. It is much more classical in design than the Peshawar casket. Coins dating from about 50 B. C. were also found on the same spot. (vide Birdwood, "Industrial Arts of India"). The thorny problem of Kanishka's exact date may be here left out of discussion. This much is certain however that whatever patronage Kanishka and his successors may have extended to Buddhist buildings, the great flourishing period of Gandhara art had then passed away. The figures on the casket are in very high relief and the design as a whole is admirable in the highest degree. The Sun-god on the casket is shown in the act of crowning Kanishka with his wreath, a well-known conception of Greek and Persian Art (compare the figures of Shamash and the king at the head of the Hammurabi Stele). In point of execution, as pointed out by Dr. Marshall (in the Report of Archæological Survey of India, 1908-9), the casket shows manifest proofs of artistic decadence, and thus enables us to affirm with certainty the theory held by some writers that the Buddhist art of Gandhara owed its origin to, or at least reached its prime under Kanishka, is no longer tenable. That this is a definite step in advance is obvious. Kanishka's casket was certainly not produced until the School of Gandhara was already on the wane and the only possible conclusion that can be drawn from this fact is that in its origin, the School was much older. For there can be no doubt at all, that this is Kanishka's casket, from the similarity of images occurring on the coins.

The occurrence of the Greek name Agisāla, found in the inscription on the casket, "Dāsa, Agisāla navakarmi Kanashkasa Viharè Mahâsenasa Sangharāmê" (The slave Agisala, the overseer of works at Kanishka's Vihara in the Sangharam of Mahâsena) already referred to above, is another interesting point. That artisans did find their way to Indian courts from the Occident in the first century A. D. is also well-illustrated by the legend of St. Thomas, who is said to have been ordered by Christ to proceed to the Court of Gondophares : and indeed nothing could have been simpler than the employment of Hellenistic workmen by the Greek principalities of Bactria in the immediate neighbourhood. For, even if Greek rule in Bactria did disappear with Hermæus, there is no reason to suppose that the Greek population disappeared at the same time. The prevalence of the Hellenistic art of Gandhara under the Kushana rulers shows conclusively that such artists or artisans were employed ; accordingly, the mention of a Greek on Kanishka's casket entirely agrees with the facts as we know them. But that such employment of Greek workmen must have been more common, in the first century B. C. or in the first Christian century than in the third, is obvious and the definite mention of a Greek in Kanishka's employ may reasonably be looked upon as a slight confirmation of the view held by those scholars who prefer to date Kanishka's career, somewhat earlier. It would certainly be surprising to find a Greek at Kanishka's court, if as Sir Ramkrishna Gopal Bhandarkar thinks that Kanishka reigned from 278 A.D. As for the name Agaisāla, we should note the following : The form Agesilas occurs in the last paragraph of Chapter 18 of the viiith Book of Pausanias, where he is mentioned as a man of Lusi, who was a victor in the Pythian festival held by Amphictyons. The forms, Agesilas and Ageisilas also occur, the latter in a Bœotian inscription from Northern Greece (Liddel and Scott, "Greek-English Lexicon")

Another interesting find, made during the excavation of Besnagar in the year 1914-15 by Professor D. R. Bhandarkar, consisted of twenty-six pieces of clay-tablets bearing impressions of seals. From the shape and marks at the back, it is clear that with one exception, they were all attached to letters or documents on small wooden boards. The majority contain the names of private individuals, but one bears the designation of office: *hayahasty adhikari i.e.* an officer in charge of the horses and elephants. The only seal which does not bear the marks of strings or wooden boards at its back, bears the legend in two lines, which Professor Bhandarkar reads as follows: (1) *Timitradatrisya* (*sa*) *ho* (*ta*)-(2)-*p* (*o*) *ta-mantra Sajana.* "The meaning of the legend," says Professor Bhandarkar, "is not yet quite clear to me, but the words, hota, pota and mantra, which are technical to sacrificial literature, indicate that the seal was really connected with the Yajnasala; and the import of the seal appears to be, "of Timitra, the donor, accompanied by the Hota, Pota, hymn-kinsmen and ...." Timitra appears to stand for the Greek name Demetrius, and it appears that the Greek was the Yajamāna who instituted the sacrifice." Another indication of Greek influence is found in a mould of steatite stone for preparing medals, on one face of which is what looks like the obverse of an Indo-Bactrian drachma, exhibiting the bust of a king, diademed and turned to the right. On the face of the mould is the caduceus of Hermes. The workmanship of the mould and the carving of the bust and caduceus show distinct Hellenistic influence.

SECTION III.

The Indo-Hellenistic Sculptures of the Mathura School [The Kanishka Statues of Mathura]: its relationship to the Gandhara School; the two theories.

The most distinct and conspicuous remains of the Indo-Hellenic Art in the interior of India are those which have been discovered at the ancient city of Mathura, situated on the Jamuna. A group in sandstone, found near Mathura, was described and figured more than fifty years ago by James Prinsep, as representing Silenus with his attendants. The following is a description given by Cunningham in the Archæological Reports vol. I, p. 243: "In the front group, the principal figure is a short semi-nude man, resting on a low seat with a vine-crowned brow, out-stretched arms which appear to be supported by figurines male and female, standing one on each side. The dress of the female is certainly not Indian and is almost as certainly Greek." Prinsep agrees with Stacey in considering the principal figure to be Silenus. His portly frame, drunken lassitude and vine-wreathed brow, stamp the individual, while the drapery of his attendants, pronounce them to be at least foreign to India, whatever may be thought of Silenus's own costume, which is certainly highly orthodox and Brahminical.

Thus the first recorded discovery of Sculpture at Mathura is that of the so-called Silenus-group, obtained by Colonel Stacey in 1856 and now preserved in the Calcutta Museum. In 1853, regular explorations were started by General Cunningham in the Katra and continued up till 1861. They yielded numerous sculptural remains, the most important among them is an inscribed standing Buddha image, now in the Lucknow Museum. In 1869, Mathura was visited by Dr.

Bhagawânlâl Indrâji, who on this occasion made two important discoveries. The first was that of a life-size female statue, which he excavated at the Saptarshi Tila. It is now in the Lahore Museum. The remarkable point about this image is that both in style and material, it proves to be a Gandhara Sculpture, a circumstance of great importance and interest for the history of Buddhistic Art. Not far from this, Dr. Bhagwânlâl discovered the famous lion-capital with its 18 Kharosthi inscriptions which throw considerable light on the history of the Northern Satraps, who ruled in Mathura before the time of the Scythians. In 1881-2 when Cunningham revisited Mathura, he discovered another sculpture no less remarkable for the classical influence it betrays. Its subject is Herakles strangling the Næmean lion ; or it would perhaps be more correct to say, it appears to be an Indian adaptation of the subject. (It should be noted however, that a hero strangling a lion is also found in Assyrian bas-reliefs and sculptures, vide G. Maspero's "The Struggle of the Nations"). Of the other finds, we need only mention a railing pillar, with a dedicatory inscription in Brahmi of the Maurya period. To these is to be added the Parkham image, now in the Mathura Museum. The last archæological explorations were carried out by Dr. Führer between the years 1887 and 1896. The inscriptions and some of the most remarkable sculptures obtained by him were fully discussed by Hofrath Dr. Bühler. Subsequently Mr. Vincent A. Smith published a series of 108 plates, which had been prepared under Dr. Führer's supervision. Fertile though the Mathura explorations have been, it is to be deplored that they were not carried out on more systematic lines.

The attempts made by Cunningham and Growse to identify some of the Mathura sites with localities mentioned by Hiouen Tsang signally failed owing to their identifications having been based on a wrong location of the city. All we can deduce with certainty from past explorations is the following: The Katra must have been the site of a Buddhist monastery named Yasi-Vihara, which was still extant in the middle of the sixth century. The Kankali Tila contained a Jaina Stupa named "Vadra-Stupa" and apparently was of considerable age, as at the time of Huvishka's reign its origin was ascribed to the gods (Dowson, "Ancient Inscriptions from Mathura"). On the Jamalpur site, there once stood a Buddhist monastery founded by Huvishka in the year 47 of Kanishka's era, and no doubt connected with a stupa, as we may infer from the discovery of the railing-pillars on this site. The Indian Museum at Calcutta contains 28 sculptures from Mathura, which include the so-called Silenus and Herakles strangling the Næmean lion. They are fully described in Anderson's Catalogue.

The vast amount of sculptural remains discovered at Mathura would suffice to show the importance of this place in the history of Indian art. It is remarkable that the only statue, which on the strength of the inscriptions, can be assigned to the Maurya period is found at Parkham, half-way between Mathura and Agra. The Satraps, who ruled at Mathura in the first century B.C., patronised the arts of architecture and sculpture, as appears from the inscribed lion-capital in the British Museum. "The great flourishing period of the Mathura School undoubtedly coincides with the reign of the great Kushana rulers, Kanishka, Huvishka, and Vasudeva" (vide Dr. Lüders' article in the Indian Antiquary, vol. xxxiii). The bulk of the inscriptions found on or in connection with Mathura Sculptures are written in Brahmi of the Kushana type.

The startling discovery of a statue of King Kanishka in the neighbourhood of Mathura had already been announced to the learned world. The statue together with the lower half of a divine image and an inscribed pedestal was found, a little to the north of Mathura, in the village of Mat, on the left bank of the river Jamuna. The lower half of another colossal statue of the Kushana King, seated on his throne, was also found at a little distance. The first image of King Kanishka is a life-size statue of which the head and both the arms are lost (vide Plate LII, Arch. Surv. Report, 1911-12). It shows the king standing, his right hand resting on a mace and the left clasping the hilt of a sword. Kanishka is clad in a tunic reaching down to the knees and held round the loins by means of a girdle of which only the square plaques are visible in front. These plaques must have been of metal, perhaps of gold. The remainder of the plaques is concealed by a long upper garment, which falls below the knees and is consequently somewhat longer than the under-garment. Both garments are plain, only the seam being shown. The folds of the robes are indicated by very shallow lines, a reminiscence of the Hellenistic influence. Most conspicuous are the very heavy boots with straps round the ankles similar, as Sir M. A. Stein points out, to those worn now-a-days in Turkestan. Regarding the identity of the figure there cannot be the slightest doubt, because across the lower portion of both garments, there runs the following inscription in Brahmi script:

Mahārāja rājātirāja devaputro Kanishka.

"The King, the king of Kings, his Majesty Kanishka.

Of no less interest than the Kanishka statue is the colossal image of a king, seated on the throne (Ibid, Plate LIV). The king is seated in European fashion on the throne or *Simhā-sana*, as indicated by two lions placed on either side. Only the front portions of the lion-figures are shown, the rest being concealed by a cloth hanging down on both sides from the seat of the throne. This colossal seated image also bears an inscription on the top of the base between the feet. The character is Brahmi of the Kushana period. It reads:—

1. Mahārāja rājātirāja devaputra
2. Kushānaputra (Shahi Vamataksha) masya
3. Vakānapatina Huma......(devakulu) karita
4. Arāma pushkarini udapāna (cha) sa-da (kothako)

The inscription records the construction of a temple, tank and a well. The name of the donor is unfortunately lost, but seems to have commenced with a syllable Huma. The preceding word Vakānapatina is probably a title. The inscription further mentions a Kushana king, whose name is indistinct, but appears to be Varmataksahuma. This name is unknown to history, the first portion reminds one of the name Wema Kadphises, the Oohmo Kadphises of the coins.

The sculptor of the above two Kanishka images has shown considerable skill in faithfully portraying the great King. But the maker of the images whatever his nationality may have been, was certainly not inspired with the ideals of Grecian art. The indication of the drapery alone seems to retain a faint recollection of classical sculpture. The characteristic features of the statues are their rigidity and strict symmetry. The pose is singularly ungraceful and the whole sculpture is flat. "It is difficult to believe," says Dr. J. Ph. Vogel, "that this barbarian statue is contemporaneous with the graceful Bodhisattwas of Gandhara, which with some propriety used to be described as 'royal figures'". So the eminent archæologist concludes, "A study of the Mathura School of Sculptures has led me to the conclusion that the great flourising period of the Gandhara School must have preceded the reign of the great Kushana rulers, Kanishka and his successors." Several of them are dated in the reign of one of those three kings; and we know that the monastery which once stood on the Jamalpur site was built in the days of Huvishka. That the Mathura School still existed at the Gupta period is attested by some inscribed Buddhist images, two of which are dated in the Gupta 135 (A.D. 454-5) and 230 (A.D. 549-50) (vide Dr. Fleet, Cor. Ins. Ind. Vol. III). But the production of the period is small as compared with the Kushana times. After A.D. 600, the Mathura sculptures apparently ceased, as hardly any inscription of a subsequent period is met with. We may perhaps connect this fact with the fall of the Gupta Empire and the decline of Buddhism (vide Vincent A. Smith, "The Jaina Stupa and other Antiquities of Mathura").

There can be little doubt however that the influence of the Mathura School, made itself largely felt throughout the period of its existence. "Everywhere in the Northwest", says Cunningham, "I find that the old Buddhist statues are made of Sikri sandstone from which it would appear that Mathura must have been the great manufactory for the supply of the Buddhist sculptures in northern India". This observation is remarkably corroborated by epigraphical records which have since come to light. Likewise the classical influence, which permeated from Taxila into the neighbouring hills of Kashmir, is well-illustrated by a fine collection of terra-cotta heads and other figures belonging to the Kushana and early Gupta epochs, which Rai Saheb Daya Ram Sahni found at Ushkur, near Baramula. The modelling of the first is highly naturalistic and perfect in the treatment of the lips, chin and cheeks; they recall to mind many Mathura images of the Kushana period (Annual Rep. Arch. Sur of India, 1916-17). The colossal Bodhisattwa image, erected at Benares in the third year of Kanishka's reign, and the contemporaneous Srâvasti statues are not only carved in spotted red-sandstone of the Mathura Sculpture but both were the gift of the Buddhist friar Bala whose name occurs also in an inscribed image from that place. The famous Nirvana Statue of Kasia, which may be assigned to the fifth century, appears to have been the work of Dinna of Mathura, the only one of those numberless artists, whose name, though imperfectly, has been preserved. (Dr. Bühler, "Specimens of Jaina Sculptures of Mathura," Epigraphia Indica Vol. II p. 311 et seq; Dr. Vogel, "Epigraphical Discoveries at Sarnath," Ep. Ind. Vol. VIII, pp. 166 ff; Dr. Bloch, "Two Inscriptions on Buddhist Images" Ibid, pp. 179 ff).

A circumstance which from the beginning attracted the attention of the European scholars to Mathura sculptures, is the Greek or rather Hellenistic influence which some of them clearly betray. The first piece of sculpture at Mathura (as we have already noticed above), the so-called Silenus in the Calcutta Museum, was at once described "as a relic of Grecian Sculpture and attributed to an able artist who could not possibly have been a native of Hindusthan". Prinsep refers to it "as a piece of sculpture bearing reference to Greek mythology, if not boasting as unequivocally of the beauty and perfection of Grecian sculpture." "There can be no doubt", he says, "as to the personage represented by the principal figure". It was at once apparent however that though the sculpture was classical in character, it by no means reached even the lowest standard of Greek or Hellenistic Art. For this reason, Mr. Growse rejected Cunningham's theory about "the existence of a small body of Bactrian sculptors, who found employment among the wealthy Buddhists at Mathura, as in later days Europeans were employed under the Moghul Emperors." Growse, moreover, after comparing the group with the one, found by him in the Pali Khera mound, came to the conclusion, that in neither case did the main figure represent Silenus (vide Growse, "Mathura : a district memoir"). While attempting to find an Indian subject disguised in a classical form, he was the first to recognise the true nature of Hellenistic influence on Buddhist Art. On both sculptures, which apparently belonged to Buddhist monuments, the main figure is not

Silenus. This view of Mr. Growse was endorsed by Mr. Vincent A. Smith.

A question of considerable interest is the relationship between the Mathura sculptures and those of the Peshawar districts (the ancient Gandhara), which as we have already seen show distinct traces of classical influence. On this point, two widely different theories have been advanced. Mr. V. A. Smith expressed the opinion that "the Mathura sculptures have very little in common with those of Gandhara and seem to be the work of a different school. It is difficult to fix their dates with precision. It cannot be well later than A. D. 300 and the style is not good enough to justify the suggestion of a very early date. For this School, he adopts the term Indo-Hellenic to differentiate it from the Græco-Buddhist School of Gandhara". The most distinctly Hellenistic sculpture from Mathura, according to him, is the mutilated group 2 feet 5 inches high, known as 'the Herakles and the Næmean lion,' discovered by Cunningham, now in the Indian Museum, Calcutta. The hero grasps the beast with his left arm and presumably threatens it with a club in the missing right arm. He is fairly well-modelled in a way that, "suggests Greek reminiscences," but the lion so far as can be seen, is a poor feeble creature. The only other Indian work of art resembling the group is the corroded bronze or copper statuettes treating of the same subject, which were discovered in a mound at Quetta in Beluchistan. This motive is however of great antiquity going back to Assyrian art, which represented Gistubar, "the Assyrian Hercules," clubbing and strangling a lion in the same way. The Mathura group was believed by Cunningham to date from the time of either Kanishka or Huvishka. Certain groups and statuettes from Mathura or its neighbourhood, all dealing with strong drink and intoxication, which has been classed together by the

Orientalists as Bacchanalian, have excited much interest and discussion. The supposed Greek character of the composition first discovered, was much exaggerated by the early commentators, while some of the connected sculptures have nothing Hellenistic about them. These so-called Bacchanalian sculptures of Mathura cannot be at all understood if considered by themselves. They evidently belong to a large class of Buddhist works of art represented by the "scénes bacchiques" of Gandhara—which fill two plates of M. Foucher's excellent book (Figs. 128, 129, 130, 131),—several reliefs on the railing-pillars at Mathura, the Indian Bacchus of the Tonk silver-dish and the festive scenes depicted in Aurangabad Bagh caves.

Prof. Grünwedel followed Mr. Vincent A. Smith in assuming the existence of an Indo-Hellenic School, and which in his opinion flourished in Mathura prior to the Græco-Buddhist School in the North-west. He remarks in his "Buddhistische Kunst in Indien," that the Mathura School represented pure Greek subjects, among which he ranks the representation of Māra with bows and arrows. Yet Dr. Grünwedel observes, that "some Buddha statues found at Mathura have also the robe laid over both shoulders and the folds executed on the dress point to Gandhara sculptures as models." Both in Gandhara and Mathura, Buddha is clad in the garment of the Buddhist monk. It is of interest that the folds of the upper garment in the Gandhara sculptures (Sanskrit, Sanghati) are clearly marked and in a much more classical manner than at Mathura. From the treatment of the dress, it has been rightly inferred by M. Foucher that Mathura has borrowed its Buddha image from Gandhara. The same is true with regard to the Buddha figure of Amaravati. It should be noted that this treatment is un-Indian, and though continued in Mathura in the Gupta period, disappears again in the mediæval Buddhist Sculpture. The

Gandhara influence is also clearly expressed in many of the interesting fragments preserved in the Mathura Museum. One of them consists of the lower portion of a figure seated in the European fashion on a wicker-work chair. The sandaled left foot is placed on an ornamental foot-stool at the side of the empty right sandal. Evidently the right which is broken, was drawn up. This peculiar position which has become typical for the Bodhisattwas of mediæval art is first found in Gandhara. It is obvious that the Mathura fragment is a copy of Græco-Buddhist sculptures, like the inscribed Bodhisattwa from Loriyan Tangai in the Calcutta Museum (vide Prof. Sergius D' Oldenburg, "Notes on Buddhist Art," translated by Leo Weiner, p. 185). Again in the Mathura representation of the four great events of Buddha's life, not only the Gandhara influence is traceable in every individual scene, but their general arrangement is evidently derived from the North-west. In the Gandhara examples, however, the classical character is much more clearly expressed, and those from Mathura are mere worthless imitations.

Thus we see that Mr. V. A. Smith and Prof. Grünwedel are not quite correct in holding that the Mathura School exhibited an earlier Greek influence than that of Gandhara. Indeed the opposite view, which has been propounded by M. Foucher with great lucidity and is endorsed by such eminent archæologists of the present day, as Dr. J. Ph. Vogel and Sir John Marshall, seems to be plausible. "The Mathura School" says Dr. Vogel, "far from being a direct and early expression of Greek influence, received its classical inspiration indirectly through Gandhara. The influence of the Græco-Buddhist School in all later Buddhist sculptures has so clearly been shown in M. Foucher's standard work that no doubt can subsist on the point. Mathura owing to its geographical position and to its political importance during the Kushana period was the first to feel that influence. This explains the mixed character of the Mathura School in which we find on the one hand, a direct continuation of the old Indian art of Bharut and Sanchi and on the other hand, the classical influence derived from the Gandhara". Sir John Marshall in his most recent work, "A Guide to Sanchi" (1918) lends support to this theory. "The art of Mathura during the Satrapal and Kushana periods," says the distinguished archæologist, "resulted from a combination of two Schools the Early Indian on the one hand, and the Semi-Hellenistic school of the North-west on the other. Owing to the close connection of Mathura first with the Scytho-Parthian kingdom of Taxila, and afterwards with the Empire of the Kushanas, the influx of the pseudo-classical art was strong enough to interrupt and enervate the older traditions of Hindustan, but at the same time too weak in its environment to maintain its own individuality. It was no longer a case of Indian art being vitalised by the inspiration of the West, but of its being deadened by its embrace." (Vide also Foucher, "L'Art Gréco-Bouddhique du Gandhara," Tome I. p. 322 et p. 615 and "The Beginnings of Buddhist Art.").

SECTION IV.

Criticism on the Indo-Hellenistic Sculptures in general.

The general impression produced by the study of Gandhara Sculptures is that they form a class standing to a considerable extent apart from the main current of the evolution of art within the limits of India. M. Foucher has succeeded in demonstrating clearly that "the Gandhara School has no direct filial relations with the earlier art of Maurya and Sunga times, notwithstanding the appearance in both of certain elements common to the Hellenistic art of Western Asia. The artists of the North-west were masters of the technique of Asia Minor and had no need to copy tritons, centaurs and so forth from the works of their humbler predecessors in the interior." The true view seems to be that whatever may be the extent and sources of foreign influence on the work of early Indian Sculptors, the rapid development of the Gandhara School during the first century B. C. and the first century A. D. was the direct result of a fresh importation into the frontier regions by accomplished artists, introduced from outside, of Hellenistic ideas expressed in the forms then current throughout the Roman Empire ; such importation of artists and ideas appears to have been closely associated with and dependent on the extension of the foreign Kushana or Indo-Scythian Empire, as it gradually advanced its borders from the Oxus to the Ganges and possibly as far as the Nerbudda. All the evidence we have leads to the inference that the rapid development and extension of the distinct Gandhara School with its characteristic Indo-Corinthian capitals, were effected under the patronage of the great Kushana kings and their immediate predecessors, who must have imported foreign artists and through their agency have applied the Hellenistic technique to Indian subjects, much farther than had ever been done before. Such foreign artists, accredited by royal authority and fashion of the Court would have been readily accepted as teachers by the local Indian sculptors, who in their usual way would have proceeded to adapt the new methods to their own purposes, sometimes perhaps improving on the instructions of their masters.

It is obvious that the foreign .elements in the art of Gandhara tended to diminish as time went on, and that generally speaking, the sculptures with a most clearly marked

Greek character should be considered ancient and those most Indianised as comparatively of recent date. But this criterion, it must be admitted, affords no infallible test of age. Some of the best finished works may have been executed in Hellenistic style by clever Indian imitators, long after its introduction just as in the Moghul paintings of the 16th century A. D., we find close imitations of Persian models side by side and contemporary with paintings profoundly Indianised.

Most European critics, convinced of the unapproachable excellence of the highest type of Greek art, the model of the less beautiful Hellenistic art, see in the process of gradual Indianisation, a marked decadence. But the critics of the new "nationalist" School are persuaded that this view is erroneous and that the process of Indianisation is in itself an artistic improvement. Mr. E. B. Havell, in general agreement with Dr. A. K. Coomarswamy, teaches us that the earliest Gandhara Sculptors were no better than mechanical craftsmen, hirelings following more or less impure Hellenistic traditions, engaged by frontier kings in the manufacture of inferior objects of handicraft, which are mere "soulless puppets, debased types of the Greek and Roman pantheon posing uncomfortably in the attitudes of Indian asceticism, and tarred with vices of commercialism, insincerity and want of spirituality conspicuous in the earliest examples." The indictment continues :—"The insincerity and want of spirituality typical of nearly all the art of Gandhara are most conspicuous in the earliest examples, or those which are attributed to the first century of our era when the Roman influence was strongest. Two centuries later, in the sculptures of Loriyan Tangai Monastery, which Professor Gründwedel describes as belonging to the best period of Gandhara, the art had become more Indian, more national and more spiritual, but it has not yet achieved the true ideal of Indian art. Since, however, it is

Indian influence, Indian thought which has so far perfected the style, it is surely incorrect to say that the ideal of Indian Buddhist art has been created by foreigners. Foreign hands may have had the tools, but the influence which have dominated the art have been throughout Indian..............The perfected ideal of Indian art is far in advance of the Gandhara type, as the art of the Parthenon surpasses the art of Gandhara. Neither artistically is it possible to place the best Gandhara sculpture on the same plane with that of Borobodur, Elephanta or Ellora or with the best modern Nepalese metal-work." ("Indian Sculpture and Painting," pp. 45 et seq.). Again, Dr. Coomarswamy declares that "just as through all the Indian Schools of thought, there runs like a golden thread, the fundamental idealism of the Upanishads—the Vedanta, so in all Indian art there is a unity that underlies all its bewildering variety. This unifying principle is here also Idealism, and this must of necessity have been so, for the synthesis of Indian thought is one, not many" (vide "Aims of Indian Art").

The substance of these criticisms seems to mean that all high-class Indian Sculpture must be an expression of Brahminical metaphysics, nothing else being truly Indian or national. But the Gandhara artists who certainly did not worry themselves about "a superhuman transcendental body," or take any interest in the Upanishads, agreed in those respects with the artists of all the early Buddhist Schools, who were nevertheless just as Indian and national, as any 9th century Brahman could be. Although the technique of Gandhara differed widely from that of Bharut, Sanchi and the rest, all the early Buddhist Schools, that of Gandhara included, were animated by the Buddhist kindly humanistic spirit as different as possible from the Tantric notions dominating mediæval art, both Brahminical and Buddhistic, but equally Indian. We are not entitled to denounce Gandhara Art as "lacking in spirituality" merely because it does not express the ideas of Ellora and Elephanta. As a matter of fact, many of the good Gandhara sculptures may be fairly held to express with admirable feeling and sincerity, the ideal of a saintly Indian and to be not "lacking in dignity." For instance, the beautiful Bodhisattwa image (now in the Berlin Museum) is very far from being a "soulless puppet"; the Kuvera, in the Lahore Museum, has a good share of "restrained dignity." The best works of the Gandhara School are deserving of high commendation for their æsthetic, technical and plastic qualities to use Dr. Fergusson's terminology; or in other words, because they are intrinsically beautiful, skilfully executed, and well adapted to express both the ideal of the artist and the religious sentiment of the patrons.

Thus, one cannot but feel sorry that in attacking the older school of critics—already be it said, sufficiently discredited—Mr. Havell and Dr. Coomarswamy should go to the opposite extreme. For by doing so, they undoubtedly weaken a good case and give a handle to their opponents for justifiable criticism. Let us take for example, Dr. Coomarswamy's special pleading in support of the proposition that Gandhara art played no part in evolving the ideal type of the Buddha. If Indian art owed nothing to Hellenistic influence in the invention of these types, how comes it that no trace of such types existed in India before the advent of that influence? We do not wish to imply for one moment, that Greek art pointed the way to transcendantalism. That was a peculiar quality of Oriental Art, and Greeks themselves would no doubt have ridiculed the idea of suppressing physical beauty in order to express the beauty of the soul. But the conclusion, to which all the evidence now available, leads us is that it was under the influence of Hellenistic iconism that the chief standard types of Buddha were first evolved, and it was reserved for Indian artists to infuse into those types their own spiritual conceptions. Of a truth, it was no reproach to Indian art that it was thus able to borrow forms and ideas from the Greeks. On the contrary, it was its particular merit that it had strength enough to assimilate those forms and ideas so completely to its own purpose without losing its own vitality and character. So says, M. Maurice Maindron in his "L'Art Indien", "L'influence hellénique, ne resta pas prépondérante son action éphémère ne modifia en rein le génie artistique hindou. Il à été jugé par la plupart des auteurs avec une injustice dont la seule excuse paraît être l'extraordinaire naïvête quand ce n'est pas le rigorisme piétiste aussi exagéré qui le fanatisme des conquérants musalmans." At present, owing to æsthetic bias or to nationalist rancour, it is the fashion to make the school of Gandhara concede its manifest superiority by a systematic blackening of its noblest productions. We refuse in this connection to share either the unjustifiable contempt of the old criticism for native inspiration, or the ill-disguised spite of the new against the foreign make. It is not the father or the mother who has formed the child ; it is the father *and* the mother. The Indian mind has taken a part no less essential than has Greek genius in the production of the Gandhara sculptures. It is a case where the East and the West could have done nothing without each other.

As we have already more than once pointed out that within the limits of India however, the art of Gandhara was not widely propagated. Perhaps the only place where the influence can be traced clearly is Mathura. Political conditions seem to have been responsible to a great extent for the failure of the art of the North-western frontier to penetrate deeply into the interior.

The disappearance of Hellenism in the Far East is

intimately connected with the problem of Kanishka. Greek was understood, as we have seen, in Kanishka's dominions; "Yavanas" ruled in Kabul up to or almost up to the commencement of Christian era. A quarter of a century later, Alexandropolis in Arachosia was still an autonomous Greek city (vide Isidore, Mans. Parth). If we can determine the time when Hellenism disappeared in those regions, we can state definitely when Hellenism ceased to exercise its influence on Indian Art. Now, the barbarism of invaders from Central Asia, and the consequent isolation of the Greek colonists, were the main causes for the extinction of Hellenism in the East. At the commencement of the 2nd century A.D., the rule of the Greek princes in the Kabul valley was finally extinguished. The Kushana Empire broke up in the time of Vasudeva, the successor of Huvishka and was probably followed by a period of anarchy, of which there are no records. The next empire of the Guptas, who completed the conquest of the Gangetic valley, about the middle of the 4th century A.D., produced an indigenous School of Art, without any reference whatever, to Hellenic ideas and Hellenic models.

BIBLIOGRAPHY

1. Fergusson ... "The Cave-temples of India."
2. " ... ... "History of Indian and Eastern Architecture."
3. " ... ... "Tree and Serpent Worship"
4. Cunningham, A. ... "Ancient Geography of India."
5. " ... ... "Reports of the Archæological Survey of India," vol. V.

6. Cunningham, A. ... "The Bhilsa Topes."
7. " ... ... "The Stupa of Bharut."
8. Grünwedel ... "Buddhistische Kunst in Indien."
9. Perrot and Chipiez ... "History of Art in Persia."
10. Langles, L. ... "Monuments anciens et modernes de l'Hindoustan."
11. Griffin ... ... "The Famous Monuments of Central India."
12. Gustave le Bon ... "Les Monuments de l'Inde."
13. Foucher, A. ... "L'Art Gréco-Bouddhique du Gandhara."
14. Curtius ... ... "Die Griechische Kunst in Indien."
15. Lübke, Wilhelm ... "Geschichte der Plastik."
16. Rājendra Lāla Mitra ... "Buddha-Gaya, the hermitage of Sakya Muni."
17. Smith, V. A. ... "A History of Fine Art in India and Ceylon."
18. Havell, E. B. ... "Indian Sculpture and Painting."
19. Stein, M. A. ... "The Sand-buried Ruins of Khotan."
20. Fr. W. Von Bissing ... "Prähistorische Topfe aus Indien und aus Aegypten."
21. Prinsep, J. ... "Notes on the discovery of a relic of Grecian Sculpture in Upper India."
22. Burgess, J. ... "Ancient Monuments."
23. Growse ... ... "Mathura, a district memoir."
24. Dowson ... ... "Ancient Inscriptions from Mathura."
25. Bühler, G. ... "Mathura lion-pillar inscriptions."
26. Indrāji, B. ... "The Northern Kshatrapas."
27. Führer ... ... "Indo-Scythic Architecture and Sculpture of the Mathura School."
28. Smith, V. A. ... "The Jaina-stupa and other antiquities of Mathura."
29. Lüders ... ... "Epigraphical Notes" in Indian Antiquary, vol. xxxiii (1904.)
30. Bühler, G. ... "Specimens of Jaina Sculptures from Mathura" in Epigraphia Indica, vol. II. p. 311 ff.
31. Vogel, J. Ph. ... "Epigraphical Discoveries at Sarnath," in Epigraphia Indica, vol. viii.

32. Bloch, T. ... ... "Two Inscriptions on Buddhist Images" in Epigraphia Indica, vol. viii, pp. 179 et seq.

33. Foucher, A ... "Les Bas-reliefs du stupa de Sikri" in Journal Asiatique (1905) p. 313.

34. Lefmann ... ... "Lalita-Vistāra."

35. D'Oldenburg, Sergius ... "Notes on Buddhist Art" translated by Leo Weiner.

36. Maindron, M. ... "L'Art Indien."

37. Spooner, D. B. ... "Handbook to Sculpture in the Peshawar Museum."

38. Birdwood, G. ... "Industrial Arts of India."

39. Mitchell ... ... "History of Ancient Sculpture."

40. Cole ... ... "Græco-Buddhist Sculptures from Yusufzai."

41. Coomarswamy, A. K. ... "Mediæval Singhalese Art."

42. " ... "Viswakarma; Examples of Indian Architecture, Sculpture, Painting, Handicraft etc."

43. Strzygowski, J. ... "Hellenistische und Koptische Kunst in Alexandria."

44. Griffiths ... ... "Buddhist Cave-temples of Ajanta."

45. Stein, M. A. ... "Ruins of Desert Cathay."

46. Mazeliére ... ... "Moines et ascetes Indiens."

47. Le Grande Encyclopédie, Arts. "Inde," "Art."

48. Actes in Sixième Congrés international des Orientalistes tenu en 1883, a Lèide, Part III, Sec. ii pp. 142 ff.

49. Epigraphia Indica, Vol. ix, pp. 136 et seq.

50. Journals of the Royal Asiatic Society, 1894, pp. 525-54; 1871 (N. S.) pp. 182 ff.

51. Burnell ... ... "Elements of South-Indian Palæography." 1911, 1912 pp. 1012-18.

52. Anesaki, M. ... "Buddhist Art."

53. Gardner, E. ... "Handbook of Greek Sculpture."

54. Ram Raz ... ... "Essay on the Architecture of the Hindus."

55. Okakura, K. ... "The Ideals of the East with special reference to the Art of Japan."

56. Lévi, Sylvain ... "Quid de Græcis Veterum Indorum Monumenta Tradiderint."
57. Harris, George ... "Theory of Arts."
58. Gopinath Row ... "Elements of Hindu Iconography."
59. Finot, Louis ... "Les Lapidaires Indiens."
60. Foucher, A. ... "Notes on Ancient Geography of Gandhara."
61. " ... ... "The Beginnings of Buddhist Art."
62. Stein, M. A. ... "Explorations in Central Asia," 1906-8.
63. Deniker, J. ... "The Gods of Northern Buddhism."

CHAPTER III

PAINTING

SECTION I

Indian Painting: Probably of Native Origin. "Indian Fresco-buono." Ajanta Caves.

NATURALLY there are no surviving examples of primitive work of this character in India where earth and leaves supply the pigments and materials. We are forced to rely upon inference and literary evidence for anything even as old as the oldest stone-sculptures, at which time equally developed Schools of Painting must also have existed. Painting was one of the sixty four arts and sciences practised according to the tradition in ancient India. It is frequently referred to in the Ramayana and the Mahabharata. It may have been known in a primitive form to the Indians before the invasion of Alexander the Great. It is very likely indeed that the foundation of the craft as now surviving in Western India, dates like many other things of Græco-Buddhistic culture, from the time of the spread of Art in the reigns of Maurya Kings and that of the great intellectual stimulus resulting from the contact of the art of Bharut with the more primitive art of which we have scarcely any remains, but which may have existed in ancient India. Thus it is easily understood that owing partly to the destructive influence of a tropical climate acting on materials ordinarily much less durable than stone or metal, and partly to the greater facilities which they offer to the destructive propensities of the Vandal and Philistine, the existing records of pictorial art are much fewer than those of Sculpture.

The oldest Indian pictures, perhaps the most ancient extant specimens of Oriental painting, excepting the Egyptian, are found in the Jogimāra Cave of the Ramgarh Hills in the Surguza State, a wild region lying to the south of Mirzapore District and now attached to the Central Provinces. The early date of these Paintings which are fairly well-preserved, is attested by inscriptions evidently contemporary, and by the style which recalls that of the sculptures at Sanchi and Bharut. They probably date from the second century before Christ.

"One of the oldest pictorial processes", writes Mr. Havell, in his "Indian Sculpture and Painting" (p. 155), "in India as in Egypt was fresco-painting, that is painting on a prepared surface of lime spread on a wall, brick or stone". The true process of fresco-painting—"the fresco-buono" as it is called in Italy,—in which the painting is begun and finished piece by piece on a section of a wall seems to have been practised in India from very early times but tempera painting was more common, as it is still in the present day. Indian "fresco-buono", when the wall is a suitable one, is an exceedingly permanent process for interior decoration and much more durable in a tropical climate than oil-painting. But as it was largely used in exposed situations or in buildings which were not in themselves of a permanent nature very few of the early Indian fresco-paintings have survived except those in the Ajanta Cave-temples (the earliest of which is said to have been executed in the second or first century B.C. but most of which were undertaken under the Gupta Dynasty) and in a few similar ones in Ceylon."

Buried in the dry sands of Egypt which are a wonderful preservative of antiquities, fresco-paintings have retained their freshness in tact for thousands of years (compare the wonderful and varied colours employed in the decoration of the Hypostyle Halls at Karnak, Luxor, Thebes and Memphis, vide Perrot and Chipiez, "History of Ancient Egyptian Art"). No painting had been discovered from Indian deserts, except in recent years; the sand-buried ruins of Khotan and Turkestan have yielded numerous fresco-paintings of extraordinary interest and almost as perfect in colour as when they were painted *e.g.* in the Buddhist Shrines at Ming-Oi site in the prefect of Kara-Shahr (vide M.A. Stein, "Ancient Khotan"; and "The Ruins of Desert Cathay"). "The Græco-Buddhist Sculpture of Gandhara" says Sir M. A. Stein, "has been known to abound in exactly corresponding examples of poses and drapery, borrowed straight from classical modelling. But it was reserved for the fresco fragments brought to light at this most distant corner of Tarim basin to prove that this dependence on Western art was at first equally close as far as Painting is concerned and traceable even in the methods of technique. In the latter respect, no more striking testimony could be desired than that supplied by the regular employment of methods of "light and shade" wherever flesh is painted in the frescoes. The use of "chiaroscuro", so well-known to classical painting, had never before been observed in the old pictorial works of India, Central Asia or the Far East. The frescoes of Miran display it invariably in all the exposed portions of the body. Many other details of the technique make it obvious that the painters of those Miran frescoes had inherited from their Western masters methods of producing a finished effect with such economy of work as constant application demanded." These tell us a great deal of the pictorial art of the Indian Buddhist monasteries in the early centuries of the Christian era and of its progress eastwards into China and Japan. (The most important of these are now preserved in the Ethnographical Museum at Berlin). The description and illustration of them however must be left to their fortunate discoverers, Dr. Von Lecoq, Professor Grünwedel and Sir Marc Aurel Stein. Many of these relics are evidently of exceptional interest and value, notably those which came from that rich storehouse, the walled-in rock-chamber of the Grotto of the Thousand Buddhas at Tun-huang, where they had remained, undisturbed by man and unharmed by time during nine or ten centuries. These include the oldest existing specimens of Chinese Buddhist pictorial art; Runic-Turki, Tibetan and Manichean writings; illuminated temple-scrolls, banners and ex-votos on silk and brocade, all miraculously preserved for their pre-destined resting place in the British Museum. "It seemed," pertinently observes Dr. Stein, "as if three civilisations, from the East, West and South had combined to leave their written traces at this lonely watch-station in the desert."

But the earliest paintings actually surviving in India are the famous Ajanta paintings of the 4th century A.D. This period was one of great artistic activity, which began in India in the fourth century under the Gupta Dynasty and absorbed Dravidian tradition into its own. The excellent character of the art of the period may be judged best from the Ajanta wall-paintings and Ellora sculptures. The early Chinese historians speak in rapturous terms of the images made in Southern India and it is clear that the fourth and fifth centuries were one of the great periods of Indian art (vide Dr. A. K. Coomarswamy, "Viswakarma; Examples of Indian Architecture, Sculpture, Painting, Handicraft"). Dr. Fergusson who visited the Buddhist cave-temples of Ajanta in 1838-39 wrote: "The style of the paintings cannot of course bear comparison with the European painting of the present day, but they are certainly superior to the style of Europe during the age in which they were executed; the perspective grouping and details are better and the story better told than in any painting anterior to Orcagna and Fiesole. The style however is not European, but more resembles Chinese art, particularly in the flatness and want of shadow". With regard to the painted ornament, the same authority said, "It is not at all unlike that still existing in the Baths of Titus".

Yet while the touch and convention are Eastern and the decorative accessories of the hieratic art of the farther East are used, one is not chilled by its rigid formalism. In Buddhist pictures of Tibet, Nepal, China, Japan, Java and Burma, there is at first sight a marvellous unity of style, resulting in part from the use of the same symbolic and decorative materials, the same positions and arrangement of figures which bear a striking resemblance to the Ajanta work. As in other early work much of the later science of art is absent; figures are crowded into the subjects, while the constant efforts to reproduce the incidents consecutively and to tell the story at length, leads to a bewildering repetition of the leading figure in the same picture. The considered verdict of Mr. Griffiths who spent 13 years in the close loving study of the Indian Paintings, may be accepted as a sound general criticism.

"It is not surprising," says Mr. Griffiths in "The Buddhist Cave-temples of Ajanta," "that paintings on stucco all over the world should bear a certain resemblance to each other. Egyptian tombs, Etruscan frescoes and painted stuccoes of Herculaneum and Pompeii furnish examples almost identical with those of Ajanta in technical details.

But as a readily available example, the fragment of the fresco-painting by Ambrogio Lorenzati (14th century) of heads of nuns in the National Gallery is singularly like the Ajanta work in colours, execution and treatment, the forms being drawn with a delicate brown outline and the flesh-tints and drapery flatly put in with very little modelling. The Ajanta workmanship is admirable, long subtle curves are drawn with great precision in a line of unvarying thickness with one sweep of the brush, both on the vertical surface of the walls and on the more difficult plane of the ceilings, showing consummate skill and manual dexterity. The touch is often bold and vigorous, the handling broad and in some cases the impaste is as solid as in the best Pompeian work" (see the excellent plates in Mr. Griffiths' volume and in Mrs. Herringham's Frescoes of Ajanta).

"For the purposes of art-education", asserts Mr. Griffiths "no better example could be placed before an Indian art-student than those to be found in the Caves of Ajanta. Here we have art with life in it, human face full of expression, limbs drawn with grace and action, flowers which bloom, birds which soar and beasts that spring or fight or patiently carry burdens; all are taken from Nature's Book—growing after her pattern."

Section II

Indian Painting, mainly religious: employment of vivid colours. Ajanta Caves and Roman Catacombs. The indigenous School of Painting in Buddhist Monasteries (Universities).

If one wants to form an idea of the original painting of the Hindus, he should do well to study not only their miniatures and their portraits, ancient and modern, but even their figurations of Pauranic divinities as executed in paints or in varnish applied on glass. There were also reproduced scenes from ordinary life. These paintings were ordinarily sketched upon strong paper or upon sheets of talc. The productions of this ordinary art are far from being despicable; the gods and godesses are here represented with great care, with a knowledge of anatomical details, and a understanding of colours that deserve high credit. Since the bygone ages, Indian paintings representing the conventional types along with sculptures on the temple-walls, have preserved for us the traditions of Hindu Mythology. The proportions of the figures, their attitudes, their expressions, their attributes are invariably in these two processes, the same. As a sign of supernatural power, the divine personalities are supplied with many pairs of limbs; above all, they have numerous arms to wield the diverse weapons, an inseparable symbol of divinity. Seated upon a galloping ram, the double-faced Agni holds in his six hands either weapons or liturgic objects. The Vedic Surya, as represented in the ancient Indian sculptures, drives the Chariot of Helios whose only horse possesses seven heads, executed by a theoretical simplification.

In these paintings, the coloration is more vivid and more glaring than in ordinary ones. M. Emile Senart tells us with good reason: "La magnificence orientale oscille communiment entre l'accumulation de richesses tres positives, entassement de perles et des pierres précieuses, et un déploiement de splendeurs plus voyantes que coûteuses, dont quelque coleurs éclatantes et un peu de clinquant font le frais". It is this richness that the Indian artists were fond of representing ; they used their skill in this direction without ever for a moment thinking to give life to those hieratic figures which they reproduced from generation to generation, since time immemorial. So M. Gustave le Bon declares with reason, "Dans sa peinture comme dans la litterature l'Inde en est demeurée a une phase d'evolution correspondant à peu près ou moyen âge".

The mention of an Indian School of Painting must seem absurd to a reader, acquainted only with modern India, where no trace of the existence of the pictorial art can be discerned except "the pretty though conventional miniatures," which a few craftsmen at Delhi and Agra are still able to execute. But whatever may be the merits and demerits of modern productions, ancient India, as we have already noticed, certainly produced paintings which deserve to be ranked as works of art. "Cependant", says the brilliant French Orientalist, M. Sylvain Lévi, "dans l'Inde ancienne, la peinture a brillé du plus vif éclat elle y fut cultivée avec passion. Les palais avaient des vastes galeries ornées des tableaux qui retracaient les plus fameux episodes de la legende et de l'épopée, une personne d'une bonne education, sous distinction de rang et de sexe, sovait peindre un portrait".

The bas-reliefs in different colours were developed independently apart from the paintings, at an early period. At the first appearance, the paintings in the caves of Ajanta seem to be somewhat of a clumsy style ; the landscapes are puerile, the figures are without models, the visages are copied with care but without life. But then we come to a period, when more finished art was produced : *e.g.* in the mystic scene, where Buddha is represented as preaching to the Apsaras. It is curious to observe however, that the closest parallels to Ajanta paintings are to be found among the remains of the early Christian art. These parallels are to be found in places where we should hardly expect them, the Catacombs of Rome. Dr. Fergusson quotes with approval the following criticism of Mr. Griffiths on a painting depicting flying figures in the so-called Zodiac Caves, "whether we look at its purity of outline or the elegance of the grouping, it is one of the most pleasing of the smaller paintings at Ajanta and more nearly approaches the form of art found in Italy in the 13th or the 14th centuries than any other example there. For pathos and sentiment and the unmistakable way of telling stories, I consider it cannot be surpassed in the history of Art. The Florentines could have put better drawing, and the Venetians better colour, but neither could have thrown greater expression into it".

The obvious comparison with ancient Italian art made by Dr. Fergusson, who considered the Ajanta paintings to be better than anything in Europe before the time of Orcagna in the 14th and even Fiesole (Fra Angelico) in the 15th century, speaks volumes with regard to the originality and exquisite beauty of the Indian Paintings. Similarly, Mr. Havell, who selects the charming "Mother and Child" in Cave xvii (Griffiths, Fig. 76) as the most attractive specimen of Ajanta art, finds on the frescoes the same intense love of Nature and spiritual devotion, as are noticeable in the sculptures of Borobodur and compares the "exquisite sentiment" of the picture selected, with the wonderful Madonnas of Giovanni Bellini. But historically the most interesting of these paintings is a large one in the First Cave, representing an incident in the reign of Pulikesin II, in whose kingdom of Maharashtra, Ajanta was situated. Mr. Vincent A. Smith says of this

Painting, "It is still easily recognisable as a vivid representation of the ceremonial attending the presentation of their credentials by the Persian Envoys from Khushru II to Pulikeshin in the 36th year of his reign. A.D. 625-6. This picture in addition to its interest as a contemporary record of unusual political relations between India and Persia, is of the highest value as a landmark in the history of Art. It not only fixes the date of some of the most important paintings at Ajanta and so establishes a standard by which the date of the others can be judged, but it also proves or goes a long way towards proving, that the Ajanta School of pictorial art was derived directly from Persia and ultimately from Greece" (Early History of India, p. 325). In the last sentence, Mr. Vincent Smith shows the unconscious bias of the European Orientalist. The Ajanta School, according to eminent archæologists, had been in existence 3 or 4 hundred years before this particular painting was executed, a length of time which is surely sufficient to establish a right to be considered Indian.

But, Sir M. A. Stein's recent remarkable explorations in the old Buddhist monasteries of Turkestan have brought to light the affinities of art of north-western India, with that of China and Central Asia. When this unwearied traveller plunged into Seistan in November 1915, he discovered the remains of a large Buddhist monastery—the first ever traced on Iranian soil—on a hill called Kohi-Khwāja. Hidden behind later masonry, there came to light remarkable fresco-remains, dating back undoubtedly to the Sassanian period (226 A.D.-641 A.D.). Wall paintings of a distinctly Hellenistic style and probably *older*, were found on the wall of a gallery below the high terrace, bearing the main shrine. The importance of these pictorial relics, protected from the ravages of man and atmospheric moisture, is great. They illustrate for the first time *in situ* the Iranian link of the chain which, long surmised by conjecture, connects the Græco-Buddhist art of the extreme north-west of India with the Buddhist art of Central Asia and the Iranian plateau. "The style of these art-relics," says Sir Aurel Stein in his "Explorations in Central Asia," "displayed quite as clearly as the works of ancient Khotan, the predominant influence of Græco-Buddhist models, brought from the extreme north-west of India." Hiouen Tsang, the Buddhist pilgrim from China, who visited India in the seventh century, says that artists from Bactria were employed to paint the Buddhist monasteries during the time of Kanishka, King of Gandhara, about the first century of the Christian era, and that the convent of Serika was famous for its mural paintings. But we must not conclude from this that the traditions of Indian Painting were entirely confined to foreign products. The Universities of ancient India, like those of Taksashila (Taxila) near modern Peshawar, Nalanda in Bengal and Sridhanya Kataka oṇ the banks of the Krishna comprised Schools of religious painting and sculpture ; and in these great culture-centres of India, all foreign artistic ideas were gradually transformed by Indian thought, and nationalised.

Yet in an essay on the Indian Schools of Painting (J.A.S.B. Vol. lviii, p. 117) Mr. Smith said that "whoever seriously undertakes the critical study of the paintings of Ajanta and Bagh, will find, I have no doubt, that the artists drew their inspiration from the West, and I think he will also find that their style was a local development of the cosmopolitan art of the contemporary Roman Empire". Here again we venture to point out that Mr. V. A. Smith, like Professor Grünwedel and others, confuses the assimilation of foreign technique by Indian traditional craftsmanship with artistic inspiration. The Buddhist monastic Schools of Northern

India, from which the art of Ajanta was derived, were sufficiently cosmopolitan in character to account for all the foreign details which were found in these paintings, but their title to be considered Indian is just as valid as that of the Schools of Athens to be called Greek, those of Italy to be Italian and perhaps stronger than that of the Schools of Oxford to be called English.

BIBLIOGRAPHY.

1. Griffiths ... "The Buddhist Cave-temples of Ajanta."
2. Binyon, Laurence ... "Painting in the Far East."
3. Coomaraswamy, A.K.... "Mediæval Singhalese Art."
4. " ... "Viswakarma : Examples of Indian Architecture, Sculpture, Painting, Handicraft etc."
5. Mosso, Angelo ... "The Dawn of the Mediterranean Civilisation."
6. D'Oldenburg, Sergius... "Notes on Buddhist Art", translated by Leo Weiner.
7. Maindron, Maurice ... "L'Art Indien".
8. Fr. W. Von Bissing ... "Prähistorische Topfe aus Indien und aus Aegypten."
9. Stein, M.A. ... "Ancient Khotan."
10. Havell, E.B. ... "Indian Sculpture and Painting."
11. Smith, V. A. ... "A History of Fine Art in India and Ceylon."
12. Maisey, F.C. ... "Sanchi and its Remains."
13. Cunningham, A. ... "Excavation of Ellora."
14. Gustave le Bon ... "Les Monuments de l'Inde."
15. Daniell ... "Oriental Scenery."
16. Langles, L. ... "Monuments anciens at modernes de l'Hindoustan."
17. Muller ... "Ancient Art and its Remains; or a Manual of the Archæology of Art."

18. Fergusson ... "Tree and Serpent Worship"
19. Grünwedel ... "Buddhistische Kunst in Indien."
20. Perrot and Chipiez ... "History of Art in Persia."
21. Kügler ... "Handbook of Painting," trans. by Layard.
22. Foucher, A. ... "Catalogue des Peintures Nepalaises et Tibetaines" (à la Bibliothéque de l'Institute de France).
23. Mrs. Herringham ... "The Frescoes of Ajanta" (Burlington Magazine, Vol. xvii).
24. Martin, F.R. ... "The Miniature Painting and Painters of Persia, India and Turkey," 2 Vols. London, 1912.
25. Okakura, Kakasu ... "The Ideals of the East with special reference to the art of Japan."
26. Venkatasubbiah, A. ... "The Kalas," Madras. 1911.
27. Foucher, A. ... "The Beginnings of Buddhist Art."
28. Deniker, J. ... "The Gods of Northern Buddhism", 1914.

CHAPTER IV

COINAGE

SECTION I

First discovery of Greek Coins in Beghram.

ABOUT twenty miles east of the modern city of Kabul, there is a level piece of tableland extending over six square miles, called the plain of Beghram. The surface was strewn over with fragments of pottery, metals and sculptures. Here and there arose solitary mounds of stone and brick, which seemed to indicate the remains of human habitations. The happy situation of this plain at a spot where rivers meet and where the main-roads and mountain passes converge from all the four quarters and the interesting vestiges visible on the surface of the ground—all this would unmistakably show that here had once existed a great capital. In modern times, the plain had become a sheep pasture. A vague avarice prompted the shepherds to scratch up the soil in search of treasure. Soon they found seals, rings, bits of metals and coins in vast quantities. The coins which were principally copper, they would hawk about the city of Kabul. As these "treasure-troves" became frequent, the trade began to thrive. And soon the mint-masters and the copper-smiths of the city repaired to the great plain, visited the tents of the shepherds and purchased the coins by weight. It was estimated that 30,000 coins a year, used to be procured in this manner and melted down. And thus were consigned to indiscriminate destruction, myriads of coins, which the greatest academicians in Europe would have honoured with a place in their cabinets and which might have told us more about Central Asia, than all the histories that ever were written. At last in July 1833, Mr. Masson being engaged in searching for the site of one, among the many "Alexandrias" founded by Alexander the Great, happened to visit this plain. He first met with eighty coins. These specimens appearing to be valuable, he prosecuted the search, until he had got together upwards of 30,000 coins of which the greater part was copper and the remainder silver and gold. From this collection, were evolved the annals of Indo-Bactria and the history of Greek connection with the East. The Asiatic Society's Journal was the organ through which these results were announced to the public. Mr. Masson himself contributed a great many papers. But the most elaborate analysis was made by James Prinsep (vide Journal of the Royal Asiatic Society, vols. I-VII *passim*). A great discrepancy arose at the outset. The inscriptions on the obverse of the medal were Greek, but on the reverse, an unknown character presented itself. The first object was to decipher this character. Mr. Masson had pointed out some Pehlvi signs, which had been found to stand for certain Greek names. "It struck me," wrote Mr. Prinsep, "that if the genuine Greek names were faithfully expressed in unknown character, a clue through them might be formed to unravel the value of a portion of the alphabet, which might in its turn be applied to the translated epithets and thus lead to a knowledge of the language employed." This plan was followed out with infinite labour and skill and met with complete success. The interest attaching to these discoveries was not confined to India. The news spread to Europe and created a sensation in the academic circles of London, Paris, Vienna, Berlin, Göttingen and Bonn. The first great scholar who took up the subject was M. Raol Rochette. He was followed in his own country, by M. Jacquet and in Germany by the Grotefends, Müller and Arseth. The Journal des Savans, the Journal Asiatique, the Vienna Jahr-Bucher, the Vienna Oriental Journal, the Göttingen Anzeigen, and the Numismatic Journal of London, all vied with the Calcutta Journal in disseminating the results of Mr. Masson's discoveries and Mr. Prinsep's interpretations. Prof. Wilson's Ariana Antiqua, and Prof. Von Lassen's Geschichte der Griechischen Könige in Baktrien, Kabul und Indien, gave us learned dissertations on Bactrian and Scythian coinage and thus our knowledge of the early Indian Coinage was first gained.

Section II

Coinage: purely of indigenous origin, developed by the Greeks. The Greek Invasion and the Græco-Indian Coins.

The opinion expressed by M. Lenormant that the mechanical process of coining money properly so-called, was unknown to the Indians until they learned it from the Greeks after the invasion of Alexander, was vigorously combated by the late Mr. Thomas with considerable success. The truth seems to be that though all ancient Indian coinages, with the slightest pretensions to artistic merit, are ultimately traced to Greek origin, yet the idea of coining money and a knowledge of the simple mechanical processes necessary for the production of rude coins originated independently in India, or at least were not borrowed from the Greeks. Sir Alexander Cunningham asserted that the "so-called" punch-marked coins were "as old as 1000 B. C. and perhaps even older." The most ancient coinage of India, which seems to have been developed independently of any foreign influences generally followed the native system of weights as given in Manu Chapter VIII, verses 132 ff. Thus the valid reason for denying the Greek origin of the art of coinage in India is that, several classes of early Indian coins do not exhibit a single clear trace of Greek influence, whereas they are distinctly marked by special Indian characteristics. The coinage of India in its most primitive forms consisted of small, oblong, roughly rectangular plates of silver, without any impression on the surface, but struck to a definite standard of weight *viz.*, 32 ratis or 58½ grains. A slight improvement was made when these little plates of silver were stamped with rough devices of stars, trees and so forth. These devices were impressed by means of small punches not covering the face of the coins (vide Plates in Rapson's Indian Coins in "Grundriss der Indo-Arischen Philologie und Altertumskunde"). These punch-marked coins are destitute of legends and the purely Indian character of the devices and the Indian standard of weight, render it incredible that they should be the result of the Greek influence. The symbols, found on "the punch-marked" coinage, were used simply as the marks of localities and of individuals without any special religious significance. They were used primarily to denote either the localities at which the coins were struck, the authorities responsible for their issue, or the money changers through whose hands they passed (vide V. A. Smith, Ind. Mus. Cat. I. p. 131 : Thomas, E. "Ancient Indian Weights," p. 52). The earliest inscribed coins are proved by the characters used to belong approximately to the period of Asoka, whose inscriptions are the earliest examples of the use of alphabet, which afterwards developed into Devanagri.

The allusions to money, however, in the sacred literature of Sakya Muni are so frequent, and their occurrence in the

Vedic writings so rare that it would almost seem superfluous to seek for confirmatory Greek authority as to the evidence of the antiquity of the art of coinage, and the existence of coined money in that country. The classical writers, who quote or epitomise the narratives of the earlier eye-witnesses of Alexander's progress, and the more mature enquirers into the Indian civilisation are profuse in their references to the laws, manners and customs of the indigenous races ; and without doubt, the absence of metallic currency would immediately have struck observers, with whom in their own hemisphere, such a means of commercial exchange had become a fiscal necessity. We quote the subjoined statement from Pausanias in order to show how far it may be accepted as probable. Towards the end of the second century A. D., we know that north India was in possession of an ample currency, in the form of Græco-Bactrian and other silver pieces, combined with an unlimited supply of gold and copper from the mint of the Indo-Scythian kings. The observation might apply with equal justice to some of the nations on the south coast, who avowedly dispensed with a coinage till a later period. "But on road, I have observed the Lacedæmonians have a place which they call Booneta. This was once the house of King Polydorus, and after his death was bought off his wife for certain oxen, for at that time there was not any coin (*nómísma*), either of silver or gold, but according to ancient custom, they mutually gave and received for what they wanted, oxen and slaves and rude silver and gold. Indeed, even at present those that sail to the Indus report that Indian rewards are given for Grecian commodities which are carried thither, but the inhabitants are unacquainted with money (*nómísma*) though their country abounds with gold and brass." (Pausanias, III. xii, 3 ; translated by T. Taylor). But there occur incidentally palpable proofs of the use of coined money, in its advanced sense, in the texts of the best authorities, which may be well to cite with a view to dispose of obsolete objections and to preclude their revival. The first extract alludes to Alexander's entry into the capital of Sambus and the offerings of absolute money and elephants then presented. The next contribution to the test of monetary civilisation of the Indians at Taxila is even more emphatic and distinct in its terms. It is embodied in the text of Quintus Curtius : " Omphis permettente Alexandro, et regium insigne sumsit, et more gentes suæ nomen quod patris fuerat, 'Taxilen' appellonere populares, sequente nomine imperium en quemcumque transiret 15 Ergo cum per triduum hospitaliter Alexandrum accepisset, quarto, die, et " quantum frumenti copiis, quæs Hephæstion duxerat, prœbitum a se asset astendit, et aureas coronas ipsi amicisque omnibus, præter hæc signati argenti lxxx talenta dono dedit " (Q. Curtius, VIII. cxii, 14, 15). Such a theoretical stage of advanced development in the local currencies is practically supported by the ready adoption, on the part of the occupying Bactrian Greeks, of so many of the devices and peculiarities of the national coinage. Thus Agathocles and Pantaleon in Arachosia imitated the square form of piece, accepted the current Indian Pali alphabet of Asoka's inscriptions, the essential symbol of pre-Aryan civilisation, and in some cases to the exclusion of their ethnic Greek, adopted a new metal in the nickel, which we must suppose to have been indigenous in those parts. Mr. Prilaux adds in a note to his "Apollonius of Tyana," that the Indian money is "metal refined and prepared" (vide J.R.A.S. xviii, 72). The larger division of the Bactrian Greeks, who took the direction of the south-east, in a similar spirit submitted themselves to the square sections of metal, incorporated the official alphabet of their new dominions—in this instance, the contrasted Aryan adaptation of an early form of Phœnician (J.R.A.S.

viii, 333; Numismatic Chronicle iii, 1863), which they carried with them beyond the vanishing point of the Vedic Aryans without regard to local preferences, in the city of Mathura (Arrian, Indica viii, 318; Pliny vi, 22, 19). This city, judging by the deposited coins of the later Greek dynasties and the extant remains of the succeeding Indo-Scythians, must have been a place of considerable importance at this period (J.R.A.S., vol. 5, New Series, p. 182).

In the text of Yājñavalkya, the advanced authority on Hindu Law, who deals with a period when the Greeks had altogether passed away from the Indian stage and the Kadphises Yue-chi had been supplanted *inter alia* by their Kushana successors, we find mention of coins "with the mark of Siva" on one side, and with their scarcely recognisable Greek letters on the other. It should be noticed here, that all the Greek princes of Bactria made use of the Indo-Pali alphabet on the reverses of their coins in conjunction with their own proper Greek epigraphs on the obverse faces; and it was this combination of names and titles, which in the first instance encouraged Prinsep and Lassen to investigate into the nature of the alphabet itself and to lay the foundations of a decipherment of Asoka's bilingual inscriptions.

The Indians had their own coinage before the advent of the Greeks, for had the Indians waited till the Macedonians came to teach them, they would have spared themselves all those manifest efforts at invention and humbly have essayed to copy the perfect coins of Alexander now ready to their hands. "On a dit que," says M. Drouin in his "Monnaies Anciennes de l'Inde" (p. 107), "si c'etaient les Grecs qui avaient donné l'idée de la monnaie en général aux Hindus, ceux-ci auraient adopté le type rond de leur modêle au lieu de la forme irreguliére, qui, par consequent, la monnaie carrée existait avant Alexandre dans l'Inde." "A good deal of interval must have elapsed," says Mr. Edward Thomas in "Numismata Orientalia," vol. I, "between the original date of the issue of these punch-coins and the intrusion of the Greeks, as testified by the discovery of associated specimens of the local and exotic currencies, the former of which had been "much worn" in the ordinary traffic of the country, while the Greek pieces were so to say, new from the mint".

But at an early period, 'the owls of Athens' were carried in course of commerce to the East when the supply from the Athenian mint grew less (i. e. for about a century before 322 B. C.), and when that mint was closed, imitations were made in northern India. Some of these are merely attempts to faithfully reproduce the originals, others probably somewhat later in date, substitute for the owl on the reverse, an eagle. From the latter class, the coins of Sophytes, who at the time of Alexander's invasion (326 B.C.) ruled over a district on the banks of the Acesines, seem to be copied. It is probable that certain copper coins of square Indian form bearing the name Alexandrou were struck in India by Alexander the Great (M. Dannenberg who first noticed these coins attributed them to Bactria). With the appearance of Greek armies on the shores of the Indus, everything changed. It is to that period that one is able to refer the drachma of Sophytes and the square pieces of copper with the legend Alexandrou, which were probably coined in India by the conqueror himself. "Quoi qu'il y ait des doutes," writes M. Drouin. "sur ce dernier point, rein ne s'oppose cependant à considerer cette pièce carrèe comme étant le point de départ du monnayage indien *avec légendes.* Nous ne ferons donc aucune difficulté d'admettre, que les premières inscriptions sur les monnaies indigenès (comme *dajaka* negama, vatasvaka), de même que les caractères alphabetiques painçonnées sur les sigles perses," (vide Rapson, "Countermarks on Early Persian and Indian Coins," J.R.A.S. 1895, p.

865) remontent au IIIe siècle de 300 à 250 av : J.C., mais il faut bein le dire, nous n'entrons dans le domaine de la certitude, qu'avec l'apparition des monnaies gréco-bactriennes frappées un siècle plus tard sur le type carrèe indien. On connait les pièces carrèes de Pantaléon, d'Agathoclés, d'Eucratides, qui portent des légendes en grec et en Kharosthi et dont on peut placer la date à l'an 200 environ av : J.C." (Monnaies Anciennes de l'Inde).

In short, and in absence of certain proof of the existence of coins with legends before the 3rd century B.C., it appears to us wiser to stick to the period truly historic, which commences only with the monuments having certain dates, as for example, the Inscriptions of Piyadasi and the Græco-Bactrian coins. Beyond these, it is only vague and hypothetical. On the contrary, from the time of the establishment of the Greeks in Bactriana, in Kabul and in the Punjab, the indigenous coinage became more and more numerous and there appeared in the history of the coins of Taxila, of Oudumbara, of Kuninda, of Kausambi, of the Sunga Kings, of the Andhras, characters, sometimes in Kharosthi, sometimes in Brahmi, sometimes bilingual with both the alphabets, which one might without danger place in the second half of the first century B.C. It results from these summary considerations that this account of the origin of Indian coinage is more favourable to the opinion that places the creation of the two alphabets after the arrival of Alexander in the Kabul valley and on the shores of the Indus.

From the date of the eastern expeditions of Seleucus and his alliance with Chandragupta in 306 B.C. (Appian, Syr. 56), a constant intercourse was maintained between the Seleucid kingdom of Syria and the Maurya Empire of Northern India, as is conclusively shown by the Seleucid embassies and from the mention of Greek names in the inscriptions of Asoka (vide M. Emile Senart, "Les Inscriptions de Piyadasi"). The adoption of the elephant as a type on Seleucid coins and the similarity between certain coins of Seleucus (compare Babelon, "Rois de Syrie," Pl. I. 15) and those of Sophytes are due to this intercourse. It has been generally assumed (vide Gardner, "The Catalogue of Coins of the Greek and Scythic Kings," p. xx) that the coins of Sophytes were copied from those of Seleucus, but the opposite may have been the case or perhaps both these classes may have been derived from the same originals. But until the beginning of the 2nd century B.C. no extensive modification of the native Indian coinage had been caused by foreign influence. It was from the kingdom of Bactria established by Diodotus, who revolted from the Seleucid sovereign, Antiochus II (B.C. 248 *circa*), that there came eventually the influence which completely changed the form and character of the coinage of north-western India. Parthian characteristics, due no doubt to the contact between the Parthians and Sakas in Bactria, are found on Saka coinages of India; the earliest of which, those of Maues, belong to the latter half of the second century B.C. The dynasty of Vonones, which seems to have exercised a sort of suzerainty over the successors of Maues in the first century B.C., is very probably Parthian in origin. The later dynasty of Gondophares is certainly Parthian.

The Greek Invasion: The incursions of the Bactrian princes into the Kabul valley and northern India must have begun about the beginning of the second century B.C. The war between the Seleucid Antiochus III and the Bactrian Euthydemus ended in an alliance between them (206 B.C.). Probably in the same year, Antiochus crossed the Paropanissus and renewed friendly relations with the king then reigning in the Kabul valley, Sophagasenus or Subhaga Sena, who has been identified with Jaloka.

Euthydemus and Demetrius: It was during the reign of Euthydemus and perhaps under the leadership of his son Demetrius, that the first Indian conquests were made (Gardner, Ibid p. xxii). As an evidence of this settlement in India, there exists a coin of Demetrius, which is perhaps the first to show the result of a compromise between the Greek and Indian methods of coinage. The regular types of Greek system are retained, but the coin is of square Indian form and on the reverse is added an Indian translation in Kharosthi characters with a Greek legend on the obverse.

Eukratides: Next in point of date, come the Indian conquests of Eukratides (c. B.C. 190-160), the rival and conqueror of Demetrius (Justin xli, 6). His coins are found at Balkh, in Seistan, in the Kabul valley and more rarely, in the Punjab.

Dates on Græco-Indian Coins: Important for the chronology of this period is the unique tetradrachm of Plato, copied from the tetradrachm of Eukratides bearing date 147 of the Seleucid era = B.C. 165. The occurrence of other dates on Bactrian coins is less certain.

Pantaleon, Agathocles: Contemporary with the reign of Eukratides in India are those of Pantaleon and Agathocles, whose coins are found both in the Kabul valley and in the Western Punjab—those of Agathocles also, as far as south of Kandahar. The Indian coins of these two rulers are the only coins of Greek princes which bear inscriptions in Brahmi characters. Certain copper coins of Agathocles have legends on both obverse and reverse, in Kahrosthi letters.

Agathocles: Certain medals of Bactrian fabric struck by Agathocles, bear the portraits, types and inscriptions of Alexander the Great, Antiochus "Nicator", Diodotus and Euthydemus; similar medals of the Bactrian prince, Antimachus also bear those of Diodotus and Euthydemus. "The beautiful coin of Alexander, was struck not only by Alexander himself," says M. Foucher in his "Beginnings of Buddhist Art," "but also in imitation of his, by king Agathocles whose name and title encircle the image of Zeus on the obverse. Everything in this medal is still purely Greek".

Antimachus: The types of coins of Antimachus point to some naval victory won by him, perhaps on the Indus or some other large river.

Heliocles: After the reign of Heliocles (*circa* B.C. 160-120) the transference of the Greek power from Bactria to the territory south of Paropanissus was complete. Until his time, many of the Greek princes had ruled both in Bactria and in India and had struck coins both of Bactrian fabric, bearing purely Greek legends and of Indian fabric, bearing bilingual inscriptions. Up to this date all the silver coins were struck according to the Attic standard. The Attic standard gradually gives place to Persian standard. Heliocles himself, Apollodotus I and Antialkidas use both standards; all the later Greek princes use the Persian standard only.

Heliocles' successors: The reigns of all the Greek princes who ruled after Heliocles, (they are about twenty in number according to the coins) must be confined within about a century, that is from *circa* 120 B.C. to 20 B.C., when the Kushanas completed the conquest of India. There were undoubtedly for a considerable portion of this period, two or more distinct dynasties of Greek princes ruling at the same time, and varying greatly from time to time in power and extent of territory. No perfectly satisfactory arrangement of these different families or of their chronology has yet been proposed.

For a century or more the Punjab was thus a Greek

colony, in the same sense in which it afterwards became Scythian, then Mogul and finally English. That is to say, a handful of foreigners, supported by mercenary troops, mostly recruited in the country itself, became masters there, and levied taxes. It is easily perceived that this kingdom of Bactria was a centre of attraction for Greek adventurers of all kinds, beginning with soldiers of fortune and mountebanks and passing by way of merchants to the artists who took upon themselves, among other tasks, that of making the superb coins, to which we are indebted for the survival of the classically sounding names and the energetic features of those so-called "Basileis" changed into very authentic rajas.

SECTION III

Greek Language: Indian language: Scythian language. Greek type: Semi-Hellenic Type. Indo-Parthian Coins: Kushana Coins.

Greek Language: Greek language in Greek characters: On the coins of earlier kings from Diodotus to Demetrius, Greek legends only were employed. After that time we find usually Greek on one side of the coin only. It is however quite evident that Greek letters and Greek language were generally understood in northern India and in Kabul as late as the second century A.D. This fact clearly established by the testimony of coins confirms the otherwise not untrustworthy testimony of Philostratus who represents that Apollonius of Tyana, when he visited India, had no difficulty in making himself generally understood there by speaking Greek. During the Hindu revival under the Guptas the Greek language was probably swept away with other traces of Greek culture.

Notable is the use by some of the later rulers, of poetic Greek words.

Indian Language : Indian language in Indian characters : These last are of two sorts. The square letters of the so-called Indian Pali are used by Agathocles and Pantaleon only and the more cursive characters called the Arian Pali are used by all other kings down to the latest times. In the case of the Edicts of Asoka, the Arian characters are used only in the Kabul valley and the Indian characters elsewhere ; and this fact which is proved in many other ways shows, how completely the Greek and Scythian power in India centred in the Kabul valley.

Scythian Language : Scythian language in Greek characters : These are the inscriptions on coins of the late kings of Kanishka group such as PAONANO, KOZOVAO, KOPANO and specially the deities on the reverses. These words, so far as at present identified, are of non-Scythic origin, borrowed from the languages of India, Persia and Greece and only bearing the Scythian stamp in their termination O and in the modifications of the forms of words.

Types :—Types of Greek Kings : In the types used by the Greek kings, we find a great variety and they often present to us quite a new chapter of Greek art, offering fresh proof of the remarkable originality of the artistsof the Hellenistic age. In regard to their style, we may note the two important points : (i) The extraordinary realism in their portraiture. The portraits of Demetrius, Antimachus and of Eukratides are among the most remarkable that have come down to us from antiquity (vide Gardner, Plates), and the effect of them is heightened in each case by the introduction of a peculiar and strongly characteristic head-dress, that is rendered with scrupulous exactness of detail. (ii) The decidedly Praxitelean character of the full-length figure of the deities on the reverse.

The figures of Herakles, of Zeus, of Poseidon, of Apollo are all in their attitudes characteristic of the school of Praxiteles. The types of Greek deities which we find on them sometimes are more distinctive than the style in which they are rendered. Thus on the coins of Demetrius, Artemis is sometimes radiate : on the coins of Agathocles, Zeus bears in his hand the three-headed Hekaté, Herakles crowns himself with a wreath, Pallas appears in a short skirt and many such strange forms of Greek deities appear.

The influence of Greek religious ideas was extended to India chiefly through the invasions and conquests of the Greek kings of Bactria. These began about 200 B.C., ; but the evidence of Indian literature and inscriptions shows that the communities of Greeks (Yavanas or Yonas = Ionés) were settled in North-west India at an earlier period. And it is quite possible that these may date from the time of Alexander the Great (see Rapson, "Andhra Dynasty" in B.M. Catalogue p. xcviii). The divinities represented on the coins of the Greek princes who ruled in the Kabul valley and the Punjab during the period c. 200-25 B.C., are Greek—Zeus, Athené, Apollo, Herakles, the Dioscuri and other types, are with a few exceptions drawn exclusively from Greek mythology. Historically and geographically important are the representations in Greek fashion of the tutelary divinities (Sanskrit, Nagaradevatâh) of two Indian cities of Kapisa, the capital of the kingdom Kapisa-Gandhara, on a coin of Eukratides, and of Pushkalāvati, the Peukelaotis of Alexander's historians, on a coin of both uncertain date and attribution (vide Rapson, J.R.A.S., 1905, pp. 783, 786). Distinctively Indian religious types seem to occur on the coins struck by two of the Greek princes—"the tree within a railing" and the "chaitya" on certain coins of Agathocles and the "Wheel" which has been reasonably identified with "the wheel of the Law"

(Dharma-chakra) of Buddhism, on one of the numerous currencies of Menander (see Gardner, B.M. Catalogue, Plate, xii, 7; Rawlinson, Bactria, p. 121). If this identification is correct, it must be supposed that the coinage in question was struck in some district of Menander's Empire in which Buddhism prevailed; but there is also some reason to suppose that Menander was himself a Buddhist and identical with King Milinda of the Buddhist apologetic work, Milindapañha (Dr. Rhys-Davids in S. B. E. Vol. xviii). The further suggestion that the title which Menander bears on his coins *dikaioe*-Prakrit, Dhramika, Sans. Dharmika—is intended to have a specially Buddhist connotation, Follower of the Law; Dharma is improbable, since this is a common epithet borne by a number of Hellenic kings, Bactrian, Indian, Parthian and others; in whose case any such special meaning would seem to be impossible.

But already in the second-half of the 2nd century B.C. began the attacks on the Greek dominions in northern India, of invading Scythians (Sakas) and Parthians (Pahlavas) who had already annihilated the Greek power in Bactria. The coins, literature and inscriptions alike indicate a close connection between these two nationalities, and historically, it is not always easy to distinguish between them. The history of these Scythic tribes, which came in contact with the Greek kingdoms in Bactriâ and India, is partially known from Chinese sources however (vide Drouin, Rev. Num. 1888. p. 13). To this period of Saka rule in Bactria, belong the barbarous imitations of Macedonian, Seleucid, Bactrian and Parthian coins. These coins are in general, mere imitations and their inscriptions are debased copies of the Greek inscriptions; but on a few specimens, there are legends which have been recognised as the most ancient examples of Aramæan writings of Turkestan. The coins show the transition from

Greek to Scytho-Parthian rule in different districts of northern India and inscriptions also afford some information as to the Satrapal families who ruled over some of the provinces (vide Rapson, B.M. Catalogue, pp. xcviii-ciii). The inscriptions show that these invaders had embraced Buddhism (Cf. the Taxila copper-plate of Patika—Bühler, Epigraphia Indica, iv. 54 F); the mythology on the coins is almost entirely Greek.

Semi-Hellenic type: The earliest of the clearly Indian types to make its appearance is a dancing-girl wearing long hanging ear-rings and oriental trousers, on the money of Pantaleon and Agathocles. As we come to a later period, non-Hellenic types or types in which there is a non-Hellenic element gradually appear on the coins. On the coins of Philoxenes and Telephus, we find a radiate figure of a Sun-god standing, holding a long sceptre. On those of Amyntas and Hermæus, we find the head of a deity wearing a Phrygian cap, whence issue rays; of all the coins of barbarous rulers, those of Maues are the earliest in style. Von Sallet in "Die Nachfölgers Alexanders des Grossen in Baktrien", remarked that the copper coins of this king were like those of Demetrius and Apollodotus, and belong to a period not much later than that of those kings. In the forms of Greek letters and the style of art, his coins were superior not only to those of Hermæus, but also to those of Zoilus and Nicias. King Maues reigned about the middle of the second century B.C., and it is an interesting fact, noticed by Cunningham, that his coins are found in the Punjab only, specially in the north-west of it and not in Afghanistan. The coins struck by King Maues bear most remarkable and original barbaro-Hellenic figures: a radiate Artemis with veil flying round her head; a draped goddess bearing a crescent on her head and standing between two stars; and under several other Maues' successors, Azes and Azilises, are there types of the same class.

A careful consideration of these facts will convince us that by some means or other, Maues and his race secured the services of artists who had been instructed by the Greeks, but were not fettered by Greek traditions. It would further seem that the kings, who were patrons of art and understood the Greek language, must have been considerably softened and refined by contact with their civilised neighbours.

The first Indian deity, however, to claim a place in the coins, is Siva, who seems to make his appearance on the coins of Gondophares, though it must be confessed that the figure may with equal possibility be called a Poseidon, for the characteristic marks of Siva are absent. But on the coins of Kadphises II, the bull which appears beside the God, sufficiently proves him to be Siva.

Such were the interesting results of the extension of Greek dominions from the Caspian to the Indus. The political supremacy perished, but the moral influence survived. The dynasties which we have spoken of just now are interesting because they used the Grecian language, adopted the imagery of the Grecian religion and venerated the Grecian art. They exhibited also in the last instances, the symbols of Greece which were blended in the same coinage with those of India. And thus in these kingdoms we still behold Greece faintly imaged, though "living Greece no more." Yet we shall see further, how Greece "could brokenly go on." The Scythians, who overthrew the Bactrian kingdom, were urged on not only by love of conquest, but also by the spur of necessity. Scythia proper was not large enough to hold all the nomad hordes that were congregated within it. At this period, it was a kind of political volcano. Within its bosom were stirring and heaving all the elements of mischief. At length, with a tremendous eruption there issued forth a fiery stream of barbarous horsemen, that burst irresistibly upon the fertile plains of Central Asia and North-western India. The Sakas were the first tribe that were driven out to seek their fortunes in the south ; these were the destroyers of the once flourishing Bactrian Empire. The ancient records of India, when collated with the Chinese and Classical histories, leave little room for doubt that these Sakas, after having subdued first Bactria and afterwards the Soter dynasty of Menander in the Paropanissus, brought all Upper India under their dominion (see H.H. Wilson, Ariana Antiqua). The Sakas were eventually overthrown by Vikramaditya, King of Ujjain in B.C. 56. This monarch, who is a Hero-divinity of the Hindus, was surnamed "Sakâri" or the foe of the Sakas. But his successors were forced to submit to the Yue-chis, a second tribe of the Scythians, (vide V.A. Smith, Early History of India), still more powerful than the first. These Yue-chis founded a most important kingdom, generally styled the Indo-Scythian.

The Coins of the Indo-Parthian Dynasties : It should be noted that a series of Indo-Parthian coins have been found, which would show that for a short time, some Parthian princes must have ruled in the region of Paropanissus. In all probability, when the Bactrian Empire was despoiled, they managed to seize a moiety of the plunder. But the Indo-Parthian coins present many difficulties. The historical relations between kings and satraps, whose coins we possess, are explained at length in an article, entitled "The Indo-Parthian Dynasties", from about 120 B. C. to 100 A. D. published in Z. D. M. G., Jan. 1906. Here, only the results of the discussion are given. The key to the chronology is to be found in the history of Parthia, that is to say, the Arsakidan kingdom of Persia ; and if that history had been more fully preserved than it has been, the position of the Indo-Parthian dynasties would no longer be obscure.

The statement of Orosius that Mithridates I (Arsakes VI) of Parthia annexed the country between the Indus and the Hydaspes (Jhelum) or in other words, the kingdom of Taxila, towards the close of his reign, in or about 138 B.C., is far from untruth. That kingdom, the western Punjab, seems to have formed an integral part of the Parthian dominions for a few years, but during the troubles which ensued upon the death of Mithridates I, about 136 B.C., the control of the central government over the outlying provinces was relaxed and about 120 B.C. a chieftain named Maues (Moa) made himself king of Taxila and enjoyed practical, if not nominal, independence and assumed the title "Great King of the Kings" (*Basilieos Basilion Megalon*). About the same time, a few years later, a Parthian chief named Vonones became king of Drangiana (Seistan) and extended his authority over Arachosia (Kandahar) and the Indian borderland. These latter provinces were administered by the relatives of Vonones, first by his brother, Spalahora and then by his nephew, Spalagodama, son of Spalahora (vide Jour. Roy. As. Soc. 1902, p. 105, note 2). When Vonones died he was succeeded by his another brother, named Spalirisha, who continued to administer Arachosia by a viceroy named Aya or Azes, perhaps his son. But when Spalirisha died he was not succeeded by Azes; and this fact may be explained by the supposition that Mithridates II, suppressed the independence or quasi-independence of Seistan with its appanages, and incorporated those provinces directly in the Parthian Empire. Azes, however, although deprived of Arachosia was permitted to succeed Maues at Taxila and to establish a dynasty there. He was succeeded after a long reign by Azilises, presumably his son, who was followed by Azes II. To him succeeded Gondophares, who reigned prosperously for many years and about 40 A.D. extended his authority over Arachosia, Seistan and the valley of the lower Indus, probably by taking advantage of the weakness of the central Parthian government at that period.

When Gondophares died about 60 A. D., his extensive dominion was broken up into smaller states. Orthogones, perhaps his brother, succeeded to his Arachosian provinces, while Abdagases, son of an unnamed brother, obtained the kingdom of Taxila. At that time, the Sakas Yue-chi and other nomad hordes from the steppes of Central Asia were swarming down upon the north-western frontier of India. Abdagases reigned for a short time and apparently had no successor of his lineage, his kingdom probably passing into the hands of the foreign invaders (Mr. Rapson has lately discovered coins of a son of a chief named Bagapharna, which come from the Jhelum district. *Vide* J. R. A. S., 1905, p. 790). In Arachosia, the Parthian power endured for a few years longer, and Orthogones was succeeded by Pakores and Arsakes Dikaios. But about 90 A. D., the Yue-chi monarch Kadphises II became master of the Punjab, Arachosia and Sind, the Parthian chiefs being restricted to a narrow territory in the Delta of the Indus. The victorious reign of Kadphises II undoubtedly was prolonged. Cunningham assigned it a duration of 40 years. The extent of the conquests made by Kadphises II and the large volume of his coinage are certain indications that his reign was protracted. The inferiority of characters in which the Greek inscriptions are engraven and of the style of coinage of the Parthian Dynasty, would show that the coins belong to the later and declining period of Græco-Asiatic mintage and the Arianian inscriptions on the reverse would mark an Indian locality.

The coins of the king Gondophares are distinguished by a peculiar monogram in Sanskrit language on the reverse : *Mahārāja rājādirāja trādata devarāta Guduphāra* (vide Gardner, "Catalogue of Coins of Greek and Indo-Scythic Kings," p. 103). Ecclesiastical history corroborated most singularly the numismatic evidence regarding this prince. Saint Thomas is said to have received a divine commission to visit the Indians, who were ruled by a prince named Gondoforus. (vide Sharon Turner's History of the Anglo-Saxons, Vol II ; and Tischendorf, "Apocalypes Apocryphæ"). The coincidence is somewhat striking. Another prince, styled Abdagases on the coins, is connected with Gondophares by uniformity of monogram. There are several other princes included in this dynasty. But we do not know much of their reigns except in faint outlines and we must close our account of this distant Indian offshoot of the Indo-Parthian dynasty. And while we refer to the Indo-Parthian dynasties and reflect how Buddhism and Brahminism with their sister Mithraism grew up under the shadow of Greek civilisation, till they overspread the extreme East, we should not forget that Buddhism made converts in high plateaux of Central Asia, later on.

The Date of Kanishka.—Kanishka the Great, alone among the Kushana Kings, has left a name cherished by tradition and famous far beyond the limits of India. Notwithstanding the widespread fame of Kanishka, his authentic story is scanty, and his chronological position is strangely open to doubt. Unluckily no passage in the works of the accurate Chinese historians has yet been discovered which synchronises him with any definite name or event in the well-ascertained history of the Middle Kingdom. The dates moreover in the ample storehouse of epigraphic materials, are recorded in such a fashion as to be open to various interpretations, and eminent scholars assign the date of Kanishka's accession between 58 B.C. to 278 A.D. Dr. J. F. Fleet maintains the 58 B.C. date and Messrs. Bhandarkar have advocated the late date 278 A.D. But the latter theory is clearly indefensible. The substantial controversy is between the scholars who place the date of the accession of Kanishka in 58 B.C. and those who date it in or about 78 A.D. It is possible that the Kushana kings may have used a special era distinct from the Saka, but it is unlikely. If such an era was used, it began after, not *before* 78 A.D. Sir John Marshall, has been convinced by direct evidence of the stratifications of the remains at Taxila that Kanishka reigned in the second, rather than in the first century of the Christian era and it is quite impossible, according to him, to accept Dr. Fleet's date for his accession. Dr. Fleet (in J.R.A.S. 1903, 1905, 1906, 1913) as well as Dr. O. Franke of Berlin (Beiträge aus Chinesischen Quellen zur Kenntnis der Türkvölker und Skythen Zentralasiens) and Mr. James Kennedy are of opinion that Kanishka, Vasishka, Huvishka and Vasudeva preceded the Kadphises kings, and that the Vikrama era of B. C. 58, either marks the accession of Kanishka or coincides with that event. It seems to us that this theory is quite plausible. Mr. Vincent A. Smith on the other hand is not correct in holding that the Kadphises kings preceded Kanishka, and that he came to the throne about 78 A. D. Dr. Fleet (J. R. A. S. 1907. pp. 1048-9) evidently attaches much weight to a tradition that Kanishka lived 400 years after the death of Buddha and to Dr. Franke's opinion. He further argues that his theory supplies a regular series of epigraphic dates and that the absence of the Roman *H* from the coins of Huvishka indicates an early date for that king. The last two arguments cannot be discussed here, but it is interesting to note that another tradition places Kanishka 700 years after Buddha (vide Indian Antiquary, xxxiii, 1903,

p. 382). One such tradition is as good as another and none is of value. Various traditions place him, 150, 300 or 500 years after the Mahāparinirvāna of Buddha. Dr. Franke lays stress on the fact that Chinese historians, as distinguished from Buddhist writers, never mention Kanishka. But he himself sufficiently answers this argument by the remark that "by the year 124 A.D. the source was dried up from which the chronicler could draw information concerning the peoples of Turkestan". The other argument on which he relies, is based on the well-known story telling how in 2 B.C. a Yue-chi king communicated certain Buddhist books to a Chinese official. The inference drawn is that the king in question, must have been Kanishka. But this conclusion drawn by Dr. Franke and M. Sylvain Lévi, is unsupported by any corroborative evidence. In India, his coins are however found constantly associated with those of Kadphises II, from Kabul to Ghazipur on the Ganges e. g.

(*i*) in the Gopalpur Stupa, Gorakhpur District—coins of Kadphises II, Kanishka, Huvishka and of a much earlier prince, Arya Mitra (vide Proc. A. S. of Bengal, 1896, p. 100).

(*ii*) Benares hoard of 193 pieces, *viz.*, 12 of Kadphises II and the rest (4 not read) of Kanishka and Huvishka (see Thomas Prinsep's Essays, I p. 227 note).

(*iii*) Masson's collections from Beghram, near Kabul. (see Ariana Antiqua.)

The reign of Kanishka appears to have lasted some 45 years. Very little is known about the successors of Kanishka. Vashishka and Huvishka were the sons of Kanishka, who both acted in succession as viceroys of Upper India. Vashishka of whom no coins are known, seems to have predeceased his father, who was succeeded in his whole Empire by Huvishka. The whole series of coins of Huvishka may have been issued after his accession to the Imperial throne.

Vashishka presumably was not empowered to coin in his own name. If he had ever issued coins, it is hardly possible that some specimens should not have been discovered by this time. The reign of Huvishka undoubtedly was prolonged, but all memory of its political events has perished. His abundant coinage is even more varied than that of Kanishka, with which it is constantly associated and like the contemporary sculpture, testifies to the continuance of Hellenistic influence (vide Gardner, "British Museum Catalogue of Greek and Indo-Scythic kings," Pl. xxvii, 9; V. A. Smith, "Catalogue of Coins in the Indian Museum," Plates xi and xii).

"The gold-coins of Huvishka," Cunningham observed, (Num. Chron, 1892, p. 98), "offer four different busts of the king," which may be referred to conveniently, as A, B, C and D respectively and described as follows :—

A.—is a very rare large head (or bust not showing the arms or hands) of the king covered with a round jewelled helmet with spreading crest and the ends of diadem hanging down behind. A large ornamental earring is in the ear, and flames spring from the shoulders. The legend of all varieties in badly formed Greek letters is PAONANO PAO OO HPKI KOPANO (Shaonano Shao Huveshki Koshano), "The King Kings, Huvishka, the Kushana."

B.—Half-length figure of the king to the left (rising from clouds) with pointed helmet, thickly jewelled, holding a sceptre in the left and a club in the right hand before the face. On some coins the sceptre is changed for the "*angkus*" or elephant-goad, which refers to the king as an elephant-rider, as seen on his copper coins.

C.—Half-length figure of the king (rising from clouds, richly dressed, sometimes with flames, springing from his shoulders) with round jewelled helmet to *left*, club and "*angkus*" in hands. This is the most common form.

D.—The same half-length figure of king to the *right*.

On some of the coins, the king's name is O H O H P K I, 'Huveshki'. Cunningham is followed by Dr. Stein in reading O in some cases as aspirate and in some cases as a semi-vowel.

From the point of view of religious history, the coinage of the Kushanas is important in several respects. The Kushana conquerors imitated the Greek coins, but substituted the figure of Herakles for that of Zeus as a reverse type (Cf. Gardner, Ibid, Plates xv and xxv). This exchange of one Greek divinity for another had not been explained, but it seems possible that the figure of Herakles may have been intended to represent Siva, since Megasthenes seemed to indicate that these two deities were popularly identified with each other in India (vide, Ind. Ant. Vol. vi, p. 122). Moreover, Vima-Kadphises, the immediate successor of Kujula-Kadphises was undoubtedly a follower of Siva as he bears the title of Māhiswara, (worshipper of Siva), on his coins and his coin-types, Siva alone or accompanied by his bull and Siva's emblem, the trident, bears witness to the same fact. (For the interpretation of the term, Māhiswara, see M. Sylvain Lévi, Journal Asiatique, new series, ix, 21 ; for the name Vima, see Rapson, Actes du xiv Congrés du Orientalistes, Algiers, 1905, vol. I, p. 219). The inscriptions of King Kanishka show that he himself was a Buddhist, and he is famous in Buddhist literature as the great patron of Maháyána. His coin-types and those of his successor Huvishka, however represent no fewer than five of the faiths professed by nations and peoples included in their vast empire. Greek religion is represented by Helios, Silene (C A A H N H) and Herakles (H P A K I L O); Persian by Mithra etc. (vide Grundriss d. Iranischen Philologie, ii, 75); Scythian by Nana or Nanaia ; Brahman by Skanda-Kumāra, Visaka and Mahāsenā and Buddhism by Buddha (see Gardner, loc. cit. pls. xxvi-xxix). Rapson asserts that it has been held hitherto that the coins of the Kushana kings, Kanishka and Huvishka "show a remarkable eclecticism, for on their reverses are represented Greek and Scythic divinities, dieties of the Avesta and of the Vedas and Buddha, and the Kushana monarchs have been credited with the profession of all or any of the different forms of the faiths indicated !" (Indian Coins, 73). The natural conclusion of this diversity of types is that these various classes of coins were current in the different provinces of a large empire. On the coins of Vasudeva, (BAZOΔHO) the last of the Kushana sovereigns, whose name is at present known, only two dieties appear, the Indian Siva and the Scythic Nana. The coins of the later Kushanas, whose names being probably indicated merely by two initials, fall into two chief classes, distinguished by the diety who appears as the reverse-type : one class with Siva seems to have been current in the Kabul valley, while the other with the goddess APΔOXPO (Ardoksho), who has been identified with the Persian Ashi Vanguhi (Grund. Iran. Phil. ii, 75), belongs rather to the more eastern portions of the Kushana dominions.

Since we are forced to touch upon the question of chronology, we find that it is only in the first century A.D. that the type of Buddha at last makes its appearance on the reverse of the coins. And certainly his name is still written there, in Greek characters "Boddo". But on the obverse, instead of an elegant Greek, we perceive the figure of the bearded Kushana Emperor, Kanishka, whom Mr. Sylvain Lévi has surnamed the "Clovis" of northern India. For, just as the Frank Clovis had no part in the development of Gallo-Roman Art, the Indo-Scythian Kanishka had no direct influence on that of Indo-Greek Art ; and besides, we have now the certain proofs that during his reign this art was already stereo-typed, if not decadent.

BIBLIOGRAPHY.

1. Gardner ... "Catalogue of Coins of the Greek and Indo-Scythic Kings".
2. Thomas ... "The Earliest Indian Coinage" in International Numismata Orientalia, Vol. I.
3. Rapson ... "Indian Coins" in Bühler's Grundriss der Indo-Arischen Philologie und Altertumskunde.
4. Wilson, H. H. ... "Ariana Antiqua".
5. Lassen, Christian ... "Beiträg zur Geschichte der Griechischen Könige in Baktrien, Kabul und Indien".
6. Von Sallet ... "Die Nachfolgers Alexanders des Grossen in Baktrien".
7. Cunningham ... "Numismatic Chronicle," vol. viii 1868, p. 282; 1873, p. 188.
8. Drouin, E. ... "Quelques Mots sur les monnaies anciennes de l'Inde, à propos de la question de l'origine de l'écriture" (Melanges Charles de Harlez).
9. Lenormant, François ... "Monnaies et Medailles".
10. Babelon ... "Rois de Syrie," Pt. 1.
11. Neibühr ... "Lectures on Ancient Ethnography and Geography".
12. Chabouillet ... "Revue Numismatique," 1867 p. 302.
13. Journals of the Royal Asiatic Society, 1889, 1895, 1902, 1903, 1905, 1906, 1913.
14. Journal Asiatique, 1890 (xv), p. 327.
15. Indian Antiquary, 1879, p, 199.
16. Z.D. M.G. 1906 (January).
17. Drouin ... "Les Legendes des Monnaies Sassanides" in Revue Archèologique, 1898.
18. Vincent A. Smith ... "Catalogue of the Coins in the Indian Museum," Calcutta, Vol. I.
19. Rapson ... "Andhra Dynasty" in B.M. Catalogue.
20. Rhys-Davids ... Sacred Books of the East, Vol. xxxv.
21. Bühler ... Epigraphia Indica, Vol. iv.
22. Actes du xiv. Congrès du Orientalistes, Algiers, 1906.
23. Hill ... "Handbook of Greek and Roman Coins."

24. Schlumberger ... "Numismatique de l'Orient latin." Paris. 1878.

25. B. V. Head ... "Hist. Numorum" Oxford, 1887.

26. Franke, O. ... "Beiträge aus Chinesischen Quellen zur Kenntniss der Türkvölker und Skythen Zentralasiens.".

27. Rapson, E. ... "Ancient Coins collected in Seistan."

28. Prokesh-Osten, Count A. ... "Les Monnaies des rois parthes."

29. Wroth, W. ... "Catalogue of the Coins of Parthia."

30. Theobold, W. ... "Notes on some of the Symbols found on the punch-marked Coins of Hindustan."

31. Macdonald, G. ... "The Evolution of Coinage".

32. Gardner, P. ... "A History of Ancient Coinage," Oxford 1918.

33. Rodgers, E. ... "Catalogue of the Coins."

BOOK THREE

THE EVOLUTION OF SCIENTIFIC AND LITERARY CULTURE IN INDIA AND HELLENISM.

CHAPTER V

ASTRONOMY

The antiquity of the Indian Astronomy: Its scientific development due to the Alexandrian Schools. The Romaka and Puliça Siddhantas. Dr. Thibaut's opinions.

THE history of Sciences is a Sciences itself; and one of the most interesting and important of them all. To trace the stream of discovery from its lofty fountain-head, to follow its various windings, to mark its frequent disappearances, its rapids and its stagnancies, is a work at once of greatest interest, and of greatest difficulty. In examining the antiquity of Hindu Astronomy, we must first take into account the fact that the Hindus had amongst them, a considerable amount of astronomical knowledge as testified by their accurate calculation of the eclipses of the sun and the moon. But for a long period they made no advancement but rather retrograded in their knowledge of the principles of the science. Astronomy was cultivated among them at an early period, and the question is whether the birth of the science is due to the contact of Greece with India.

The author of 'Mecanique Celeste' writes, "The origin of astronomy in India, as among all other nations, is lost in obscurity in the first period of their history." The Indian tables however indicate a state of considerable advancement in astronomy, but everything else leads us to believe they are not of very high antiquity. The ensemble of the Indian tables and especially the impossibility of the general conjunction which they suppose, prove that they have been constructed or at least corrected in modern times. This fact is further borne out by the mean motions, which they assign to the moon with reference to her perigee, her nodes and the sun, which being more rapid than that given by Ptolemy, prove that the tables containing them are subsequent to that astronomer; for we know that these motions are subject to an acceleration from age to age.

In this connection it is well to note, that even before the name of the "middle kingdom" had ever been uttered in the learned halls and avenues of the Athenian Academy, even before the eagle of the Roman legions thirsting for universal sway, had attempted its earliest flight across the Central Appennines, before the English of that ancient world, the colonising merchants of Phœnicia had unfurled their sails upon the waves of the Atlantic and trafficked in precious metals on the coasts of the Albion and Ierne, large communities of settlers, stretching far across the plateau of Upper India were already living under the patriarchal rule of great and powerful princes, and cultivating at this early period, the science of astronomy for the regulation of time. In fact, it is well-known that the Hindus were in possession of an important body of astronomical knowledge for centuries before they came in effective contact with European nations and as also undoubtedly is the case, before the Muhammedans established themselves in India and brought with them their own astronomical knowledge and skill, which are generally acknowledged to rest on the basis of Greek science. Broadly characterising the amount and kind of astronomical knowledge which the Hindus were found to be in possession of by the European nations, we may say that the Indian astronomers were able to accomplish on the whole as much as the Greek astronomers of Alexandria, in the first centuries of the Christian era. They knew that the earth is a sphere freely suspended in space. They had a very accurate knowledge of the length of the mean revolutions of the planets. They knew how to calculate the true position of the planets (as distinguished from the mean ones), and they were acquainted with the two inequalities of the planetary motion which had to be distinguished for that purpose. And like the Greek astronomers and in fact all astronomers previous to Kepler, they employed for the calculation of the true position of the heavenly bodies, the hypothesis of eccentric cycles and epicycles. They were in possession of the true theory of solar and lunar eclipses, and hence capable of calculating those phenomena beforehand with a fair amount of accuracy. They employed the same sexagesimal division of the sphere and of time, which the modern western nations have taken over from the Greeks. "They generally carried on their calculations according to certain practical concise rules given in astronomical manuals of comparatively recent date, such as the Grahalâghava (1442 Shaka) and the Tables of Makaranda; but the better informed section of the Jyotishis were also fully acquainted with the theory of the subject as contained in an important group of earlier works, viz., the so-called astronomical Siddhantas, of which three enjoyed the highest authority and were prevailingly studied viz., the Surya Siddhānta, the Siddhānta Shiromoni and in Southern India, Ārya-Siddhānta" (vide "Indian Thought", ed. by Drs. G. Thibaut and Ganga Nath Jha, Vol. I., 1907, p. 82).

The astronomical system as propounded in the pages of the Surya-Siddhānta and similar works was after all comparatively simple and primitive. Not only was it immeasurably less complicated than modern European astronomy, but if once freed from certain peculiarities of exposition which in no way touched the essentials of the doctrine, exhibited a marked resemblance to the teachings of the great Greek astronomers. Thanks to the labours of such men as Colebrooke,

S. Davies, Bentley, J. Warren, Bailey, Delambre and others, the theories and processes of Indian astronomy thus came to be analysed and understood about the end of the 18th and the beginning of the 19th century, already with an accuracy and completeness which have left comparatively little to be accomplished by later researches.

Various hypotheses on the historical aspect of Indian Astronomy, were already set forth by early inquirers. The great French astronomer, M. Bailey was inclined to view the Indian system as embodying elements established at a very early period, long anterior to the rise of the Greek astronomy. J. Bentley going to the other extreme, maintained that the Siddhāntas are quite recent fabrications, mistakenly or rather deceitfully assigned to early periods. Others again, struck by the fundamental similarity above referred to between the Hindu methods and those of the Greek astronomers, favoured the view that the Hindu system is at any rate posterior to the developed Greek system, which was for the first time fully explained in the great astronomical treatise of Ptolemy (Klaudios Ptolemaios, 140 A.D.). It is, as may be here mentioned at once, the latter view which has in the course of the last century established itself more and more firmly among the Western scholars. And as in the course of the 19th century, the entire literature of ancient India came to be studied with increasing thoroughness and width of outlook by Western *Savans* as well as by Hindu scholars of the modern type, in connection therewith, passages of astronomical bearing and interest were collected from all the branches of that vast literature including the large mass of Vedic writings.

Of the great antiquity, not only of the Hindu nation but of Indian astronomy generally, the first definite evidence was afforded to European investigators by the publication of certain astronomical tables in the "Memoirs of the Academy of

Sciences" in 1687, which were brought from Siam by M. de Loubére of the French Embassy, and subsequently examined and explained by the celebrated Cassini. They were and are known as the "Tables of Siam". Two other sets of tables were afterwards received from French Missionaries, then in India. These were called the "Tables of Crishabouram and Narsapur." But they remained unnoticed till the return of the French astronomer Le Gentil, who had been in India, for the purpose of observing the transit of Venus in 1769. During his stay there, he employed himself in acquiring a knowledge of Indian astronomy, being instructed by the Brahmins of Trivalore, in the method used by them, of calculating the eclipses ; and they communicated to him their tables and rules which were published by Le Gentil, as the "Tables of Trivalore", in the memoirs of the Academy in 1772. It is however to another Frenchman M. Bailey, the author of "Traité de l'astronomie Indienne", that we owe the full discussion regarding the antiquity of the four tables referred to, and to which he devoted an entire volume. Professor Playfair made an elaborate investigation into Bailey's work and presented it to the Royal Society of Edinburgh in 1790. Thus in Europe, the knowledge about the Hindu astronomy was first dessiminated.

Colebrooke in his "Miscellaneous Essays" II., p. 447 said long ago, "The Hindus had undoubtedly made some progress at an early period in the astronomy cultivated by them, for the regulation of time. Their calendar, both civil and religious, was governed chiefly not exclusively by the sun and thé moon ; and the motions of these luminaries were carefully observed by them and with such success, that their determination of the moon's synodical revolutions, which was what they were principally concerned with, is a much more correct one than the Greeks ever achieved." But "whatever may have been the period," pertinently remarked Prof. Max Müller in his 'Ancient Hindu Astronomy and Chronology,' "when the notion was first obtained, that fore-knowledge of events on earth might be gained by observations of the planets and stars and by astronomical computation wherever that fancy took its rise, certain it is that the Hindus have received and welcomed communications from other nations on topics of astrology; and although they had astrological divinations of their own as early as the days of Parāsara and Garga, centuries before the Christian era, there are yet grounds to presume that communications subsequently passed to them on the like subject either from the Greeks or perhaps the same common source (perhaps that of the Chaldæans), whence the Greeks derived the grosser superstitions engrafted in their own genuine and ancient astrology which was meteorological" (p. 45). Applying this indication to that of the division of the Zodiac into twelve signs, represented by the same figures of animals and names, by the words of the same import with the zodiacal signs of the Greeks and taking into consideration, the analogy, though not identity, between the Ptolemaic system, or rather that of Hipparchus, and the Indian one of eccentric deferents and epicycles which in both serve to account for the irregularities of the planets or at least to compute them, no doubt can be entertained that at some time or other the Hindus received hints from the astronomical schools of the Greeks.

L. von Schroeder in his "Indiens Literatur und Cultur," discusses the question thus: "Ein wirkliches Aufblühen der Astronomie in Indien beginnt jedenfalls erst mit der Zeit des griechischen Einflusses und es ist dies die einzige Wissenschaft, in welcher wir unzweifelhaft starke Beeinflussung von seiten der Griechen nachweisen können. Die Indischen Astronomen geben denn auch durchweg die Yavana (d. i. die Jonier oder Griechen) als ihre Lehrer an. Deiser Einfluss springt vor Allem deutlich in die Augen durch die zahlreichen griechischen

Bezeichnungen, welche sich in den astronomischen Schriften der Inder vorfinden. So werden uns Z. B. (in Varâhamihira's Horâçastra) die griechischen Namen der Zodiakalbilder und Planeten vollständig aufgeführt und zum Theil neben den indischen und ebenso häufig wie diese, gebraucht: So Ara-Ares; Heli-Helios; Jyau-Zeus; Asphujit-Aphrodite; Kriya-Krios; Tavuri-Tavros; Pathona-Pardenos u. s. w. Es finden sich ausserdem noch eine Menge termini technici bei den Indern (so namentlich bei Varâhamihira) im Gebrauch, welche direkt den astronomischen Werken der Griechen entnommen sind; so z. B. Kendra-Kentron; Apoklima-Apoklima; Trikona-Trigonos; Jamitra-Diametron; Dyutum-Duton; Panapharâ-Epanaphora; Liptâ-Lepte; Anaphâ-Anaphe; Sunapha-Sunaphe; Drkana-Dekanos, u. s. w."

Parāsara is considered to be the most ancient of Hindu astronomers and second in order of time is Garga. Of Parāsara, we know very little, except that his name is connected with the Vedic Calendar. The work which professes to contain Parāsara's teachings is called the Parāsara Tantra. It was held in high esteem in the Pauranik period and Varâhamihira often quotes from it. As the Yavanas or Greeks are placed by Parāsara in Western India, the date of the work cannot be much earlier than the second century B. C. Of Garga, we know something more and he is one of the few Hindu writers, who tells us something of the Greek invasion of India in the 3rd century B. C. He had regard for learned men among the Greeks—although they were considered Mlechchhas—and the following passage of his, is well-known and often quoted: "The Yavanas (Greeks) are Mlechchhas, but amongst them this science is well-established. Therefore they are honored as Rishis; how much more then an astrologer, who is a Brahmana." Speaking of Sālisuka, Garga says: "Then the viciously valiant Yavanas after reducing Sāketa (Oude), Pāñchala country and Mathura, will reach Kusumadhwaja : Pushpapura (Patna) being taken, all provinces will undoubtedly be in disorder". Dr. Goldstucker found mention of this invasion of Sāketa or Oude by the Greeks in Patañjali and thus fixed the date of Patañjali, the author of the Mahābhāsya and the Yoga Philosophy.

Now, the whole of the astronomical and astrological science of the Hindus, as fixed at the time of the Varâhamihira and indeed long before him was divided into three branches. So we know from Brihat Samhitā, Chapter I, verse 9, "The Jyotihçāstra treating of several subjects is contained in three branches. The treatment of the whole is called by the sages, Samhitā. In the Jyotihçāstra, in one branch are to be found the movements of the heavenly bodies as determined by calculation (Ganita); this is called Tantra. The second branch is horoscopy or the casting of horoscope. Different from both is the third branch." The whole knowledge of celestial phenomena, of chronometry, of omina and portents, of augury, in short, natural astrology went under the name of Samhitā, before each of the three branches attained its full development; when in course of time, the Hindus through the Greeks became acquainted with two separate branches of the knowledge of the stars (the one really scientific, the other quasi-scientific) they must have felt some difficulty in incorporating the mathematical astronomy and the so-called judicial astrology into the Samhitā.

Dr. Kern remarks in his Introduction to "Brihat Samhitā", that as the Greek historians ascribe the greatest conquest to Demetrius and Menander, [Demetrius reigning according to Lassen, 205-165 B. C.] and as Sālisuka is midway between Asoka's death 226 B. C. and Brihatdhrata's death 178 B. C., it would not appear very far from the truth to place the conquests of the Greeks about 195 B. C. [But the only Greek word in the Samhitā is 'Hora']. The Gargi Samhitā proceeds: "The unconquerable Yavanas (Greeks) will not remain in the middle country. There will be a cruel, dreadful war among themselves. Then after the destruction of the Greeks at the end of the Yuga, seven powerful kings will reign in Oude." We are then told that after the Greeks, the rapacious Sakas were the most powerful and we have little difficulty in recognising in them the Yue-chi invaders, who destroyed the kingdom of Bactria at the middle of the second century B. C. These new conquerors continued to repeat their depredations and the annals of Garga here come to an end. From the details given above, we would agree with Dr. Kern in placing Garga in the first century B. C.

It is now generally conceded by the European scholars that the 'scientific' Hindu astronomy has been originally based on that of the Alexandrian Greeks, who had brought the study with them from the Ionian lands, where it had been early cultivated by Thales (*circa* B. C. 636-570); by Anaximander (B. C. 610-547), who declared that the earth moved round its axis and that the moon reflects the sun's light, and who invented the gnomon, observed the solistices and equinoxes, measured the obliquity of the ecliptic, noted the morning setting of the Pleiades on the 29th day before the equinox and made the first geographical charts; by Pythagoras (*cir.* 570-490 B. C.); by Anaximenes (*cir.* 550-470 B. C.), who taught gnomonics; and by Anaxagoras (*cir.* 499-472 B. C.), who ascribed the cosmical adjustments to intelligent design. Eudoxos of Knidos (*cir.* 370 B. C.) introduced the sphere, observed and recorded the places of fixed stars and determined the tropical year at 365¼ days. Phænos, Euktemon, and Meton (432 B. C.), observed the solistices, laid down the places of the four tropical circles and introduced the cycle of

19 years. Plato proposed the representation of celestial motion by circles, which has been so prolific of scientific results. Aristotle wrote a work on astronomy, now lost. Hipparkhos of Bithynia (*circa* 160-120 B. C.) "the lover of truth and labour", made his observations at Rhodes, but except his commentary on the poem of Aratos, all his works have perished and it is to Ptolemy, his great admirer, that we owe our information about the extent and importance of his researches ; to him is also due the reconciliation of observation and theory, the procession of the equinoxes, etc. After him Geminer, Kleomedes, Theodosios, Menelaos, Hipsikles, Strabo, Cicero, Hyginos, and Pliny all bear testimony to the continuity of astronomical research down to the time of Claudius Ptolemy (100-160 A. D.), whose *syntaxis* with the commentary on it by Theon, was so long the standard text-book on the subject.

"How far however, during the first five or six centuries of the Christian era", says Dr. Burgess in the Journal of the Royal Asiatic Society, 1893, p. 718, "such works of later Greek astronomers reached India, we shall never probably know for certain. We know this much that the forms and methods of the Hindu Siddhāntas are so evidently borrowed from the Greek sources, that apart from the admission in some of these works respecting the teaching of the Yavanas, there could be no doubt as to their source." Professor Weber in 1865 (Ind. Stud. vol x. p. 264 et seq) had already drawn attention to the Suryaprajñapti, a Jaina astronomical treatise, which from the resemblance its elements bear to the system of the Jyotisha-vedānga, naturally suggests to us the main features of Hindu science before it was modified and affected by the Greeks. This new line of research was followed by the eminent *savant* Dr. G. Thibaut in the Journal of the Bengal Asiatic Society for 1877, vol. xlvi pp. 107-127 and 181-205.

It needs only to be added that as it is to Ptolemy that the sexagesimal division is ascribed, there can be little doubt that Paulus or Pulisa was one of those who introduced the Greek system of astronomy into India. Dr. Thibaut considers that the Romaka and the Paulisa Shiddhāntas must have been composed not later than 400 A. D. The name Paulisa from which Pulisa seems to have been derived as an author of the Siddhānta, has an un-Indian sound and Alberuni, who did not have the original Siddhānta before him, attributes the teaching of the Siddhānta to a Greek, named Paulus. That the work might be connected with Paulus Alexandrinus, who is well-known as the author of an astrological hand-book, cannot be proved and besides it is not very probable; because the various Paulisa Siddhāntas, which are known to us, seem to deal purely with astronomical discussions. The Romaka-Siddhānta is ascribed both by Brahma-Gupta and Alberuni, to Sri-Shéna. Except the quotations given by Utpala, we are not able to give any further details about it; whether it is still in existence, is extremely doubtful, it must have been scarce, if indeed not wholly lost, long ago, for there exists a spurious Romaka-Siddhānta; besides the experiment of fabricating one would have been deemed unsafe, if the old genuine work had been known to be extant. A MS. pretending to be the Romaka-Siddhānta belongs to I. O. Library in London. It is a purely astrological, not astronomical, work. Amongst other curious things, curious in their way, it contains a horoscope of Jesus! As it speaks of the kingdom of Baber, and mentions, prophetically of course as it befits an astrologer, the overthrow of the kingdom of Sindh, which was conquered by Akbar in 1572 A. D.; so it certainly dates from 1600 A. D. or later, and not 400 A. D., as Dr. Thibaut thinks. From certain expressions in the work, Dr. Kern comes to the conclusion that the author was a Parsee and not a Hindu. He calls himself Karman-sri-Karmana. Now it is hardly conceivable, how it could enter one's head to call himself Karman "the blessed," unless one be a Parsee. The Paulisa Siddhānta, although not procurable now-a-days, is much better known than the Romaka, being largely quoted by several astronomers and their commentators: it stood manifestly in high favour as late as the date of Alberuni and was, barring the Sphuta Brahma-Siddhānta, the only Siddhānta, he could procure for himself (vide Reinaud, pp. 334 et seq). The name of the author Pulisa (it has been corrected by some *lepidum caput* as Pulastya !) points clearly to a foreigner, a Greek or a Roman. Alberuni calls him Paules, the Greek and gives the name of his birth-place in a form, which seems corrupt. His testimony of course is the testimony of Hindu astronomers of his time, and there is not the slightest reason to doubt its accuracy. Weber has made the suggestion that Pulisa the Greek may be identical with Paulus Alexandrinus, the author of an astrological work of the title of Eisagoge. In this Eisagoge, so he argues (Ind. Stud. II, p. 260), there is a passage, which agrees "almost literally" with the one found in a modern Hindu book on Nativity, the Hãyana-ratna, by a certain Balabhadra. Weber's surmise is scarcely admissible. For the passage alluded to will be found in all works on Nativity, because it is a simple enumeration of the mansions and their lords. Besides there is no indication that Balabhadra has taken this passage from Pulisa, which must be established before any conclusion can be drawn. But that Pulisa was a Greek, we do not doubt for a moment, notwithstanding that the Pulisa-Siddhānta judging from quotations rather numerous, is so thoroughly Hinduised that few or no traces of its Greek origin are left. It may be set down as a trace of foreign influence that Pulisa calls "solar" (*saura*) time, what otherwise is called "civil" (*savana*) time or as Utpala puts and exemplifies it, "what with us is 'civil time,' is with Pulisa-āчharya, 'solar time,' a solar time being with him the interval from midnight till midnight or from sunrise till sunrise." We should meet perhaps with a few more traces of Greek influence, if we had the whole work before us.

Thus, Indian astronomy in its scientific form, as in later Sanskrit text-books, is derived from the astronomy of the Alexandrian Schools and its technical nomenclature is to a large extent Greek, in a slightly disguised form.

We do not subscribe however to the opinion held by some scholars that an earlier inexact astronomy probably of Babylonian origin had been known in India, long before the work of Alexandrian professors reached her shores ; but it is certain that Indian astronomy with any claim to scientific precision is more or less Greek. This scientific astronomy was taught by Aryabhatta in c. A. D. 500, and by Varāhamihira about half a century later.

Sir William Jones was amongst the first to enter the lists against this Grecian theory ; and he thus threw down his gauntlet in defence of the antiquity and originality of the science of Astronomy in India : "I engage to support an opinion (which the learned and industrious M. Montucla seems to treat with extreme contempt), that the Indian division of the Zodiac was not borrowed from the Greeks or Arabs but having been known in the country (India) from time immemorial, and being the same in part with that used by other nations of old." Since Sir William Jones wrote this challenge, volumes of heated controversy by many authors, have been devoted to the same subject. The majority of scholars however, both European and Indian, appear to have accepted as an axiom the opinion that much of Indian Astronomy and certainly Indian acquaintance with the twelve-fold division of the Zodiac is to be attributed to Grecian influence. A minority of writers still hold the view, advocated by Sir William Jones about a hundred years ago, and it is thus reiterated by Dr. Burgess (the translator of the Indian standard astronomical work, Surya Siddhānta): "The use of this twelve-fold division and the present names of the signs can be proved to have existed in India at as early a period as in any other country." But the minority, who hold this view, are very few in comparison with those who hold the opposite view.

History does not tell us of any close communication between Greece and India, sufficient to account for this similarity of astronomical method, till after the date of Alexander's conquest, about 300 B. C. The Greeks could not at that late date have first become acquainted with the figures of the Zodiac; for in the Grecian literature of a much earlier age, the figures of the Zodiac and other constellations are alluded to as perfectly well-known. On the other hand, in the most ancient Sanskrit work in existence—the purely Indian Rig-Veda, which contains no Grecian taint, the twelve-fold division of the Zodiac appears to be unknown. This opinion as to the Rashis or constellations of the Solar Zodiac is so generally adopted, that the age of any Sanskrit work in which mention of these Rashis occurs, is at once set down as not earlier than the comparatively modern date of 300 B. C. As the Greeks could not have learnt their astronomical lore from the Indians, the Indians must have learnt something from the Greeks at some date, later than Alexander's eastern conquests.

But as regards the Indian Lunar Zodiac, it is admitted on all hands that the Nakshatra series was not derived from Grecian sources. It is contended however, that the fixation of the initial point of this Lunar Zodiac (a point at the end of Revati and the beginning of Aswini, 10 degrees west of the first point of the constellation Aries) was due to astronomical reforms of the Hindu Calendar, probably carried out under the Greek auspices at a date not much earlier than 600 A. D. A very clear statement of this opinion is given by Whitney (the editor of Burgess's translation of Surya-Siddhānta). For a further corroboration of their view, ancient Sanskrit literature is appealed to. Hymns and lists referring to the Nakshatras are to be met with in the Yajur and Atharva Vedas in which Krittika now the third Nakshatra holds the first place, containing the group of stars known to the European astronomers as "the Pleiades."

These very briefly, as far as we have been able to gather them, are the chief arguments in favour of,

(*i*) The Grecian introduction of the twelve-fold Zodiac into India about 300 B. C.

(*ii*) The date of 570 A. D. for the fixation of the initial point of the Indian Zodiacs.

These arguments are, is no doubt, cogent and have been held by very high authorities. The opponents of this modern theory, have brought forward the following consideration. "The Brahmans are always too proud to borrow their science from the Greeks, Arabs or any nation of the Mlechchas as they call those who are ignorant of the Vedas." This statement put forward by Sir William Jones is further emphasised by the high regard which the Greek writers, at the beginning of the first century A.D., had for Indian Astronomy. For instance, in the Life of Apollonius of Tyana (written by Philostratus about 210 A. D.), the wisdom and learning of Appollonius are set high above those of all his contemporaries, but he is spoken of as learning many things specially matters (Apollonius concerning Astronomy from the sages of India of Tyana, Book III, Chapter xli).

This high opinion held by the Greeks in regard to Indian Astronomy may be contrasted with the very moderate praise bestowed on the European science by Varâhamihira, the Hindu astronomer. He says : "There are the following Siddhāntas, the Paulisa, the Romaka, the Surya and the Paitāmaha, out of these four, the first two, the Paulisa and the Romaka which appear to have been European treatises have been explained by Lâtaveda. The Siddhānta made by Paulisa is accurate, next to it stands the Siddhānta proclaimed by Romaka, more accurate is the Savitra (Surya-Siddhānta, the Hindu standard work) while the remaining two are far from the truth." This moderate but reads, judicious estimate of Varāhamihira, touching the superiority of the native Surya-Siddhānta over the Paulisa and the Romaka Siddhāntas—which has been confirmed by modern European scholars—may be appealed to as conveying the impression that when Varāha wrote, his co-religionists and scientists were not accepting wholesale and with avidity, Grecian astronomical methods in place of their own native science. It is true however, that in Varāha's work, many words evidently of Grecian origin are to be met with and some scholars have claimed that "these Greek terms occurring in Varāhamihira's writings are conclusive proofs of the Greek origin of the Hindu Astronomy." That such terms should occur in a work professedly a resumé of five astronomical treatises—some of them Indian and some, European—can scarcely be considered as conclusive proof that in the writer's time no purely Indian astronomical science existed. Varāhamihira's writings suggest an author interested in comparing the points of resemblance and difference to be met with in home and foreign methods rather than one introducing for the first time important astronomical truths to the notice of his readers.

It may further be urged, that the claims to antiquity of

Sanskrit astronomical works are so well-known that those who claim the Grecian origin, must necessarily throw discredit on all ancient authors in general. Bentley's furious diatribes against the credibility of Indian antiquity, cannot, however, be looked upon as convincing argument.

The recent researches of archæologists in Western Asia, have brought to light vast amount of information, concerning the knowledge of astronomy possessed by the inhabitants of Babylonia and Chaldæa in ancient times. In 1874, a paper, entitled "The Astronomy and Astrology of the Babylonians", was read by Professor Sayce before the "Society of Biblical Archæology", and since that date, other papers by various authors dealing with the subject have appeared in the same Society's proceedings. Also in the "Zeitschrift für Assyriologie" articles have been contributed by such eminent writers as Epping, Strassmaier, Oppert, Meyer, Mähler, Jensen, Lehmann and others, in which the calendars and astronomical methods in use in Mesopotamia are discussed. All the informations gained from the cuneiform tablets, concerning the science of Astronomy in Western Asia must undoubtedly influence the judgment of inquirers as to the antiquity of the same science in India.

We will not further pursue the pros and cons of what has hitherto been said on the vexed question, of the originality and antiquity of Astronomy in India. Suffice it to say, that the Hindus did evolve the Science independently, but the 'Scientific' Astronomy of the Indians is partly due to the contact with the Greeks.

This intricate question about the Greek influence on Indian Astronomy has been finally set at rest by the most learned and weighty opinions of Dr. G. Thibaut, the greatest authority on Ancient Indian Astronomy etc., in his "Astronomie, Astrologie und Mathematik", in Bühler-Kielhorn's

Grundriss der Indo-Arischen Philologie und Altertumskunde. We wish to quote the following passages from that excellent work : "Die Frage der Entlehnung von den Griechen :—Sollte also die Indische astronomie von den Griechen entlehnt oder wenigstens beeinflusst sien ? Die Inder selbst lehnen dies ab, wenigstens soweit es sich um die Grundzüge ihres Systems handelt. Ein solcher Einfluss könnte nun kaum von irgend anderswo als von Griechenland gekommen sein—insofern wir nämlich das völlig entwickelte indische System ins Auge fassen, wie es uns im S. S. vorliegt-und der sich natürlich darbietende Schluss ist daher, dass die inder ebenso wie die Völker des westlichen Asiens und alle modernen Nationen bei den Griechen in die Schule gegangen sind.

"Dazu kommt nun der bezeichnende umstand dass Bestehen einer bedeutend entwickelten griechischen Astronomie von gewissen indischen Autoren selbst anerkannt wird, und dass sick ferner in indischen astronomischen und astrologischen Werken technische Ausdrücke vorfinden, die ganz unzweideutig griechischen Ursprunges sind. In ersterer Beziehung ist auf den schon erwähnten Passus aus Garga hinzuweisen, welcher sagt, dass "obschon Mlechhas, die Yavanas (Griechen) bei denen diese wissenschaft (Astronomie) sich wohl gegründet vorfindet, geehrt werden als wären sie Rsis". Es ist weiter bemerkenswert dass in den einleitenden versen des uns vorliegenden S. S. die wissenschaft der astronomie als eine von Surya dem Asura-Maya in der Romaka-stadt gemachte Offenbarung bezeichnet wird ; hier bleibt die Enwähnung von Romaka merkwurdig auch wenn wir nicht geneigt sein sollten, mit A. Weber anzunehmen, dass unter dem "Asura Maya" der name des Astronomen Ptolemaus verborgen sei eine Hypothese, die sich darauf gründet, dass in den Asoka-Inschriften der Name eines Gliedes

des ägyptisch-griechischen Herrschergeschlechts der Ptolemäer in der Form "Turamaya" erscheint. Im S.S. selbst finden sich schon, einige Wörter, die unzweifelhaft griechischen Ursprungs sind, darunter als das wichtigste "Kendra" womit die Entfernung des mittleren Planeten von der Apsis die mittlere Anomalie bezeichnet wird ; dieser Ausdruck geht unzweifelhaft auf *kéntron* zuruck da der mittlere Ort des Planeten zusammenfallt mit dem Orte des centrums des Epicykels."

From all these extraneous indications, coupled with the internal reasons of probability mentioned above, we conclude that the Scientific Astronomy of the Indians should be regarded as an offshoot of the Greek Science.

BIBLIOGRAPHY.

1. Thibaut, G. ... "Astronomie, Astrologie und Mathematik," in Bühler-Kielhorn's Grundriss der Indo-Arischen Philologie.
2. Max Müller, W. ... "Ancient Hindu Astronomy and Chronology."
3. Brenand ... "Hindu Astronomy."
4. Lewis, C. ... "Historical Survey of the Astronomy of the Hindus."
5. Bentley, J. ... "Hindu Astronomy."
6. Cantor ... "Geschichte der Mathematik."
7. Whitney ... "Suryya-Siddhānta" in the Journal of the American Oriental Society, Vol. vi.
8. Sachau ... "Alberuni's India."
9. B. G. Tilak ... "Orion."
10. Thibaut, G. ... "Pañchasiddhāntika."
11. Lewis, C. ... "Survey of the Astronomy of the Ancients."

12. "Indian Thought" edited by Drs. Thibaut and Jhā. Vol. I. pp. 82 ff.
13. Journal of the Royal Asiatic Society," 1893, p. 717.
14. Jones, W. ... "Collected Works," Vol. I.
15. E. M. Plunket in Actes du douzième Congrés International des Orientalistes, Rome 1899.
16. von Schroeder, L. ... "Indiens Literatur und Cultur."
17. Cantor ... "Gräko-indische Studien."
18. Garbe ... "Beitrage zur indische Kulturgeschichte."
19. von Bohlen, P. ... "Das Alten Indien," Bands I & II.
20. R. C. Dutt ... "Ancient India," Vol. III.
21. Lietner ... "Greek Influence on India," International Congress of Orientalists, 1880.
22. Steinthal in Z.D.M.G. xi. p. 396.
23. Winternitz, M. ... "Geschichte der Indische Literatur."
24. Holtzmann, A. ... "Uber den griechischen Ursprung des indischen Thierkreises."
25. H. Jacobi, ... "Astrologiæ Indicæ," "Hora appellatæ Originibus."
26. Thibaut, G. ... "On the Surya-prajñapti," J. A. S. B. 1880.
27. A. Weber ... "Indische Literatur."
28. " ... "Die Griechen in Indien."
29. Lassen, Chr. ... "Indische Altertumskunde," Bd. I.
30. Gustaf Adolf van den Bergh van Eysinga ... "Indische Invloeden Op Oude Christelijke Verhalen."
31. Kern, H. ... "Brihat Samhitā" of Varāhamihira (Bibliotheca Indica).
32. Davis, S. ... "On Hindu Astronomy" in Asiatic Researches Vol. II.
33. Whitney ... "The Lunar Zodiac."
34. Delambre ... "Histoire de l' Astronomie."
35. Playfair ... "On the Astronomy of the Brahmans."

CHAPTER VI

MATHEMATICS

The Hindu Arabic Numerals: early ideas of their origin. The invention of Arithmetic by the Indians: The independent development of Geometry and Algebra by the Hindus. The Sulva Sutras:—Dr. Thibaut's opinion. The introduction of Hindu Numerals into Europe.

It has long been recognised that the common numerals used in daily life are of comparatively recent origin. The number of systems of notation employed before the Christian era was about the same as the number of written languages, and in some cases a single language had several systems. The Egyptians, for example, had three systems of writing with a numerical notation for each, the Greeks had two well-defined sets of numerals and the Roman symbols for number varying more or less from century to century. It may be said that the Arabic numerals are only one of the many systems in use before the Christian era. In Europe, the invention of notation was generally assigned to the eastern shores of the Mediterranean, (until a critical period of about a century ago), sometimes to the Hebrews, sometimes to the Egyptians, but more often to the early trading Phœnicians (vide Bede, De Computo Diologus, Opera Omnia, Vol. I. p. 650; Ramus, Arithmeticæ libri dvo, Basel, 1569, p. 112).

The idea that the common European numerals are Arabic in origin is not an old one. The Mediæval and Renaissance writers generally recognised them as Indian, and many of them expressly stated that they were of Hindu origin. Maximus Planudes states in 1330 A. D. that "the nine symbols come from the Indians" [Waschke's German translation, p. 3]. Willichius speaks of the "Zyphræ Indicæ" in his Arithmeticæ libri tres (1540), and Cataneo of "le noue figure de gli Inde" in his Le Pratiche delle dve prime Mathematiche (Venice, 1546 fol. I). Others argued that they were probably invented by the Chaldæans or the Jews, because they increased in value from right to left,—an argument which would apply quite as well to the Roman or Greek systems, as to any other. It was indeed to the general idea of notation that many of these writers referred, as is evident from the words of England's earliest arithmetical text-book maker, Robert Recorde (c. 1542): "In that thinge all men do agree, that the Chaldays, which Fyrste inuented thys arte did set these figures as thei set all their letters, for thei wryte backwarde as you tearme it and so doo they reade. And that may appeare in all Hebrewe, Chaldays and Arabike bookes...whereas the Greekes, Latines and all nations of Europe do wryte and reade from the left hande towards the ryghte" (The Ground of Artes, fol. c. 5). Sacrobosco (c. 1225) mentions the same thing. Others and among them such influential writers as Tartaglia in Italy and Dr. Köbel in Germany admitted the Arabic origin of the numerals, while still others e. g. Glareanus Vossius left the matter undecided and simply dismissed them as "barbaric." Of course, the Arabs themselves never laid claim to invention, always recognising their indebtedness to the Hindus, both for their numeral forms and for their distinguishing feature of place value. Foremost among these writers is the great master of the Golden Age of Baghdad, one of the first Arab writers to collect the mathematical classics of the East and the West, preserving them and finally passing them to awakening Europe. This scholar was Mohammed, the son of Moses from Khowaren or more after the manner of the Arabs, Mohammed ibn Musa al-Khawarazmi (c. 840 A. D.), a man of great learning and one to whom the world is much indebted for its present knowledge of Algebra and Arithmetic (see Z. D. M. G. Vol. xxxiii, p. 224). In the Arithmetic which he wrote [and of which Adelhard of Bath (c. 1130 A. D.) made the paraphrase], he stated distinctly that the numerals were due to the Hindus. This is also plainly asserted by later Arab writers *e.g.* Abdal Kadir ibn Ali al-Sakhawi (c. 1000). Indeed the phrase *ilm hindi* (Indian Science) is used by them for Arithmetic.

Probably the most striking testimony from Arabic sources is that furnished by the Arabic traveller and scholar, Al-Beruni (973-1048), who spent many years in Hindustan. In his work on India, he gives a detailed information concerning the language and customs of the people of that country, and states explicitly that the Hindus of his time did use the letters of their alphabet for their numerical notation as the Arabs did. Leonard of Pisa wrote his Liber Abbaci in 1202 A. D ; in this work, he refers frequently to the nine Indian figures ('novem figurarum yndorum'), thus confirming the general consensus of opinion in the Middle Ages that the numerals were of Hindu origin. We are therefore forced to the conclusion that the Arabs as also the Europeans from the early ninth century onwards, fully recognised the Hindu origin of the numerals.

While it is generally conceded, that the scientific development of Astronomy (vide Chapter V) among the Hindus towards the beginning of the Christian era rested upon the Greek sources, yet their ancient literature testified to a high state of civilisation and to a considerable advance in sciences, in philosophy and along literary lines, long before the Golden Age of Greece. The importance of the Sutras as showing an independent origin of the Hindu Geometry—contrary to the opinion long held by Cantor in his 'Ges. der Math.' of a Greek origin—has been repeatedly emphasised in recent literature [*e. g.* Beppo Lévi in Bibliotheca Mathematica Vol. ix (3) pp. 97-109; A. Bürk, ibid Vol. vii (3) pp. 6-20; Max Simon, 'Geschichte der Mathematik in Altertum'], specially, since the appearance of the important work of L. von Schroeder. Further fundamental mathematical notions such as the conception of the irrationals and the use of Gnomons—all these having long been attributed to the Greeks—are shown in these works to be native to India. Absolutely absurd is the hypothesis of a Greek origin of the Hindu numerals, based on the supposition that the current symbols were derived from the first nine letters of the Greek alphabet. This difficult feat is accomplished by twisting some of the letters, cutting off, adding and effecting other changes to make the letters fit the theory. This peculiar theory was first set up by Dasypodius (Conrad Rauhfuss), and later on was elaborated by Huet in his 'Demonstratio Evangelica' (1769). This bizarre derivation is not even supported by such a pro-Hellenist as Weber. "The Indian figures from 1-9", said the author of the 'History of Indian Literature,' "are abbreviated forms of the initial letters of the numerals themselves...the Zero too has arisen out of the first letter of the word *Sunya* (empty) (it occurs even in Pingala)". It is the definite place value of these figures which gives the significance. Indeed upon the evidence at hand, we might properly think that everything points to the numerals as being substantially indigenous to India.

The decimal system as current among all the Indo-European peoples and among some other races, evidently owes its origin to the habit of counting upon the digits. If we had three or six fingers in each hand, we then would have without doubt, the chance of possessing a sexagesimal or duodecimal system. In this science too, the debt of Europe to India is considerable. There is in the first place the great fact that the Indians invented the numerical figures used all over the world. The influence which the decimal system of reckoning arising out of those figures, had on Mathematics, as well as on the progress of civilisation in general, can hardly be over-estimated. During the eighth and ninth centuries, the Indians became the teachers of Arithmetic and Algebra to the Arabs and through them to the nations of the West, and though Algebra is the Arabic name of the science, it is a gift which the Europeans received from India. In Algebra, the Hindus displayed a proficiency far exceeding anything ever achieved by the Greeks.

Colebrooke was the first European writer, who thoroughly investigated into the subject of Hindu Mathematics. He said about the Hindu Algebra : "The Hindus had certainly made distinguished progress in the science, so early as the century immediately following that in which the Grecians taught the rudiments of it. The Hindus had the benefit of a good arithmetic notation : the Greeks, the disadvantage of a bad one. Nearly allied as Algebra is to Arithmetic, the invention of the Algebraic calculus was more easy and natural, where Arithmetic was best handled. No such marked identity of the Hindu and Diophantine systems is observed as to demonstrate communication. They are sufficiently distinct to justify the presumption that both might be invented independently of each other. If however it be insisted that a hint or suggestion, the seed of their knowledge, may have reached the Hindu Mathematics immediately from the Greeks of Alexandria, through those of Bactria, it must at the same time be confessed that a slender germ grew and fructified rapidly and soon attained an approved state of maturity on Indian soil". But the recent theory, as has already been shown, is quite the contrary. "Pour tout ce que concerne l'arithmetique, l'algebra et la geometrie," says M. Woepocke in his 'Memoirs sur la propagation des chiffres Indiens,' "il est indeniable que le

Indiens se sont appliques de bonne heure à resoudre par des methodes conformes à leur genie, plus synthetique qu'analytique, les questions des chiffres et des dimensions soluvées soit par les transactions de la vie usuelle, soit par les exigencies du ceremonial religieux, soit par le calcul des observations astronomiques." It is thus that with their numeration purely oral, they had learned in the more ancient Sutras, not only to express by a word or rhythmic syllable, the numbers that required from westerners a long periphrasis, but still more to place and resolve the complicated problems relating to the permutations of syllables and to the formations of domestic altars.

Again M. D'Alviella in writing about the Mathematical Notations of the ancient Indians, states as follows: "Vers le milieu du IIIe siècle avant notre ère, on voit apparâitre, dans les plus anciennes inscriptions de l'Inde, plusieurs mode de notation qui se rattachent respectivement aux deux alphabets; l'alphabet bactrien ou kharosthi et l'alphabet indien ou indo-pali." The signs are sometimes the letters borrowed from the Kharosthi alphabet, sometimes the symbols taken from the Phœnician or the Mesopotamian alphabet or even the Egyptian, all being equally foreign to the Greek alphabet. In the Indian Alphabet properly speaking, these signs were twenty in number, serving respectively to designate, the first nine units, the first nine tenths, the number hundred and the number thousand. "Cette notation", the learned Count goes on, "qui s'est perpetuée jusqu'au VIIIe siècle de notre ère dans les inscriptions des rois Valabhis, survit encore aujourd'hui parmi les Tamouls et les Malais de l'Inde meridional. Dans l'intervalle, la table colonnes avait penetré chez l'Inde. Il est possible qui les Indiens directement reçu des Grecs. Mais il est egalement admissible qui l'importation en remonte aux temps de l'occupation Perse, voire a l'époque des relations commerciales avec la Chaldée. Quoi qu'el en soit c'est bien à l'Inde et à l'Inde seul qu'on doit les perfectionnements tire de cette elementaire machine à compter. En effet, nous savons, par les auteurs arabes, qu'on commencement du VIIIe siècle aprés J. C. ou employait ençore dans tout l'occident, l'ancien systeme du notation alphabetique on la valeur de position etait en connue."

The oldest figures directly derived from the Indian signs up to ten might well have been retained by the writers of the Arabic versions of Ptolemy, and in similar works, to designate and indeed to distinguish the sexagesimal "zero," for which 'cursive' writing was comparatively little needed. India claims the invention of the value of position of the zero and the evidence, which may be adduced in support of it, whether direct or circumstantial, is quite convincing. This invention was already an accomplished fact at the commencement of the 8th century A. D. Because Āryabhatta, as pointed out by M. Léon Rodet, applied to the extraction of square and cubic roots, a process analogous to the modern science which presupposed the knowledge of the principles of position. M. Bayley however estimated that the adoption of a symbol representing 'zero' and consequently supplanting the necessity of the 'columns' is not anterior to the first half of the 8th century A. D. Of course, it is just possible that as regards the value of position, the Indian knowledge though certainly of an early date, may relate back to a still earlier age than it is generally supposed, namely the commencement of the sixth century A. D.

In Geometry, the points of affinity between the Sulva Sutras and the works of the Greeks are considerable. The western scholars have been acquainted with the contents of the Sulva Sutras in great detail by Dr. G. Thibaut. Out of these have resulted, comparatively speaking, a very definite knowledge of geometrical relationships; although these are not essential to the theoretical scientific parts of the exposition but are entirely suggested by the practical necessity of the measurements of the sacrificial objects, still they are nonetheless important, or any-the-less noteworthy. Of special importance here, is the fact that the so-called theorem of Pythagoras is not only known to the Sulva Sutras, but plays a very important and leading part in them. Pythagoras had to thank the Indians for the greater part of his knowledge and that in Geometry, the Brahmans must have been his teachers. Hence to the Indians should be ascribed a very considerable influence in the development of Greek Geometry. This view was first propounded by von Schroeder but it has been neglected by specialists and even has met with definite opposition. Their contention is that everything depends on the question of the age of the Sulva Sutras, as far as the Geometrical portions contained in them, are concerned. Cantor had already clearly perceived this and declared that "it is as good as established that the resemblances between Greek Geometry and the Sulva Sutras are so obvious in essential particulars, that a borrowing on one side or the other is in the highest degree probable." He then said that it was Alexandrian Geometry, which at a time later than 100 B.C, had reached India, and he is of opinion that the Sulva Sutras have been influenced by Hero of Alexandria about 215 B.C. Weber also has declared that according to his opinion, there is nothing in literary history to prevent the supposition that the Sulva Sutras borrowed from the teaching of the Alexandrian Hero. This opinion is however opposed to very important considerations. The Sulva Sutras belong to the Vedic or the sacred literature of the Indian priests. It is very hard to believe, that the Greek science had penetrated even into the Vedas, when we take into account the complete isolation of India in religious matters, the great pride with which the Brahmans look upon these revealed books from time im memorial, and the deep, almost superstitious, veneration which they show for these writings. This opinion must *à priori* appear extremely improbable and moreover has not been put forward with regard to any other portion of the Vedas, in fact not even hinted at. What cannot be legitimately spoken of secular literature can hardly be applied to the religious, and the measurements taught in the Sulva Sutras in fact appertain to matters of religion, a part of Brahmanic theology. The Sulva Sutras are far anterior to the 3rd century B. C., for they form an integral portion of the Srouta Sutras and their Geometry is a part of Brahminical theology, having taken its rise in India from practical motives as much as the science of Grammar. The prose-parts of the Yajur-Veda and the Brahmanas frequently refer to the arrangements of the sacrificial grounds and the construction of altars according to very rigid rules, the slightest deviation from which might cause the greatest evil. This being the fact, it is not likely that the exclusive Brahmans would have willingly borrowed anything closely connected with their religion, from the foreigners.

"We have finally to consider," says Dr. Thibaut, in his 'Astrol. Astron. und Math.,' "the question whether the whole development of Mathematics in India is to regarded as completely independent, or it is derived from foreign sources, as influenced materially in the course of its evolution by such foreign theories. The resemblance which part of Indian Mathematics bears to part of the Greek, makes the question of obvious importance, and then besides we have already come to the conclusion that the scientific astronomy of the Indians was an offshoot of the Greek Science, and we have already indicated in what close contact the Mathematics and the Astronomy of the Indians stand. Hence it is not unreasonable to admit the possibility of the Greek influence also in the region of Mathematics. But here it is considerably more difficult to come to a final decision. For, obvious indications as exist in the case of the Indian Astronomy *e.g.* the technical terms of unmistakable Greek origin, are absent in the region of Mathematics. Also there is an absence in this case, of a common system of 'half-true' theories found simultaneously on both sides *e.g.* the theory of Epicycle in Astronomy. Of course it is evident, that an agreement of this special kind is a very convincing proof of real historical connection. The absence of such and other similar proofs is naturally to be taken to a certain extent to indicate the originality of the Indians in the domain of Mathematics. To this we might add the other circumstances, viz. that at least in Arithmetic, the Indian cannot be regarded as having originated from the Greek in any particular and that in certain higher matters, specially regarding indeterminate analysis, their works are considerably in advance of the Greeks."

Introduction of Arabic Numerals into Europe.

If then Arithmetic and Algebra had their origin in India when did the Arabs come to know of them? It is customary to say that it was due to the influence of Muhammedanism that learning spread through Arabia and Persia; and it was so, in part. But learning was already respected in these countries long before Muhammed appeared, and commerce flourished all through this region; in Persia, for example, the reign of Khashru Anushirwan, the great contemporary of Justinian, the law-maker, was characterised not only by an improvement in social and economic conditions, but by the cultivation of letters. Khashru fostered learning by inviting to his court scholars from Greece and by encouraging the introduction of culture from the West as well as from the East. At this time, the works of Aristotle and Plato were translated and portions of the Hitopodesa or Fables of Pilpay were rendered from Sanskrit into Persian. All this means that some three centuries before the great intellectual ascendancy of Baghdad, a similar cultivation of learning took place in Persia under pre-Muhammedan influences. Now the first definite trace that we have of the introduction of the Hindu system into Arabia dates from 773 A. D., when an Indian astronomer visited the Court of Caliph, bringing with him astronomical tables, which at the Caliph's command were translated into Arabic by Al-Fazari (vide H. Suter, 'Die Mathematiker,' pp. 4-5). It is asserted that at the same time, the King of Kabul offered as a present to the Khalif Al'Mansur a beautifully bound copy of Indian Arithmetic. Al'Mansur's successor, Al'Mamun, had it translated into the language of Canaan. The Arab and even the Byzantine historians attributed the invention of Arithmetic to the Indians. The Arabs again acted as intermediaries in spreading their knowledge of notation to Europe. But at first the followers of Christianity opposed this introduction. It is said that in 1299 A. D. (at such a late date !), the use of the abacus and the Roman figures was prohibited by the magistrates of Florence (vide M. Thirion, 'Histoire de l'Arithmetique,' p 132).

For over 500 years, Arabic writers and others continued to apply to works on Arithmetic, the name "Indian." The Greek monk Maximus Planudes, referred to already, writing in the first half of the 14th century followed the Arabic usage in calling his book, "Indian Arithmetic." There were many opportunities for the transmission of such knowledge to Europe, through Spain and Italy. In the first place, the Moors went to Spain to uphold the cause of a claimant to the throne and remained as conquerors. The power of the Goths, who had held Spain for three centuries, was shattered at the Battle of Jerez de Frontera in 711 A. D. and almost immediately, the Moors became masters of Spain and so remained in power for 500 years. Furthermore, there was abundant opportunities for the numerals of the East to reach Europe through the travellers and ambassadors. Charlemagne (c. 800) sent emissaries to Baghdad, just at the time of the commencement of mathematical activity there. Then too in Alfred's time (849-901) emissaries went from England as far as India. A very interesting illustration of this intercourse also appears in the 10th century, when the son of Otto I. married a princess from Constantinople. This monarch was in touch with the Moors in Spain and invited to his Court numerous scholars from the West as well as from the East. Then there were the Crusades, which in these times brought the East in direct contact with the West. Hence we find, that there was abundant intercourse between the East and West for some centuries before any reference to Hindu Arithmetic and Algebra appears in the manuscripts of Christian Europe. The Hindu numerals, moreover, must of necessity have been known to many traders in a country like Italy, at least as early as the 9th century and probably even earlier ; but there was no reason for preserving them in treatises. Therefore, when a man like Gerbert made them known to the scholarly circles by his work, "Libellus de numerarum divisione," he was describing merely what had been already more or less familiar to many people in a different walk of life (vide Bubnov, 'Gerberti hostea Silvestri II').

BIBLIOGRAPHY

1. Thibaut, G. ... "Astronomie, Astrologie und Mathematik" in Bühler-Keilhorn's Grundriss der Indo-Arischen Philologie.
2. Cantor ... ... "Geschichte der Mathematik."
3. Max Müller ... "Ancient Hindu Astronomy and Chronology."
4. Kern, H. ... ... "Brihat-Samhitä" in Bibliotheca Indica.
5. Thirion, J.... ... "Histoire de l'Arithmetique."
6. Taylor, Isaac ... "Origin of the Arabic Numerals."
7. Rodet, Léon ... "Leçons de Calcul d'Aryabhatta" in Journal Asiatique, 1879.
8. Colebrooke ... "Algebra with Arithmetic and Mensuration, from the Sanskrit of Brahmagupta and Bhāskara."
9. Wallis ... ... "History and Practice of Algebra."
10. Woepocke, J. ... "Memoire sur la propagation des chiffres Indiens" in Journal Asiatique, 1863.
11. Plunket, E. M. ... "Ancient Calendars and Constellations."
12. Weber ... ... "Die Griechen in Indien."
13. Journal of the Royal Asiatic Society, 1883.
14. L. von Schroeder ... "Indiens Literatur und Cultur."
15. Smith and Karpinsky ... "The Hindu Arabic Numerals."
16. Max Simon ... "Geschichte der Mathematik im Altertum."
17. Marie ... ... "Histoire des Sciences Mathematiques et Physiques," Vol II.
18. Kern, H. ... ... "Aryyabhatiyam."
19. Sudhākara Dwivedi ... "Lilāvati and Vijaganita."
20. Schubert, H. ... "Mathematical Essays and Recreations."
21. Whitney ... ... "Oriental and Linguistic Studies."
22. Montucla ... ... "Histoire des Mathematiques."
23. Bubnov ... ... "Gerberti hostea Silvestri II."
24. Beppo Levi, in Bibliotheca Mathematica, Vol. IX (3) pp. 97-105.
25. Z. D. M. G., Band 33, p. 224.
26. Suter, H. ... ... "Die Mathematiker."
27. D'Alviella, Count ... "Ce que l'Inde doit à la Grèce."
28. Macdonell, A. ... "Sanskrit Literature."

CHAPTER VII

MEDICINE

Section I

The Development of the Science of Medicine in India : conflicting views regarding the Age of Hindu Medicine.

In every country individuals are found to use their best endeavours to discover the means of alleviating pain and of curing diseases. In Europe especially, the different countries are so connected together as to enable the physicians to profit by the discovery of his neighbours and the historians to trace the progress of the sciences among the various races of mankind from the Mediterranean to the Atlantic, and from the time when Medicine emerged from the obscurity of ancient fables to the present age. During this long period, we know the individuals, and the people who have added to the medical knowledge, and we can prove that all these systems have a common source, being originally derived from the family of Hippocrates. Those distinguished benefactors of mankind first explained the nature and treatment of diseases, and reduced to theory the various phenomena of the human body. The Grecian philosophers were inspired at first by the Egyptian sages, who appear to have obtained much of their knowledge from the first-hand study of the human anatomy and physiology. After her institutions had been destroyed by the sword of the conquerors Egypt became the seat of Grecian learning, which was afterwards transferred to the East, and under the fostering care of the Caliphs of

Baghdad, Medicine was cultivated with diligence and success. It received a still further impetus from the East; and thus improved, it was conveyed by the Muhammedan conquerors into Spain. From thence it was communicated to other parts of Europe, where it has exercised the genius of many great men with so much advantage to suffering humanity.

Among the sacred records of the Hindus, there is a system of Medicine, propounded at a very early period, which though appears to have formed no part of the Medical Science, yet is supposed to have enlightened the other nations of the earth—a system which is certainly of great antiquity. People who had distinguished themselves at such an early age, by their power and riches as well as by their successful cultivation of sciences, may be supposed to have studied with much care, the means of succouring the wounded and the maimed, of alleviating pain and of curing diseases. The Hindu history of medicine proves this to have been the case: for one of the fourteen *ratnas* or precious gems, which the Gods are believed to have produced by churning the ocean, was a learned physician. The beginning of Indian Medicine has been thoroughly discussed by Bloomfield ("Atharva Veda" in the second volume of the Grundriss der Indo-Arischen Philologie); Hillebrandt has also given a summary of Vedic magic for illness, in the third volume of the Grundriss; Caland, in his annotations on Kausika Sutra, embodied in his important work "Altindisches Zauberritual", has compared the Indian popular system of Medicine with similar systems and methods of ancient Greeks, Romans, Germans and other peoples; Dr. Winternitz too in a small but comprehensive treatise on the "Popular Medicine of Ancient India", comes to the conclusion that in India, as elsewhere, the doctor is the direct follower of the wizard and the magician; Dr. P. Cordier in his "Etude sur la Médicine Hindoue," has collected and discussed the medical references in the Rig and Atharva Veda, as well as in the Upanishads, Epics and the Law-Books. So let us confine our attention to some new researches and the relation between the Vedic and later Medicine.

Now Folk-medicine in India is closely connected with sorcery. "The most primitive witchcraft looks very much like medicine in an embryonic state" (see Lyall, Asiatic Studies, Vol. I. p. 118). The earliest collection of charms found in the Atharva-Veda, which is reckoned as the earliest medical-book of India, is directed against demoniacal beings who are supposed to bring in the abnormal and morbid states of body and mind. So in the medical charms of Kausika Sutra, the diseases and frequently the curative agencies as well are addressed as supernatural beings. The remedies applied are based on a rude kind of homœopathic or allopathic principle. The cure of wounds and fractures is effected by incantations, which have been compared by Dr. Kuhn with the Merseburg charm of German antiquity. The second period of Indian medicine is the Buddhist period, ushered in by Jivaka Komārabhachha, the contemporary of Buddha himself, of whom the most wonderful cures are reported and whose name indicates that he was particularly famous for the treatment of children's diseases. The canonical books of the Buddhists contain a number of medical statements. Buddhist kings founded hospitals for men and beasts, and appointed regular physicians. The famous Buddhist University at Nālanda in Behar, of which some ruins are still visible, had ample accommodation in the 7th century A. D. for 10,000 students of philosophy and medicine. The third period produced the now current Sanskrit treatises of Charaka, Susruta, Mādhavakara, Vangasena, Bheda, Vrinda and others, on Medicine in general or on particular subjects, such as pathology, fever, infantile diseases, materia medica etc. Charaka is said to have lived at the Court of the Buddhist king, Kanishka ; the great work of Susruta is said to have been recast by the celebrated Buddhist sage Nāgārjuna. The connection of the modern period of medical science in India with the Buddhist epoch may be established, and the high stage of development reached by it seems to date in the main, from the Buddhist time.

In the medical Samhitās themselves, the Atharva Veda is more often referred to. Thus Susruta (1,i) speaks of the art of healing as an *upānga* of the Atharva Veda, and it is otherwise also called an Upaveda. According to Charaka (4, 8, 42) an Atharva-Vedavid Brahmin, should ward off demoniacal influences in the 'Sutikā Griha,' by means of *sānti.* Astāngahridaya (4, 5, 15) recommends as a remedy for consumption, at the end of a long list of remedies, also *atharvoktam* i.e. sacrifices etc. according to Atharva Veda. One must also bear in mind that long before the compositions of medical Samhitas, a rivalry had sprung up between the Vedas and the magic-knowing Brahmins ; and the caste of doctors is mentioned by Manu, as Vaidya, Bhisaj, Chikitsaka, Ambostha. Even as regards the contents, connection between the Vedic and later medicine is not wanting e.g. *jwara*-Ved. *takman.* In the names of the medicinal herbs, which already in the Vedas play an important part with reference to the magical formulæ and in those of the Upanishads, the resemblance is very close to the later ideals. This proves what great importance, the ancient Indians attached to the healing art, and accords with the opinion of the best informed of the foreign writers. Thus Arrian informs us that in the expedition of Alexander the Great to India, " the Grecian physicians found no remedy against the bites of snakes ; but the Indians cured those who happened to fall under that misfortune". " For this reason", Nearchus tells us, "Alexander having all the skilful physicians about his person, caused proclamation to be made throughout the camp that whoever might be bitten by one of the snakes, should forthwith repair to the royal pavilion to be cured. These physicians are said to have made other cures, but as the inhabitants have a very temperate climate, they are not subject to many varieties of disease. However if any among them feel themselves much indisposed, they apply to their sophists, who by wonderful and even more than human means, cure whatever will admit of it" (Arrian's Indian History, vol. ii, Chapter 15).

But the exaggerated theories about the antiquity of Indian medical literature, which were put forward by Dr. Hessler, the author of a Latin version of Susruta, and others have been succeeded in Europe by the hypercritical views advanced by Dr. Haas. He has endeavoured to refer the composition of Susruta's standard work to the period between 12th and 15th centuries A. D. i.e. a great deal more than 2000 years later than what Dr. Hessler had assigned (vide Dr. Haas, in Zeit. der Deut. Morg. Ges. vol. xxx, 571 ff). The ingenious theories of Dr. Haas have been refuted in their turn by Weber and particularly by Prof. August Müller, by whose elaborate investigations (vide Z. D. M. G. Vol. xxxlv), the influence of the Indian writers on Medicine on the medical literature of Arabia has been clearly established. The same influence may be traced in the contemporaneous works of Persian writers on Medicine, as may be gathered from Abu Mansur Muwaffak's voluminous works on Pharmacology. This learned composition contains references both to the medical men of India and to authorities with such unmistakable Indian names, as Sri-Fargavadat i. e. Sri-Bhārgavadatta and Jathak-Hindi i.e. the Indian work on Nativity. What is more, the 584 remedies enumerated and described in this work include many that are more or less native to the soil of India e. g. aloes, tamarind and sandalwood.

Direct proof of the existence of a native Indian system of Medicine far anterior to the Arabian and Persian treatises on Medicine has been furnished, besides those indicated above, by the discovery of the famous Bower MS. and of the two Sanskrit works on Medicine contained in it. The date of this MS. has been referred to the 5th century A. D. both by Dr. Hœrnle and Prof Bühler. Susruta and other leading authorities in the field of medical science figured as prominently in this early work, as in the hitherto known Sanskrit compositions on Medicine (vide W. Z. K. M. Vol. V. pp. 302 ff.)

Nor do the Hindus appear to have derived their knowledge of Medicine from any of their neighbours. The Greeks were the only people from whom they could have borrowed it ; but besides the immeasurable distance and absence of frequent communication between the two countries in such remote times, the Hindus were naturally so averse to travelling and so little desirous of intercourse with foreigners, that the hypothesis of their having borrowed the medical literature seems to stand on an exceedingly slender basis.

SECTION II

The Study of Anatomy, Physiology and Osteology in Greece and in India.

The venerated father of Greek Medicine, the great Hippocrates, who probably flourished before Susruta, had a much more correct conception of anatomical science than the latter ; yet neither in his time nor for two centuries later, is there any distinct record of human dissections being practised by the Greeks. It is not until after the death of Alexander the Great, and the institution of the Museum at Alexandria (304 B. C.), that the great anatomists, Erasistratus and Herophilus recorded their discoveries. In the time of Galen, none of their works remained extant. Yet the Greeks had noble witnesses of their anatomical skill. Their sculpture even to this day is unrivalled for its realism and anatomical correctness. The agonising group of the Laocoons is still the admiration of our time, as it had been of the preceding ages. Could Polydorus, Athenodorus, and Agesander of Rhodes have executed such works as this without a practical knowledge of anatomy? We believe it to be well-nigh impossible. All the great artists of our times are practical anatomists. They know that the expression is produced only by muscular action; and when a Landseer dissects the animals whose expressions and passions he so wonderfully depicts, we must conclude that a Phidias could not have worked without a knowledge of it. "But the most perfect specimens of Hindu sculpture," contends Mr. Webb in his Historical Relations of Ancient Hindu with Greek Medicine, "the relievos in their most ancient cavern temples, show nothing that for truth of form can compare with Greek specimens of art. Neither at Ellora, nor at Karli, nor at Elephanta, nor even among the fresco-buonos at Ajanta, the Hindus ever attained a great knowledge of the muscles or of their power of expression. From their writings therefcre and from their specimens of art, it may be concluded that the Hindus never attained a good knowledge of Anatomy." This captious criticism of Mr. Webb has been refuted by the weighty opinions of Sir John Marshall. "All that is best," Sir John declares, "in the details of Indian reliefs (at Bharut or at Sanchi), the wonderfully skilful and accurate modelling of animals and plants, for instance—are admittedly Indian." Probably it will come as a surprise to many to discover the amount of anatomical knowledge, which is disclosed in the works of earliest medical writers of India. Its extent and accuracy are surprising, when we allow for their early age—probably the twelfth century B.C.—and their peculiar methods of definition. The Atharva Veda evinces a very thorough knowledge of what may be called the coarser anatomy of the human body, naming its various external subdivisions and many of its external organs. Thus in ii, 33, there is a long list of the parts of the body from which disease is to be 'torn'; similar lists occur also in ix. 8, x. 2 and xi. 8. Beyond this, their knowledge, which was to a great extent a pre-historic acquisition (vide O. Schrader, "Reallex d. Indogerm. Altertumskunde") can hardly be said to go. No satisfactory knowledge of human anatomy, however, can be attained without recourse to human dissection. Of the practice of such dissection in ancient India, we have direct proof in the medical compendium of Susruta and it is indirectly confirmed by the statements of Charaka. It is worthy of note however, that in the writings of neither of these two oldest Indian medical writers is there any indication of the practice of animal dissection. Whatever knowledge of the structure of the human body they possessed, would seem to have been derived by them from the dissection of human subjects. And whether cases of dissection were frequent or not, their surprising proficiency in Osteology shows a considerable familiarity with the bones of the human body. As to the Greeks, there is indubitable evidence that an extensive practice of human dissection on dead and even upon living subjects, prevailed in the Alexandrian Schools of Herophilos and Erasistratos in the earlier parts of the 3rd century B. C. But their knowledge of anatomy in some particulars such as in the nervous and the vascular systems, appears, much less than that of the early Indians.

This conclusion is confirmed by the chronological indications, no doubt more or less vague, given to us by the Indian tradition, which places the earliest Indian medical schools of Charaka and Susruta at some time in the first century B. C. This being so and considering that we have direct evidence of the practice of human dissection in the Alexandrian School, and that of the visit about 300 B. C. of the Greeks to India, the conclusion of a dependence of Greek anatomy on that of India may be left out of question. But on the other hand, there is some indirect evidence that the Hippocratics were not entirely unfamiliar with human dissection. (On this and other points touching the Greek Anatomy, see the learned treatise, Dr. Puschmann's "History of Medical Education"), And once admitting the practice of such dissection among both the early Greeks and the early Indians, we may well conceive the general similarity of standard in their knowledge of human anatomy without assuming the hypothesis of an interdependence. In order to be able to verify their mutual dependence we require the evidence of agreement in points which are both peculiar and essential in the respective systems.

No summary of Osteological doctrines, such as we find in the writings of Charaka and Susruta, appears to exist in any of the known works of the earlier Greek medical schools. There exists however a somewhat similar Osteological summary in the Talmud (vide The Jewish Encyclopædia, s. v. Anatomy); and as the Talmudic anatomy is admittedly based on the anatomy of the Greeks, the summary in question may perhaps be taken to reflect the contemporary Greek doctrine on the subject. It is ascribed to the first century A. D., but certain points in it, such as the inclusion of the "processes" and cartileges to make up the total of 248 bones, seem to point to its being rather a survival of the system of the Hippocratic school. In any case, in its methods and details of classification, it differs materially from the Indian, and if it may be taken in any way as a representative of the Greek doctrine, it is difficult to establish any connection of the latter with the Indian. In this connection, a statement of Celsus, who is a fair exponent of the Greek Osteology of the first century B.C. may be noted. Referring to the carpus and the tarsus, he says that "they consist of many minute bones, the number of which is uncertain", but that "they represent the appearance of a single interiorly concave bone" ; and with reference to fingers and toes he says, that "from the five metacarpals, the digits take their origin, each consisting of three bones of similar configuration" (beginning of Book VIII). In the latter enumeration of fifteen joints in the hands and feet, Greek Osteology agrees with the Talmudic and the Indian. As to the carpus and the tarsus, the two views of a number of small bones and of a single bone, are also found in the Indian Osteological summaries of Susruta and Charaka respectively, and the Talmudic summary contains a reckoning of eight small bones. But many centuries ago, a misfortune overtook the Osteological summary of Susruta, the true form of which totally disappeared from all manuscripts owing to its supersession by a falsified substitute, which gained general acceptance through the great authority of Vāgabhata I, who once held the same position in India, that Galen had in the mediæval medicine of the West. At a very early period in the history of Indian medicine, owing to the ascendancy of Neo-Brahmanism, which abhorred all contact with the dead, the practice and knowledge of anatomy very rapidly declined and concurrently anatomical manuscript-texts fell into great disorder. Attempts were made from time to time to restore and edit such corrupt texts ; but divorced from and not guided by practical knowledge of anatomy, they could not but prove unsatisfactory. The earliest example of such an attempt which has survived, is what is called the non-medical version of the summary of the Osteological system of Atreya, which may be referred to the middle of the fifth century A.D.

In the days of Hippocrates, the elementary theory of Physiology was the only one known in Greece. He, as well as Plato, taught that fire, air, earth and water, were the elemental constituents of our body. His views and those, which Pythagoras entertained of health and disease, precisely accord with Plato's and Hindu Susruta's. "When we remember also that Pythagoras introduced Brahminical institutions into Greece, that he as well as Plato believed in the transmigration of souls, we are led to the inevitable conclusion that there was some Indian influence upon the medicine of ancient Greece. The analogy between the Hindu and Greek system of medicine is certainly much too close to be the result of accident" (W. Hamilton, 'History of Medicine,' vol. I., 43). We shall consider this statement later on.

Of the Greek philosophers, Thales considered water as the principal element of our bodies; Anaximenes thought air to be the chief constituent; Pythagoras mentioned fire as the main element; Xenophanes formed us of earth; Empedocles, the celebrated philosopher of Agrigentum (B.C. 578) is said to have first harmonised all these conflicting opinions and given to each element its proper share in the composition of our bodies. Thus he explains the formation of our muscles, by an unequal mixture of the four elements. The ligaments had a superabundance of fire and of earth. It appears therefore, that having found the stuff, these "wise men" hardly knew what to do with it in order to make a man. But the Greek writers became more intelligible to us through the severer abstractions of the Hindus. The Hindus for instance, boldly and fairly embody qualities: these qualities form elements of elements, they arise out of atoms or their grosser forms—fire, air, earth and water, to which the Hindus added the ether (*byoma*).

The Hindu sage, Susruta, says "when digestion is accomplished, the respective elements unite with those which had entered into the fermentation of the body; the earth unites with earth, water with water, etc., and they acting on the inherent qualities of each of the five elements, mix and increase those of the body; smell, the property of earth, with that of the body, taste with water, touch with air and sound with ether." (vide Wilson's Commentary upon the Samkhya Karika Philosophy, p. 121). This is what exactly Empedocles also taught, *viz.*, that the sensations take place only through the affinity of elements composing the object perceived with the elements of perspective organs or senses. He says, by the earthy element we perceive earth; by the watery water; the air of heaven by the aerial element and the devouring fire by the element of fire (see Kurt Sprengel, 'Histoire Pragmatique de la Medicine'.) This passage has been commented upon both by Aristotle and Galen, as being somewhat obscure, but is clearly interpreted by Hindu Philosophy (vide Webb, Pathologica Indica) and is beautifully paraphrased by Milton (Paradise Lost, Book V. verses 4-7). Both Hippocrates and Plato declare that the humors of the body consist of four ingredients, blood, phlegm, black and yellow bile. Charaka and Susruta say air, bile, phlegm, and blood are the chief humors of the body. They are called by them "pillars of the system. If they be deranged they are the causes of disease. Without these the individual could not exist." They assert also that "as long as the elements remain in due proportion the body remains in health, when any one is increased or decreased disease occurs." This causation of diseases agrees precisely with that of Hippocrates and with Plato. Plato says "the disproportion of the physical elements of the body is the proximate cause of all diseases:—since the marrow, the muscles, the bones and the ligaments consist of these elements as also the blood and humors derived from them. Disproportion of the elements produces degeneration of the humors and this degeneration again causes the different diseases" (see Timæus, c. 63). Thus about the elementary theories of Physiology, the Hindus and Greeks are in one accord.

SECTION III.

The Burning of the dead : a custom observed both by the Greeks and the Indians.

Like the Hindus, the Slavonians now-a-days burn their dead ; whilst the ancient Greeks seem to have had both customs, that of burning and that of burying. To the former method, Galen makes a distinct reference in his Commentary on the apothegms of Hippocrates, where he says "it is generally known that Asklepios was raised to the angels in a column of fire, the like of which is also related of Dionysios, Herakles and others who laboured for the benefit of mankind. People say that God did thus with them in order to destroy the mortal and earthly part of them by fire and afterwards to attract to himself the immortal part of them and to raise their souls to heaven." In these words, there is an allusion to the Greek custom of burning, but it seems to have been observed only in the case of great men among them. The Hindus expressed themselves in a similar way. There is an ethereal substance in man by which he is, what he is. This substance becomes free, when the mixed elements of the body are dissolved and scattered by combustion.

Nikolaos Damaskenos states that at Antioch near Daphné, he met with the ambassadors of the Indians, who were sent to Augustus Cæsar. The letter was written in Greek upon a skin, the import of which was that Poros was the writer ; that although he was sovereign of six hundred kings, he nevertheless esteemed the friendship of Cæsar highly. The ambassadors were accompanied by a person, who it is said, burnt himself to death at Athens. On his tomb was this inscription:—"Here lies Zarmanochegos [in Dio Cassius, 549, he is called Zarmanos, a variation probably of Sarmanos, while Zarmanochegos may be a corruption of the Indian word, Sramanāchārya (?)] an Indian, a native of Bargose (Bargose is a corruption of Barygaza mentioned in the Periplus of the Erythrean Sea, the Sanskrit Bhrigukachchha, the modern Broach), having immortalised himself according to the custom of his country." In the pre-historic tombs of Knossos, the corpse was buried in a grave, or else was laid on the pavement of the sepulchral chamber or in a sarcophagus in a larnax of clay. Burial was thus the method of disposing of the dead, followed by all the Mediterranean peoples during the Neolithic period and the same custom obtained in Greece and was continued without interruption at least until the Homeric period. That the Greeks of the pre-Mycenæan and Mycenæan civilisation buried their dead is evident from the tombs discovered in Crete, in the Cyclades, at Mycenæ, Orchomarus and Vaphio. It has also been proved that Schliemann was mistaken in believing that he found in the Mycenæan tombs indications of a partial cremation of the dead. Apparently then, the first notice of cremation occurs in Homer; it is described with grim vividness, specially in the account of the obsequies of Patrocles (Il. xxiii, 110 ff). Homer also offers an explanation of this new funerary custom, which appears to be contrary to the beliefs of the Greek people (Il. vii, 331 ff). But his reason is inadequate to account for so profound a change of custom. The change from burial to cremation must already have taken place in the Homeric age, just as it had previously been introduced in Central and in part, in Southern Europe. It was then introduced into Greece as it had been into Italy, and very probably by the same races who were afterwards known under the name of Aryan, and who originated many other changes in the customs of the people subdued by them.

While in some regions of Europe, there was a period during which cremation prevailed (and among these regions must be included Italy), in Greece the ancient and modern practices flourished for a long time side by side, just as was the case in Rome; but in Rome, from the discoveries in the Forum and from those made in other parts of the city and in Latium, we can plainly recognise the substitution of cremation for burial. This does not appear so clearly in Greece; but it cannot have happened otherwise. At the time of the Homeric rhapsodies, cremation must have been in use quite as much as burial. In succeeding epochs, both methods were employed, as may be gathered from the Greek authors, who testify to the existence now of one custom and now the other.

The usual method of disposing of the dead among the ancient Hindus, is cremation. But the well-known distinction drawn in the Rig Veda (x. 15, 14) between *agnidagdhas* and *anagnidagdhas*, shows that other forms were known and practised. It is not at all impossible that Rig Veda (x. 18.10) originally referred to the rite of burial (Winternitz, Ges. d. ind. Lit. I. 85). The data as to burial are found in the Vedic hymns and specially in the Sutras—the Grihya and the Petrimedha and kindred texts—and in the records of modern usages. But cremation of the dead was and still is, the ordinary practice.

SECTION IV

Analogy between the Hindu and Greek system of Medicine: Dr. Jolly's views.

The medical system of the Hindus like that of the ancient Greeks was for a long time crude, and as might be naturally expected was associated with religion and administered by priests. The Brahmins were the first teachers and improvers of it. They performed the same service to the Hindus, that the Hindus, the Nestorians and the Jews performed to the Arabians and the latter to the Europeans. "Not unwilling to pluck a few more plumes from those who heated their baths with the library of Alexandria," Dr. Royle thinks it probable that Geber, the earliest Arab chemist, was instructed in Rasāyan (chemistry) from the Ayûr Veda. In the earliest Arab author Serapion, the greatest of the Hindu Physicians, Charaka is mentioned by name; in the Latin translation, he is named as "Xarch Indus, or Xarcha Indus." Avicenna calls him "Apud, Sirak Indum," "Rhazes in quit Scarac Indianus," and again says "dixit Sarac" (vide T. F. Royle, 'Essay on the Antiquity of Hindu Medicine'.)

The Greeks, who may fairly boast of having produced the Father of Medicine, Hippocrates, were not slow in appreciating and acknowledging the merits of the Hindu physicians. Strabo quoting Megasthenes states that "there is a class of physicians among the Indians, who rely most on diet and regimen and next on internal application, having a great distrust of the effects of more powerful modes of treatment." In Greece, on the other hand, professors of medicine were divided into two grades, namely, those who pursued it as a profession and those who adopted it as an industrial occupation. Among the latter was Aristotle, who kept an apothecary's shop at Athens. The Ayûr Veda is the most venerable medical authority among the Hindus, for in it is embodied the ancient system of medicine. There are several other medical works based on the plan of the Ayûr Veda, such as the Charaka by Charaka, Bhilatantra by Bhila, Parâsara Samhitā by Parâsara, Hârita Samhitā by Hârita and the Susruta by Susruta. The Agni Purana also treats of medicine. The Charaka and Susruta however are the great standard works of medicine, having a permanent value. The works of these authors do not treat solely of medicine, properly speaking, but more of toxicology, of anatomy, of surgery, and of cures by magic and super-natural agents.

But the question as to whether Indian medical science in its earlier period was affected by that of the Greeks cannot yet be decided with certainty, the two systems not having hitherto been compared with sufficient care. Recently however, some close parallels have been discovered between the works of Hippocrates and Charaka. On the other hand, the effect of Hindu medical science upon the Arabs about 700 A. D. was considerable, for the Caliphs of Baghdad caused several books on the subject to be translated. The works of Charaka and Susruta were rendered into Arabic at the close of the eighth century and were quoted as authorities by the celebrated Arabic physician, Al-Razi, who died in 982 A. D. Arabic medicine in its turn remained in high authority down to the 17th century of European physicians. By the latter, Indian medical authors must have been thought highly of, for Charaka is repeatedly mentioned in the Latin translations of the Arab writers Avicenna (Ibn Sina), Rhazes (Al-Razi) and Serapion (Ibn Sarafyun), as noticed above. Even in modern days, European surgery has borrowed the operation of rhinoplasty or the formation of artificial noses from India, where Englishmen became acquainted with the art in the last century. The Indian rhinoplasty has got some reputation, because of its early introduction and because of its influence upon the plastic operations of European surgeons, such as Carpue, Gräfe, Dieffenbach, perhaps even these two, namely Branca and Tagliacozza. Although the skin of the forehead was used as a substitute for the nose in the operations performed in the 18th century by the Indian doctors, still its connection with the old method namely, where the skin of the cheek was used, could not be doubted. Dr. Haas declared Susruta's description of the rhinoplasty as an insipid modification of a similar description in Celsus (7, 9), and referred to a remark in Chakradatta's commentary on Susruta; according to which the whole of the description in Susruta is said to have been *anarsa* i.e. not genuine. But the references in Celsus have only a faint resemblance to Susruta, and Dallana, Jaiyyata, Gayadasa and others, i.e., the oldest commentators have recognised that portion of Susruta as genuine.

Now let us conclude the subject with what the eminent Indianist, Dr. Julius Jolly, sometimes Tagore Law Professor in the University of Calcutta, has to say about the analogy between the Greek and Hindu systems. "Liecht zu constatiren sind die Indischen Elemente" goes on that learned Doctor, "in dem Arzneischatz des Dioskorides und früherer Autoren, wie Pepéri—*pippali*, Peperéosriza-*pippalimula*, Costus-*kustha*, Ziggíberis—*srngavera*, Kardámomos *kardama*, (ela) hakoros—*vaca*, Bdéllion—*guggulu*, Sakkaron-*sarkara* u. a. Weit schwieriger ist es, den Ursprung der vielen anderweitigen Analogieen zwischen indischer und griechischer Medicin zu ergrunden. Ich nenne z. B. die durchgeführte Humoralpathologie, das rohe, reifende und riefe Stadium des Fiebers, der Geschwülste und anderer Leiden entsprechend der *apepsia*, *pépsis* und Krisis die Einteilung der Heilmittel in heisse und kalte, auch in trockene (ruksa) und ölige d. h. Feuchte (snigdha, picchila) die Heilung der Krankheiten durch Arzeinen von entegegengesetztem Charakter, die echt hippokratische Betonung der Prognostik, die Charakterisirung der Arzte und die an den Eid der Asklepiaden erinnernden Verhaltungsregein für deselben in der Diätetik den Einfluss der Jahreszeiten und die den religiösen Anschauungen der Inder zuwiderlaufende Empfehlung geistiger Getranke, bei den einzelnen Krankheiten das Quotidian, Tertian-und Quartanfieber, *ksaya,* Pthisis u. a., in negativer Bezeihung das Zurücktreten der Herzlieden, von den Symptomen die öfter vorkommende Empfindung des Herumkreichens von Ameisen auf dem Körper, das Essen von Erde bie Bleichsucht in der Entwicklungslehre und Geburtshilfe die gleichzeitige Anlage aller Körperteile, die Entstehung von Zwillingen durch Spaltung der Samenmenge die Bezeihung die rechten Körperseite zu dem männlichen Geschlecht des Fötus die Lebensfähigkeit des Fötus im 7.; das Gegenteil im 8. Monat, die Zerstückelung des toten Fötus und siene Herauszeihung mit einem in der Augenhöhle befestigten Haken, die Schüttelungen zur Beförderung der Nachgeburt in der Chirurgie die Methode das Steinschnittes, die Paracentese bei Wassersucht das Brennen, Atzen und Ausschneiden der Hämorrhoidalknoten die Aderlässe, Blütegel (darunter die aus Griechenland, *Yavana* Stammenden Suç. I. 13) und Cauterien, manche chirurigsche Instrumente, in der Ophthalmologie das Operiren mit der linken Hand am rechten Auge und umgekehrt und andere Details der Staaroperation. Dass in der zeit des noch starken griechischen Einflusses, aus der sich ausser den mannigfachen in Indien geprägten griechischen Münzen sogar ein in seiner Form an die Papyrusrollen, erinnerndes Handschriftfragment, erhalten hat, auch nicht naher bestimmbare medicinische Schriften der Griechen Eingang gefunden haben mögen, ist allerdings um so leichter möglich, als auch die griechische Astronomie, und Astrologie bekanntlich in Indien recipirt wurde. Doch dürfen die griechischen Elemente auch nicht Uberschätzt werden, wie z. B. die Humoralpathologie die in ihrer ausgebildeten Form so sehr an die griechische erinnert, andererseits auch mit der Harmonie der drei *guna* in der Samkhyaphilosophie zusammenhängen kann und in ihren Anfängen schon frühe nachweisbar ist. Am stärksten mag die griechische Einwirkung auf dem chirurgischen Gebeit gewesen sein. Es ist auch beachtenswert, dass B. C, noch nichts über chirurgie enthalten wie dann auch in den späteren Werken die Chirurgie wieder völlig zurücktritt." (Jolly, "Medicin" in Grund. der Indo-Aris. Phil. p. 18).

Many medical Sanskrit texts were translated into Tibetan and again from Tibetan into Mongolian and other languages of Central Asia. Recently, Mahāmohopādhyāy Haraprasād Sāstri in his "Report on the Search of Sanskrit Manuscripts" (1895 to 1900), mentions that the discoveries of manuscripts made in Nepal by Professor Bendall and himself, in 1897 and 1898, are important as regards old Sanskrit Medical Literature. A manuscript of Lañkāvatāra, a Hindu Tantrik work on Medicine, in the Durbar Library (in Katmandu), dates from the year N. S. 28—908 A. D: a MS. of the Medical Glossary, Sārottaranirghanta of Āchāryyavaryya is probably written in 1080 A. D. A important fragment of the Kāsyapa-Samhitā, dealing mainly with Fever and its treatment, has been described in greater detail. Kāsyapa has been referred to in the Bower MS. (2,1010-40) and in Charaka (1, 1, 3). To the famous Nāgārjuna has been ascribed Yogasataka, which, with a commentary by Dhanvapala, is contained in a MS. of 1415 A. D. as also the Yogasāra with its richness of contents. The Chikitsāmrita of Milhana, a splendid text-book on Medicine, was composed in Delhi in 1224 A. D. in the reign of Samsuddin Iltishmish. Naḍiparikshā (or Feeling the Pulse) of Rāmchandra Somayāji, 1348 (Samvat 1405) was also another Hindu work on Medicine. On the veterinary science there are the works of Yogamanjari of Vardhamāna, Aswavaidyaka of Dipānkara and Aswāyurveda of Gana. According to Cordier (Origines, 82, 84) references to fragments of works of Jatukarna, Parāsara, Hârita, Vaitarana, Pushkālavata and Gopurarakshita, have been found in Nepal. We wish that these discoveries are soon published, as these will undoubtedly throw much light on the antiquity of Indian Medicine in general, and will finally set at rest the heated controversy on the interrelation between the Greek and Indian medical systems.

BIBLIOGRAPHY.

1. Sprengel, Kurt ... "Histoire Pragmatique de la Medicine."
2. Wise, T. A. ... "Hindu Medicine."
3. Royle ... "Essay on Hindu Medicine".
4. Valentino ... "Notes sur l'Inde."
5. Littré ... "Oeuvres completes d'Hippocrate."
6. Cordier, P. ... "Étude sur la Medicine Hindoue."
7. Z. D. M. G. vol. xxvi pp. 448-9; xxx. p. 651.
8. L. von. Schroeder ... "Indiens Literatur und Cultur."
9. Jackson, A. V. ... "History of India," vol. ix.
10. Rudolf Hœrnle, A. ... "Studies in the Medicine of Ancient India.
11. Gerrish ... "Text-book of Anatomy."
12. Cordier, P. ... "Recentes Decouvertes"
13. Jolly, J. ... "Medicin" in the Encyclopædia of Indo-Aryan Philology.
14. Lietard ... "La Doctrine Humorale."
15. Haser ... "Lehrbuch der Geschichte der Medicin."

16. Stenzler ... "Zur Geschiche der Ind. Medicin."

17. Wilson ... "On the Medical and Surgical Sciences of the Hindus", Works 3, pp. 269-73.

18. Brian ... "Coup d'œil sur la Medicine des anciens Indiens."

19. Pagel ... "Geschichte der Medicin."

20. Wickremasinghe ... "Catal. Sinh. Manus." British Museum.

21. Munck, E. ... "Geschichte der griechlschen Literatur."

22. Dahlmann, J. ... "Das Altindische Volkstum."

23. Winternitz, M. ... "Geschichte der Indischen Litteratur."

24. Weber, A. ... "Die Griechen in Indien."

25. " ... "Indische Litteratur."

26. Grill in Z. D. M. G. vol. xxvii p. 425.

27. Bühler, G. ... "Indian Studies," vols. i, ii, iii

28. Weber, A. ... "Indische Skizzen."

29. P. von Bohlen ... "Das Alte Indien", Bands I & II.

30. Schmidt ... "Liebe und Ehe in Indien."

31. Journal of the Royal Asiatic Society, 1897, pp. 227.

32. Cantor ... "Gräko-indische Studien."

33. Jolly, J. ... "Early Medical Literature of India" (Transactions 9. Orient. Cong. London 1893).

34. Zimmer ... "Altindisches Leben"

35. Chevers ... "Diseases of India."

36. Vullers ... "Altindische Geburtshilfe."

37. Webb, A. ... "The Historical relations of ancient Hindu with Greek Medicine."

38. Mukherjee, G. ... "Surgical Instruments of the Hindus."

39. Henry, V. ... "La Magie dans l'Inde antique." Paris, 1904.

40. Caland, W. ... "Altindische Zauberie."

CHAPTER VIII

ART OF WRITING

The Origin of the Devanagri Alphabet ; Indigenous or Foreign ? A similarity of form between some of the Greek and Sanskrit Alphabets : The Kharostri writing and its Cradle.

IT has been a matter of considerable dispute whether the Devanagri alphabet is of indigenous or foreign origin. The majority of oriental scholars have held the latter view and have based their theory on the resemblances of the Devanagri to some of the foreign alphabets. Those letters of the Devanagri which stood the test, have been supposed to have undergone modifications, due either to the cursive hands or to the intentional changes made by the borrower. Hofrath Dr. Bühler was of opinion that the alphabet imported into India was made to assume native Indian forms very cleverly.

Before we enter into the discussion, we should note that nothing in the Vedas nor even in the Brahmanas permits us to believe in the existence of the art of writing at the epoch, when these Indian religious literature were composed. There is no mention of writing-materials even, whether paper, bark, or skin, at the time when the Indian Diaskeuasts collected the songs of the Rishis ; nor is there any allusion to writing during the succeeding period. This upsets the common theories about the origin of the prose literature, for, according to Wolf, prose composition is a sure sign of a written literature. It was not so in Brahminical India. "The whole of the Brahmana literature, however incredible it may seem", remarked Prof. Max Müller in his 'History of Ancient Sanskrit Literature', "shows not a single vestige of the art of writing, nay more than this, even during the Sutra period all the evidence we can get would lead us to suppose that even then though the art of writing began to be known, the whole literature of India was preserved by oral traditions only." If letters had been known in India during the period, when men were still able to make gods, a god of letters would have surely found his place in the Vedic pantheon, side by side with Saraswati, the Goddess of Speech and Learning, and Pushan, the God of Agriculture. No such god is to be found in India or in any of the genuine mythologies of the Aryan world.

But there are stronger arguments than these to prove that before the time of Panini and before the first spread of Buddhism in India, writing for literary purposes was absolutely unknown. "Panini," says M. Sylvain Lévi in Quid de Græcis, p. 18, "mentionnè l'écriture grec la yavanani." "But if writing," said Prof. Max Müller, "had been known to Panini, some of the grammatical terms would surely point to the graphical appearance of words. I maintain that there is not a single word in Panini's terminology which presupposes the existence of writing." Yet if one maintains, that at that epoch, the term yavana served to designate all the occidentals in general, "il n'en reste pas moins ce fait que du temps de Panini, l'existence de l'écriture n'ètait plus en connue dans l'Inde."

But writing was certainly practised in India before the time of Alexander's conquest; and though it may not have been used for literary purposes, we can hardly doubt that a written alphabet was known during the greater part of the Sutra Period. Nearchus himself ascribes to the Indians, the art of making paper from cotton. In the Lalita-Vistāra, we read that the young Buddha is learning to write. There are no

Brahmanic inscriptions however, earlier than the Buddhist inscriptions of Asoka on the rocks of Kapurdigiri, Dhauli, Jaugada and Girnar, which belong undoubtedly to the 3rd century B.C. This contradicts the theory of M. D'Alviella that "L'étude des documents indigénes tend d'ailleurs a reporter bien en deça d'Açoka, et même d'Alexandre l'emploi de l'écriture dans l'Inde." In the Lalit-Vistāra too, where all possible alphabets are mentioned, nothing is said of 'yavanani lipi' or Greek alphabet. "The Sanskrit alphabet though it has always been suspected to be derived from a Semitic source has not certainly been traced back to the Greek source. It shows more similarity with the Aramæan than with any other variety of the Phœnician alphabet. 'Yavanani lipi' most likely means that variety of Semitic alphabet which previous to Alexander and previous to Panini, became the type of the Indian alphabet" (Lepsius). But according to the opinion of competent scholars, the time does not appear to have come for deciding at what exact date, by what route, nor even under what form, has penetrated into India the Semitic writing. We shall now examine how far the theory of Lepsius is correct.

An independent and indigenous origin for the Indian alphabet has however been suggested by Sir Alexander Cunningham, Prof. Dawson and others ; Prof. Dawson even goes so far as to assert that the nature of phonetic lessons given by the Sutras required the help of the art of writing. But since their suggestions are not so much based upon positive historical evidence, it found a few supporters. Mr. Isaac Taylor nicely summarises the different theories of the origin of the Devanagri alphabet in his work on "The Alphabet." Three theories have been propounded :—

(i) Prinsep following Otfried Müller was inclined to attribute the peculiarities of the Asoka alphabet to Greek influences,—an opinion upheld by M. Emile Senart and M. Joseph Halévy. Dr. Wilson's guess was that Buddha's followers derived their letters from Greek or Phœnician models.

(ii) A Semitic origin had however already been suggested by Sir William Jones in 1806 and was supported by Kopp in 1821. In 1834, Lepsius declared his adhesion to this opinion, which was afterwards espoused by Weber, who was the first to bring forward in its favour arguments of real cogency. Benfey, Pott, Westergaard, Bühler, Max Müller Friedrich Müller, Sayce, Whitney and Lenormant have given a more or less hesitating adhesion to the Semitic hypothesis, but without adding any arguments of importance to those already adduced by Weber. Benfey's conjecture that it came direct from the Phœnicians is open to fatal objections: "the trade of the Phœnicians with India which commenced at the time of Solomon" said Benfey, "might have been supposed to give India her alphabet." But Mr. Edward Thomas rejects a Semitic origin of the Asoka Alphabet,

(*a*) because of the different directions of the writing :

(*b*) because of the insufficient resemblance of the forms of the letters :

(*c*) because the Indo-Bactrian, which is of Semitic origin, is inferior to the Asokan for the expression of the sounds of Indian Language.

Professor Bühler, on the other hand, marshalled powerful arguments to identify all the 22 Semitic letters in the Brahma alphabet and to explain the formation of numerous derivative signs, which in his opinion the Indians were compelled to add (vide Bühler, 'The Origin of the Brahma Alphabet', p. 58). It is merely an appearance of resemblance on which he has based his theories however. Dr. Gustaaf Adolf van den Bergh van Eysinga, in his well-known work entitled "Indische Invloeden op Oude Christelijke verhalen," at p. 111, follows in the same strain : "Reeds in 1857 had Weber Babylonischen invloed op Indii meenen to herkennen in de Indische astrologie in het Indische schrift. Ein nieuw onderzoek omtrent dit laatste punt leidde Bühler tot de Stotsom, dat de Indeirs hun zoogenaamd Brahmi lipi of Maurya Alphabet, aan de Semeitin hebben ontleend, iets wat ten opzichte van het andere alphabet, het kharosthi lipi van den aanvang of door de geberden is irkend. Dr. Bühler acht involer van het Brâhma lipi uit Mesopotamië over den zeweg reeds in de 8 ste at 9 de eeuw voor christus waarschijnlyk". (On the Origin of the Indian Brahma Alphabet in Sitz. der Philos. Hist. classe der Kais. Ak. der Wissenschaften, Band 132, Wein 1895). The most recent advocate of this theory is Dr. Deeke.

(*iii*) A third theory, that of an indigenous origin, is upheld by specialists of nearly equal authority. This solution was first suggested by Christian Lassen, (Lassen and Karl Ritter, the most industrious encyclopædists had by their epoch-making researches contributed greatly to our scientific and accurate knowledge about Indian antiquities). Lassen was followed by Mr. Edward Thomas who definitely rejects the Semitic source, attributing the invention to the Dravidian races of Southern India. General Cunningham has propounded an elaborate scheme as to the mode in which, as he considers, the Asoka alphabet may have originated out of a primitive Indian picture-writing. The final contribution to this argument is from the pen of Prof. Dawson, whose opinions are entitled to great consideration. His conclusion is "that the peculiarities of the Indian alphabet demonstrate its independence of all foreign origin," and that "it may confidently be urged that all probabilities and inferences are in favour of an independent invention." The Southern Indian alphabet, the oldest form of which we possess in the Maurya and Andhra periods (Nânâghât, Nasik, Karli and Amarâvati inscriptions) no doubt comes before us as a fully developed system about 300 B. C. and is accompanied both in certain Maurya and in certain Andhra inscriptions by an equally developed system of numeral figures, which are clearly syllables. "As far as I can see," said Dr. Bühler, "there can be no doubt that this alphabet was an old institution in India about 300 B. C. and that it owed its development to the grammatical schools of the Brahmans". Now, there is no other alphabet in the world which has developed such a number of signs for nasals; most alphabets have only two, some like the Greek three. If the Indian alphabet is derived from a Semitic source, these nasals must be mostly an Indian invention. The inference as to a very early cultivation of the art of writing in India at a time much anterior to 300 B. C. is strengthened by the consideration of the Northern (Baktro-Arian) alphabet which was clearly worked up by the same class of people, who fashioned the southern system of characters.

The theory of the indigenous origin of the Devanagri Alphabet is based not so much on negative evidence, disproving the theories of foreign origin held by others, as on positive documentary evidence. Prof. R. Shāmasāstry of Mysore throws a flood of light on the origin of the Tântric literature, not inferior in its bulk to any branch of Sanskrit literature, which provides us with a fairer and more reliable clue as to the origin of the Devanagri alphabet than the Egyptian papyrus scrolls do regarding the rise of Phœnician or Semitic alphabets. Prof. Shāmasāstry then goes on to discuss the origin of the Sanskrit alphabet from the Tântric or Āgama literature, taking each letter by itself. Different kinds of hieroglyphs, according to this learned scholar, are derived from the description of the mystic figures in the literature of the Sakti worshippers, the Saivas, the Vaishnavas, the Jainas and even the later Buddhists (vide Indian Antiquary, 1906, p. 258).

"A Greek source", says Prof. Shāmasāstry "may be dismissed without serious examination, as it is beset by difficulties both chronological and phonological of a most formidable nature." But it must be added here that there is a striking similarity of form between some of the Greek and Sanskrit alphabets. Regarding this similarity, James Prinsep observed as follows : "This striking similarity becomes more palpable the farther we retire into antiquity, the older the monuments we have to decipher ; so that even now, while we are quite green in the study, we might almost dare to advance (with the fear of M. Raoule de Rochette before us), that the oldest Greek (that written like the Phœnician, from right to left) was nothing more than Sanskrit turned topsy-turvey." It is not absolutely necessary to contest in this correction, an influence of Hellenic culture. It is to a large extent possible that the Brahma lipi were at first written from right to left, and that its change in direction is attributable to the contact with the Greek mode of writing. "It is equally probable that the Indians borrowed from the Greeks, the usage of the feather, of the tablets, even of the book, if we can infer from the names which they had given to these diverse objects such as ink (melán), kalama (kâlamos) pustaka, book (in Aristophanes pyzion, tablets to write upon) perhaps also phalaka (plakos, plaque) and even pitaka (pittakion, tablet). Finally it is perfectly admissible, that India had taken from the Greeks the idea of the inscriptions on stone, and of the legends on money." (D'Alviella). But this borrowing does not contradict the anterior existence of other indigenous processes of writing to indicate by signs the transmission of thought and to preserve the documents.

The Kharostri Writing: In the north-west of India and

in some neighbouring territories, there was in use in ancient times, an alphabet best known perhaps from its occurrence in some of the records of Asoka and on certain coins, the characters of which were written from right to left, instead of from left to right, as was the case with its contemporaneous Indian script, and to which had been attached the name of Kharostri. The name of this writing was early familiar to Indianists from being placed second, immediately after the Brahmi, in the list of 64 forms of writing in the Lalita Vistâra. In 1886, M. T. de Lacouperie pointed out a passage in the Fa-yuan-shu-lin, in which the Kharostri is contrasted with the Brahmi writing. Savants, relying on this information, applied the name Kharostri to the "alphabet employed in the Gandhara country from the 3rd century B. C. to the 3rd century A. D." The traditional interpretation, preserved by the Chinese compilations and commentaries, where Kharosthi is always translated as "ass-lip" (Sans. *Khara* and *ostha*), seemed to justify this preference for Kharosthi to Kharostri. In support of this etymology, Chinese tradition traces the invention of Kharosthi to a Rishi called Kharostha. But European scholars have made ingenious comparisons to Kharostra particularly with such names as Zaradusht, Zarathustra (vide Weber, Ind. Striefen, Band III s, 8-9). In his "Indische Palæographie," Dr. Bühler writes, "The Kharostri as at present known is an ephemeral alphabet, almost purely epigraphic, of the North-West of India. Its proper domain lies between 69° and 73° 30′ E. long. and 33°-35° N. lat." But the Kharostri manuscript, discovered in the environs of Khotan, of the Dhammapada, and acquired partly by the mission of Dutreuil de Rhins, partly by M. Petrovski, at once confuted these two assertions ; the Kharostri was a writing of the scribes and copyists and was employed exactly as the Brahmi was, to reproduce literary or religious texts. "It appears more and more evident," asserts M. Sylvain Lévi, "that Kharostri was the writing of Central Asia." Sir M. A. Stein, who has explored the region of Takla Makan, announced that on the old banks of the Niya River, he had found 500 inscriptions on tablets of wood in Kharostri characters. Separated by an interval of thousand years, the Greek and Chinese evidences by their agreement show that the name Kharostri was used from the 5th century B. C. to denote the barbarian peoples, Turks or Tebetans, who lived in the north-west confines of India, scattered among the Hindukush and the Himalayas and on the slopes of the Pamirs. Hence the Kharostri must have received the name at a time when the name Kharostra was in ordinary use. Ktesias' reference to the Indian Kalystrioi (Greek Kynokephaloi i. e., Dog-headed), proves that the name was known to the Iranian world, that is in the Persia of the Achæmenides, about 400 B. C. The Greek influence could not have penetrated into India at so remote a date.

BIBLIOGRAPHY.

1. Bühler ... "The Origin of the Brahma Alphabet."
2. Taylor, Isaac ... "The Alphabet," vol. II. pp. 312 et seq.
3. Max Müller ... "History of Ancient Sanskrit Literature."
4. Bühler ... "Indische Palæographie" in Grundriss der Indo-Arischen Philologie und Altertumskunde.
5. D'Alviella, Goblet ... "Ce que l'Inde doit à la Gréce."
6. Cunningham ... "Coins of Ancient India."
7. Indian Antiquary, 1906, pp. 268 et seq.
8. Journal of the Royal Asiatic Society, 1884.
9. Journal of the Asiatic Society, Bengal, vol. III. p. 390.
10. Musée Belge, vol. II. pp. 126-152

11. Gustaaf Adolf van den Bergh van Eysinga ... "Indische Invloeden op Oude Christelijke verhalen."

12. J. Kirste in Actes, Paris, 1897, vol. I.

13. Indian Antiquary vol. xi, pp. 266 et seq.

14 D. H. Müller in Denkschr. Wein Ak. 1894.

15. Sitz. der Philos. Hist. classe der Kais. Akad. der Wissenschaften, Band 132, Wein 1895.

16. Sylvain Lévi ... "Quid de Græcis," p. 19.

CHAPTER IX

LITERATURE

The supposed Indian Origin of the Greek Romances—Resemblance between the Greek and Indian Epics—the Iliad and the Ramayana. The Great Epic, the Mahabharata : its time of composition. The Yavanas in India.—The age of the Ramayana.

Notwithstanding the wonderfully unbroken continuity of Hindu writings, the spirit of classical Sanskrit literature differs greatly from that of the Vedic. The chief distinction between the two periods is that the Veda is essentially a religious collection, whereas classical Sanskrit is with rare exceptions, such as the Bhagavat-Gita, profane. In the Veda, lyric poetry as well as legendary and expository prose mainly deal with prayer and sacrifice ; in classical literature, epic, lyric, didactic, and dramatic forms are all used for the purpose of literary delectation and æsthetic or moral instruction. In classical Sanskrit moreover with the exceptions of the grand compilations of the Mahabharata and the Puranas, the authors are generally definite persons, more or less well-known, whereas the Vedic writings go back to families of poets, or schools of religious learning, the individual authors being almost invariably submerged.

Now, every form of artistic literature, whether epic, dramatic or confessedly lyric, has a strong lyric cast. At the bottom, these three kinds, in the Hindu poets' hands, are but thematically differentiated forms of the same poetic endowment. Ornate figures of speech, luxuriant richness of colouring, introduced into literary composition from the gorgeous climate, flora and fauna of India, subtle detail-painting of every sensation and emotion—these are the common characteristics of classical Sanskrit literature. But even in erotic lyrics the Hindu's deep-seated bias for speculation and reflection is evident. It is Hindu 'minne-song' tinged with the universal, though rather theoretical, Indian pessimism. A few of the Indian lyrists, however, treat love from the romantic or ideal point of view, for it is almost invariably sensuous love. Similarly, the poetic treatment of love in Greece was usually confined, as for instance, by Mimnermus and Anacreon to its sensual aspect and it is clear from the history of the Greek tragedy that a serious pre-occupation with the causes, symptoms or effects of love was considered unworthy of a poet, who aspired to be true to his calling. But Euripides was the herald of a new development in imaginative literature, of which the climax has probably been reached later on, in the romantic novels which became highly popular during the last hundred years. Pathos and sentiment however, were entirely alien to the cold atmosphere and artificial mechanism of these writings. A new tone—that of sympathy with the fortunes of the lovers—asserted itself for the first time in some of the masterpieces of Alexandrian literature. Whether this was merely the result of the diffusion of the Hellenic spirit outside the confines of the city communities through the countries which then constituted the civilised world or more specially of closer acquaintance with popular Eastern tales, it is impossible now to determine.

It is asserted also that the most of the Greek romances were written by authors who hailed from the East. M. F. Lacote, in his "Sur l'Origin indiènne du roman grec dans les Mélanges Indiènne" discusses the question thus : "In India we have been unable to render a satisfactory account of the progressive development of the system of romance-writing. It had never ceased to exist, but extended to all the narratives in prose and perfected itself with regard to the process so well, that the Kathās when most rigorously constructed were nothing but romances. The Greek romance on the contrary, had not delayed to out-strip its primitive type and to approach the ordinary standard of a narrative epic, and at the same time the erotic element was present in it in a more marked degree. The influence other than that of the Indian romances, that may have given to the Greeks the idea of composing "a romance of episodes," we have not been able to trace however. We could think of that of Egypt, of a still more high antiquity, where the popular narratives had taken literary forms. Thus in one of the accounts translated by M. Maspero we see a very good sketch of a story outlined—but nothing more ; the initial scene served as a prelude to the narrative, but the analogy with the Egyptian process can not be extended further. 'Khufu and the Magicians' opened with a scene in which the Pharaoh Cheops felt uneasy, as each of his sons related to him, the miracles of an ancient magician ; then his son Dodoufru proudly mentioned of a sorcerer still alive ; but the rest of the narrative diverged from the initial story. But if one wishes to recognise the type of an Indian frame in it, he would as much be certain to find it in the Alexandra of Lycophron, and better still in the Greek Mimics."

On the other hand says another distinguished French writer, "Il existe chez les Grecs un genre littéraire, voisin de la comedie, que pourrait bien avoir fourni des modéles a des écrivains de l'Inde." It is the Romance, particularly the Erotic Romance, according to this writer, of the Milesian School of which one finds likeness in the Indian novels, written in the 7th century A. D. by such well-known authors as Bāna and Subandhu. Mr. Vincent A. Smith supposes that these tales were imbibed by the young Greeks who settled in that country and frequented the courts of the Indian princes. He also points out that in the works of Bāna, there is a formal allusion to a book written by Yavana (Yavana-prokta-Purāna). Some of the chief works of Greek literature might have been known to, and even appreciated by, a small group of men of letters in India at the beginning of the first century A. D., but they could not have found their way into Indian literature. Again, it may be noticed that about the time of the publication of Greek romance, the intellectual relations between India and Greece were not very close. India, at least the north-western part of it, may have received inspirations from Greece, but Greece likewise received from India through some other intermediary, a knowledge of her romances. In any case, a curiosity is shown by the Greeks for Indian things (Lassen, Ind. Alt. II., pp. 626-752). It is sometimes in the terms, in the descriptions, in thoughts and imageries, that we possibly find a resemblance between the Greek and Indian romances. Peterson in his 'Introduction to Kādambari', outlines a comparison in some important points between Kādambari and Leucippe and Clitephon, and holds with M. Goblet d' Alviella that the Indian romance was directly borrowed from the Greeks. This is denied by M. Lévi (vide "Quid de Græcis veterum Indorum monumenta tradiderint," p. 60). After carefully considering all the parallels between the Greek and the Indian romance we are also constrained to hold that these and many others which might be cited, do not seem to corroborate this fact. In the first place, a large number of them can be considered as such only by straining their sense ; and in the second place, they are obviously the outcome of independent, though partially similar, processes in the development of Greek and Sanskrit literature respectively and should be interpreted accordingly. But even were an essential resemblance granted, it would still be difficult to prove the dependance of the Sanskrit romance on the Greek. The romances of the two peoples are totally different both in plan and in spirit as even a cursory reading will show. The least part of the Sanskrit romance is the thread of the story or the adventures of its characters ; all the stress is laid on rhetorical embellishment, minute descriptions of Nature, detailed specification of exploits and of mental, moral and physical qualities. In the Greek romance, on the other hand, as in Latin, the story is everything. The reader is hurried from one adventure to another, the wilder and more improbable the better ; fine writing is practically disregarded ; description and appreciation of Nature, are to all intents and purposes, avoided. The only Greek romance, that can by the highest stretch of imagination be compared even superficially with the works of Subandhu and Bāna is the 'Poimeniká' of Longos ; but even there, the real similarity lies in the longing for Nature rather than for feverish adventure—a longing which might be traced back to Theokritus, Bion and Moschos on the one hand, and to Bhartihari and his congeners on the other. Even the Dasakumārcharita which, as a picaresque romance, one might be tempted to compare with the works of Achilles Tatios, Heliodorus, and Chariton, is *totally* different in plan from any Greek romance, tracing its 'box-arrangement' of stories to the peculiarly Indian scheme, which may be seen, for instance, in the Kathāsarit-Sāgara or the Jātakas, and which was subsequently carried to Persia, where it was incorporated in the famous "Thousand Nights and one Night", ultimately appearing in the Occident in the Decameron of Boccacio. The adventures narrated in Dandin's romance of roguery, moreover, bear no resemblance, either in plot or in episode, to the amorphisms of Eustathios and his fellows. To sum up, the spirit of the Sanskrit and Greek romancers is as divergent as the learned audiences on the one hand

and the uncultured mass on the other, for whom they wrote; nor can any real affinity be traced between the romances of India and of Greece.

The Epics of India.

The epic poetry in India is much older than the lyric, whose form does not contradict its complete and profound originality. The Vedas contain already the veritable heroic poems, celebrating the exploits of Indra and other divine heroes, who guided the Aryas in their struggles against the Dassyus. Next come the two epic poems, the Ramayana and the Mahabharata, which recite the *itihāses* or histories of that period and faithfully depict the state of indigenous society anterior to its first contact with the Europeans and Hellenic world. But without doubt the Ramayana, which recounts the invasion of the Aryas of the South India and the island of Ceylon, offers a curious analogy to the facts of the war of Troy. We do not think it worth our while to consider the absurd theory of certain Orientalists, who following the wild remarks of Dio Chrysostom (A. D. 117), maintain that the authors of the Ramayana and the Mahabharata were inspired by the Homeric poems, recited in the north-west of India in those centuries by a handful of Greek rhapsodists. In the Indian epic the Ramayana, a foreign sovereign surreptitiously carries off the wife of a prince, who with his allies and after many a strange adventure and numerous combats at last succeeds in recovering his wife; similar in broad detail, is the case with the Greek king and his queen. An ingenious French writer also finds curious resemblances between certain personages who figure in the Indian and Homeric epics:—Nestor and Jambubat, the king of bears,—Ulysses and Hanuman, the general of the monkeys,—Agamemnon and Sugriva,—Patrocles and Lakshmana. But this is more or less superficial analogy.

In all epic poems, one is certain to find heroes and their allies, who distinguish themselves by courage and wisdom. With regard to the heroines in the two epics, Sitā bears many privations and sufferings and is faithful to the valiant Rama to the last; so it is an injustice to compare her to the fickle spouse of good Menelaus. "That the older poem (the Ramayana)" accordingly says Dr. Winternitz, "actually served as a model to Aswaghosha, proves that long before his time, it must have been composed. This agrees well with the fact that in the older and genuine portion of the Ramayana, no trace of Greek influence or any acquaintance with the Greeks is to be found. The two places in which the Yavanas were alluded to, are probably not genuine. There can be no question about the improbability of the theory, which was brought forward by Weber, of the influence of the Homeric epic on the poem of Vālmiki. Between the carrying away of Helena and Sitā, between the invasion of Lañkā and of Troy, there is not even a distant resemblance of the motif, and between the bending of the bow by Rama and by Odysseus, there is quite a distant resemblance."

On the other hand, we may assert with good reason in agreement with Fiske ("Myth and Myth-makers") that "the elements of the myth of the Trojan war are to be found in the Rig-Veda." In the Vedas, the Trojan war is carried on in the sky, between the bright dieties and the demons of night; but the Greek poet, influenced perhaps by some dim historical tradition, has located the contest on the shores of the Hellespont, and in his mind the actors, though superhuman, are still completely anthropomorphic. Of the true origin of his epic poetry he knew as little as Euhemeros or Lord Bacon or the Abbé Banier.

But first to define the Epic. If we mean by this word the genesis of epic story, as may be gathered from the circling narration in the original Bhârati Kathâ or in the early mention of tales of heroes, who are also epic characters, the time of this epic poetry may lie as far back as 700 B. C. or 1700 B.C. There are no further data to go upon than the facts that a Bhārata is mentioned in later Sutra, the latter part of the Satapatha Brāhmana mentions the "circling narration," and that the Akhyāyana stories, some in regard to epic personages, told in prose and verse, go back to the early Vedic period (vide "On the Early prose-poetic Akhyāyana of the Vedic and Brahmanic age," the essays of Von Bradke in Z.D.M.G. xxxvi, pp. 474 ff. and of Oldenberg, ib. xxxvii. pp. 54 ff., and ib. xxxix, pp. 52 ff.). Ballad recitations and Akhyāyana are mentioned in early Buddhistic works, which we may doubtfully assign, not as Professor Dr. Rhys Davids does unhesitatingly, to the fifth century B. C. We must be content with Weber's conservative summary: "The Mahabharata Saga in its fundamental parts extends to the Brahmana period." ('Episches im Vedischen Ritual,' p. 8; "Die Mahabharata Sage reicht somit ihrer Grundläge nach in die Brahma periode hinein").

If on the other hand, we mean the Epic as we now have it, a truly synthetical view must determine the date and we shall fix the time of the present Mahabharata as one when the sixty-four *kalas* were known, when continuous iambic *padas* were written, when the latest systems of Philosophy were recognised, when the Trimurti was acknowledged, when there were one hundred and one Yajur-Veda schools, when the Sun was called Mihira, when the Greek words had become familiar, and the Greeks were known as wise-men, when the eighteen islands were known, when the whole literature comprising grammars, commentaries, Dharmasāstras, Granthas, Pushtakas, written Vedas and complete MSS. of the Mahabharata including the Harivamça was known. But this is a little too much, and even the inconsistent synthetist, who draws on a large vituperative thesaurus whenever any attempt is made to dispute its subsequent date, may well be pardoned for momentarily ceasing to be synthetic and exclaiming with reason, "Da liegt doch die Interpolation vor Augen" ! ("Gensis der Mahabharata").

That the complete Mahabharata for the most part as we have it to-day, cannot be later than the fourth or fifth century A. D. follows from the fact brought out first by the eminent Indianist, Sir Ramkrishna Gopal Bhandarkar and then by Professor Dr. Bühler, that it is referred to as a Smriti in inscriptions dated not much later than the fifth century at least, when it was about as long as it is now. Quite important on the other hand is the fact recently emphasized by Dr. Cartellieri (W. Z. xiii, p. 69, 1899) :—"Fur Subandha und Bāna was das Mahabharata...........kein Dharmasāstra, sondern ein Kavya," which the poem itself proclaims itself to be, I. 16. But we may go further back and say with comparative certainty that with the exception of the parts subsequently added, the introduction to the first book and the last book, even "the pseudo-epic" was completed as early as 200 A. D. For the Roman denarius was known to the Harivamça, and Harivamça is mentioned in the first part of the first book and the last book and is implied also in the twelfth book ; hence such parts of these books as recognise the Harivamça must be later than the introduction of Roman coins into the country (100 to 200 A. D.) ; but though coins are mentioned over and over again, nowhere even in the twelfth and the thirteenth books is the denarius alluded to by name. Another interesting item is contributed by the further negative evidence afforded in the matter of the copper-plate grants. Gifts to priests are especially urged in the Anuçāsana Parva and the gift of land above all, is praised in the most extravagant terms. We know that by the second century A. D. and perhaps earlier, such gifts to priests were ensured by copper-plate grants, bearing the technical name of *patta* or *tamra-patta*, and elaborate instructions for their making are given in the law-books of Nārada and Vishnu, while they are mentioned only in the Code of Yājnavalkya and not before. This epic speaks again of the written Vedas and recognises rock-inscriptions, but in the matter of the recorded grants to priests, says nothing at all (cp. "citrakara iva lekhyam kritvā," v. 189. 1).

"The time of the whole Mahabharata generally speaking may then be from 200 to 400 A. D.", says Hopkins. This however does not take into account the subsequent additions, such as we know to have been made in later times. For the terminus à quo, the external evidence in regard to the Pandu Epic, though scanty, is valuable. Cis-Indic evidence is negative and without weight. Megasthenes c. 300 B. C. has left no fragment of the Hindu Epic and the source of Dio Chrysostom (117 A. D.) who mentions a Hindu Homer, is unknown. The external evidence shows us, first that the Mahabharata is not mentioned in any Sanskrit literary work till after the end of the Brahmana period and only in the latest Sutras composed towards the close of the Sutra period, occur the words Bhârata and Mahabharata. Patañjali it may be admitted, recognises a Pandu Epic in the verse "Asidvityio 'nusasara Pandavam", and in his account of the dramatic representation of the sacred legend indissolubly connected with the tale (cf. Weber, Indische Skizzen, i. pp. 147-9). This takes us farthest back to the second century B. C. Pānini knows the names of the epic heroes and recognises the Arjuna-Krishna cult in giving a derivative meaning of the expression "worshipper of Arjuna" (Krishna). He also, which is more important, recognises the name Mahabharata. According to the Rev. Dr. Dahlmann as Pānini lived in the 3rd century B. C., the Mahabharata must also be as old as the 3rd or the 4th century B. C.

Again, it is one thing to say that Pānini knew a Pandu Mahabharata, but quite another thing to affirm that his Epic is the same as our present Epic. The Pandu Epic, as we have it, represents a period subsequent not only to Buddhism, (500 B. C.) but to the Greek invasion in 300 B. C. Buddhistic supremacy already decadent is implied in the passages which allude contemptuously to the *edukas* or Buddhistic monuments as having ousted the temples of Gods (cp. iii. 190, 65. "They will revere *edukas*, they will neglect the Gods)". More important than this is the evidence of Architecture, which from the places where it is found may all belong to the period of the recasting of the Epic. Buddhistic buildings with wooden fences and walls of bricks and stone are alluded to in Cullavagga (vi. 31), those of stone and metal are attributed to the demon Asura or Dânava Mâyâ, who by his magic powers erects such huge buildings. There is in India, as we have already stated, no real architecture, that goes back beyond the Buddhistic period, and in both Buddhistic and Jaina architecture, some motifs were distinctly influenced by Greek models. In ii, 4, 21, 22, the Greeks are compared to Kālakeya Asura. Here along with the king of Kambodja is mentioned one king Kampana, who was the only man who ever frightened (*kamp*) the Yavanas, though strong, heroic, and skilled in weapons. "Like the Indra he frightened the Kālakeya Asuras." [Compare also the Kālayavana, 'who had the Garga glory' (xii, 340, 95).]

The oldest instances of the use of the word Yavana or Yona in India were discussed by the late Prof. A. Weber of Berlin in his "Die Griechen in Indien" (Sitzungsberichte der Königlich Preussischen Akademie der Wissenschaften, 1890 pp. 901 ff.). He maintained that the Indians adopted the denomination of the Greeks from the Persians. He also remarked that the name was later on transferred to the Indo-Scythian successors of the Greeks in North-western India and further to the Parthians, Persians and Arabs. There can be no doubt that the word was in later times commonly used to denote the Mussalmans and sometimes also in a general way, was synonymous with Mlechchas (cp. Kielhorn, Epigraphia Indica, vol. iv, p. 246). On the other hand, its original meaning was certainly "a Greek". That is the case in Asoka inscriptions in the Besnagar column, and in some of the Nasik inscriptions and Karli epigraphs of the nineteenth year of Siri Pulomayi Vasisthiputta (E. I. vol. viii 60). We find the Yavanas mentioned along with the Sakas and Palhavas, and it is just possible that the word here denoted some Indo-Scythian tribes and not exactly the Greeks. In the Junagadh inscriptions of Rudradamana of the year 72, i. e. probably A. D. 152 (E. I. vol. viii, pp. 36 ff.), we hear of a Yavana king, "rajan" Tushāshpa, who was governor of Kathiawaḍ under Emperor Asoka. The word Tushāshpa cannot be Greek but must be Iranian. Still he is called Yavana. This shows that in the second century A. D., the name Yavana was not restricted to the Greeks only.

The word Yavana also occurs in the three Junar inscriptions, which must be assigned to second century (see Burgess and Bhagwānlāl Indrāji, "Inscriptions from the Cave-Temples of Western India", pp. 41 ff). One of them, Burgess-Indrāji No 7, does not give any further indication of what can be signified by the name. The two remaining ones both mention Yavanas who are further characterised as *gatas*.

The first of them, Burgess-Indrāji No. 5, runs thus :—

Yavanasa Irilasa gatâna deyadhâma be podhiya.

"Gift of two cisterns by the yavana Irila of the Gatas".

The second, Burgess-Indrāji No. 53 reads as follows :—

Yavanasa Citasa gatâna bhojonâmâtapa deyadhâmê sangha.

"Gift of a refectory to the community by the yavana Cita of the Gatas."

The names Irila and Cita and the word Gata do not occur in any other inscriptions, and they have not been satisfactorily explained. Professor Lüders thinks that *gata* represents Sanskrit *garta.* The only thing which is certain, is that the two yavanas are characterised as belonging to the gatas. Junar played a rôle of considerable importance under Western Kshaṭrapas. According to Sir R. G. Bhandarkar (Gazetteer of the Bombay Presidency Vol. I, pt. ii. p. 160) it was the capital of Nahapāna. "There cannot be any objection to explaining the word yavana," says Dr. Sten Könow, "in the Junar inscriptions, a name of other foreign tribes than the Greek, just as in the case of Rudradamana inscriptions, it may denote any of those tribes which formed the following of the Kshatrapas."

In the Mahabharata again, there are numerous allusions to the Yavanas. (One finds an inscription of the 2nd century B. C. dating from the reign of Dattamitra Yonaka Raja, *i. e.* the Greek king, Demetrius). The names of planets and the zodiac occurring in the Mahabharata are considered by some orientalists to have been borrowed from the Greeks : so M. le Comte d'Alviella writes : "Il n'est donc pas étonnant qu'il s'y recontre de nombreuses allusions aux Yavanas et dès lors un peut parfaitement admettre qu'il s'y soit glissé des épisodes empreuntés aux traditions populaires aussi bien qu' aux œuvres litteraires de la Grêce, sans qu'on puisse en déduere une influence quelconque de l'epopée hellénique surle développement de la poésie épique dans l'Inde." (Ce que l'Inde doit à la Gréce). The Greeks are described as a western people (north-western with Kambodjas), famous as fighters, wearing specially fine armour of metal and their overthrow is alluded to therein. The allies engaged in the epic battles are not only native princes, but also Greek kings and Persian potentates who came out of the West to wage the war. In one passage, the Greeks are described as all-knowing (cp. ii, 14, 14 ; iii, 254, 18) "sarvajna Yavana." But even if the passage mentioning the 'all-knowing Greeks' refers to the real Greeks, bearing the name Yavanas (Yavanas or Yonas xii, 207, 42-3, u. Ionians, Jacobi loc. cit.), it is a desperate resort to imagination that in all these cases the word refers to other peoples, as the synthetists assume, such as the Greeks, Bactrians, Persians, Huns and other foreigners mentioned throughout the poem. We should also notice here that the Kshudrakas and Mālavas were united into one nation for the first time by the invasion of Alexander (Lassen, Ind. Alt. ii. pp. 169-71), and that they appear thus united under the combined name Kshudraka-Mālavas in the Epic ii, 52, 15 (Weber, Ind. Stud. xiii, p. 375). The Romakas (not to be identified with the Romans, but a hill-tribe having an abundant growth of hair) are mentioned but once in a formal list of all possible peoples (ii, 51, 17) viz. Cannibals, Chinese, Greeks, Scythians, Persians and other barbarians and stand thus in marked contrast to the Greeks and Persians. The Palhavas, who are mentioned very often, though in the account of Krishna killing a Yavana, the name was Kaserumat (iii, 12, 32); it has been suggested by Weber that the name may be of Latin origin. It is clear from this that while the Greeks were familiar, the Romans were as yet unknown. Further the distinct prophecy, that "the Scythians, Bactrians and Greeks will rule unrighteously in the evil age to come" (Kaliyuga) which occurs in iii, 188, 35, is too clear a statement to be ignored or explained away. When this was written, the peoples mentioned were already rulers of some portions of Hindusthan. If this were the only place, where the names occurred, then the Mârkandeya episode might be regarded as a part of interpolation en masse. But the peoples here described as foreign oppressors are all mentioned repeatedly as barbarians and warriors, associated generally with other peoples of the West as Abhiras and Kambodjas : thus in iii, 51, 23, we have Singhalese, Barbaras or barbarians and the inhabitants of Lañkā (*i.e.*, both the native and Hindu name for Ceylon and the Greek and Hindu name for barbarians!) ["Sinhalān, Barbarān, Mlechchhān ye ca Lañkānevāsinah."] The word *barbaras* (-oi Barbaroi) occurs in both epics, but not in literature of an earlier date. Weber (Ind. Lit. p. 237 note), drew attention to the constant union of Greek with the Western people in other literature as well. The name was extended to Indo-Scythians and later even to Parthians and Arabians (Weber, loc. cit). These are grouped together along with the Western peoples, the Persians, Greeks and Scythians and the folk of Kashmere, Darades, Kirātas, Huns, Chinese, Tusâras, Indus-dwellers etc.. So in xii, 207, 43, opposed to "sinners of the south" are "the northern sinners," *i.e.* the Greeks (yavanas), Kambodjas, Gāndhāras (Kandahar people), Kirātas and Barbaras, who are said to have been wandering over this earth from the time of Tretā Age, having customs like those of the wild animals or of the lowest castes.

Such allusions as these can mean only this : The Pandu Epic in its present form was composed after the Greek invasion. As has long been suggested if the Greeks are mentioned in the epic, among the allied forces, Bhagadatta may be Apollodotus, the founder of the Græco-Indian kingdom (60 B. C.) [Weber, Ind. Lit. pp. 204 ff.] This Greek is especially mentioned not only as a "ruler of the Yavanas", but as the friend of the epic hero's father, (ii, 14, 15) [vide L. von Schroeder, "Literatur und Cultur" p. 463.] But it should be noted that the form of the name Bactrian does not compel us to accept Professor Weber's conclusion with regard to the date of the passages containing this form. If this seems inconclusive, there is no other way but to refer the epic in its present form to a post-Christian era. But even otherwise, the presence of the Greeks and Bactrians as warriors and rulers in India, cannot be explained out of the poem by a loose reference to the fact that India had heard of Yavana before the advent of Alexander the Great.

Dr. Winternitz sums up the various theories about the probable date of the Mahabharata and declares thus, in his 'Geschichte der Indischen Litteratur' (p. 395): "If however the Mahabharata already undoubtedly possessed in the 4th century A. D., the later portions, such for example, as the 13th Book and Harivamça, if at that time the epic had already become a religious and devotional book, and if a century later the MSS. of the Mahabharata had already spread up to further India and were read there in the temples, then we can with perfect justification conclude that it must have received the form which it has to day, at least one or two centuries earlier, that is, in the 2nd or the 3rd century A. D. On the other hand however, it might have received its earliest shape not only after the rise and spread of Buddhism, because it contains so many allusions to it but also after Alexander's invasion of India, because the Yavanas i.e. the Ionians or Greeks are often alluded to and there are moreover references to stone-buildings, whereas before the time of the Greeks only wooden buildings were known in India. The Mahabharata therefore in its present form could not be earlier than the 4th century B. C. and later than the 4th century A. D."

The question of the age of the Ramayana is also involved in some obscurity, because the arguments bearing on it are rather inconclusive. There is no evidence to show that the Ramayana existed even in its earliest form before the end of the Vedic period (c. 800 B. C.). The Ramayana however was, along with its later additions, a complete work by the end of the 2nd century A.D. and was already an old book by the time the Mahabharata had more or less attained its final shape in the 4th century. Various sources of evidence have been examined in order to fix approximately the upper chronological limit of the Ramayana. The history of early Buddhism supplies no decisive information. In the oldest Buddhist literature, the Pali Tipitaka, there is no mention at all of the Ramayana. It is true that in a Jataka, relating to King Dasaratha, there are twelve verses in which Rama consoles his brothers on the death of his father Dasaratha, and that one of these verses actually occurs in our Ramayana. The fact however, that there is only one verse in common indicates that some old story about Rama, other than the Epic itself, is the source of the Jataka verses; for there is not a word in the whole Jataka about Rāvana and his following, though it is full of fabulous matter and has much to say about demons and *rakshasas.* On the other hand, excepting one evidently interpolated passage, there is not the slightest reference to Buddhism in the Ramayana itself. Dr. H. Oldenberg has shown (Guru-pujākaumudi, p. 9 ff) that the metre of the Ramayana represents a later stage of development than that of the Pali poetry of Buddhism. This evidence would place the composition of the original epic, appreciably later than the rise of Buddhism, c. 500 B. C. On the contrary, Dr. H. Jacobi of Bonn adduces some arguments based upon the political conditions appearing in the epic to show that it is anterior to the rise of Buddhism. In the first place, he notes that the city of Pātaliputra (now Patna), which had become the capital of India by 300 B. C., is not mentioned at all, though Rama is described as passing by its very site and Vālmiki makes frequent allusions to the foundation of various actual cities in cast India to show how far the fame of the Ramayana had spread beyond Kosala, the country of its origin; he would certainly have mentioned it, had it existed.

He further observes that in the old parts of the Ramayana, the capital of Kosala is always called Ayodhyā, while with the Buddhists, Jains, Greeks and with Patañjali (c. 150 B. C.) its name is invariably Sāketa. In Book vii, we learn that Lava, one of Rama's twin sons, established his government in Srāvasti, a city which is not mentioned at all in the original Ramayana, but which is known to have been ruled in Buddha's time by King Prasenajit of Kosala. From these data he infers that the original epic was composed while Ayodhyā was still the capital of Kosala, before its name Sāketa was known and before the seat of government was shifted to Srāvasti. It would seem further to follow that the first and last books which also mention Ayodhyā and even when subsequently added contain no reference to the name Sāketa, must have been composed considerably before the time of Buddha. Such a conclusion is highly probable. Dr. Jacobi finally notes that in Book i, Mithilā and Visāla are twin cities governed by different rulers, while it is known that by Buddha's time they had become a single city under the name Vaisāli, ruled by an oligarchy. A further argument has been adduced to show that the oldest part of the Ramayana dates from before the time of Buddhism. The Ramayana is a popular epic and its language is popular Sanskrit. Now about 200 B. C., King Asoka used for his inscriptions not Sanskrit, but vernacular dialects resembling Pali. Buddha himself before B. C. 500 preached not in Sanskrit, but in the vernacular of the people. Hence a popular epic could not have been composed in a language that was already dead, but must have been written in one that the people understood clearly. The original form of the epic must therefore date from a pre-Buddhistic period when Sanskrit was still a living tongue. Occasionally the same verses occurring in the Mahabharata and the Ramayana are also found as Pali or Prakrit verses in Buddhist or Jain texts.

This may imply that such verses have been translated into Sanskrit from popular languages.

Accordingly, a review of all the evidence available so far, appears to indicate that the original part of the Ramayana was composed a century or two prior to the rise of Buddhism, when popular stories current about Rama and his wonderful achievements were collected and worked up into a homogeneous epic by the great poet Vālmiki ; while it may have attained its present extent by the beginning of the first century A. D. Therefore as regards the relative age of the two monumental epics of India, it is well nigh certain that the original form of the Ramayana was finished before the epic-nucleus of the Mahabharatā had assumed a definite shape. For, while the leading characters of the latter are not referred to in the Ramayana, the story of Rama is often mentioned in the sister epic.

Now about the general theme of the epic it was formerly held, especially by Lassen and Weber, that the narrative is an allegorical representation of the spread of Aryan culture to the south of India and Ceylon. This view is, however, not borne out by the statements of the epic itself. The poet is evidently unfamiliar with the south, which he peoples with fabulous beings that might easily be imagined to haunt an unknown country. There is much probability in Jacobi's theory that the second part of the original Ramayana represents a narrative of terrestrial events based on mythological elements, traceable to the earliest Veda. The name of the heroine Sitā appears in the Rig Veda as the personified Furrow, invoked as an agricultural goddess (IV. lvii. 6). In a ritual work of the latest Vedic period (Kausika Sutra, 106) she appears as the divinity of the ploughed field—a being of radiant beauty adorned with lotuses, the wife of the rain-god. In the Ramayana itself, Sitā is said to have arisen from the earth, when her adoptive father Janaka was ploughing, and in the last book she finally disappears underground, received into the arms of Mother Earth. Her husband, Rama would then represent Indra and his fight with the demon Rāvana a modification of the Vedic conflict of Indra with Vritra, the demon of draught. The abduction of Sitā by Rāvana is parallel to the carrying away by the demons of the cows later recovered by Indra. Therefore A. Weber's theory that the Greek influence can be traced in the Ramayana, referred to already, seems to be entirely baseless. The great historian Michelet has made, *à propos* the Rape of the Sabines (Histoire Romaine, livre I, Chapter i) the following reflexions : "The origin of the temptation in the traditions of all nations, the symbol of desire, which carries man beyond his own self, the occasion of war and conquest, is woman. For her, commence the heroic struggles. The wives of Rama and of Krishna had been carried away by Rāvana and Sishupāla in the Indian epics : Brunhild, by Seigfried in the Nibelungs : in the "Book of Heroes" (Livre des Héros), Chriemhild was captured by the Dragon, as Proserpine by the king of the nether worlds. Helen left Menelaus for the Trojan Paris ; the adroit Penelope eluded with difficulty the pursuit of her lovers" (Quoted by M. Leon Féer in his translation of "Cula-Padma Jātaka", Dix Septième Séance de la Congrés International des Orientalistes. Paris, 1873.)

BIBLIOGRAPHY.

1. Gustave le Bon ... "Les Civilisations de l'Inde."
2. Rhys-Davids, T. W. ... "The Questions of Milindā" (Milindāpañha) in Sacred Books of the East, vols. xxv-vi.
3. Jacobi, H. ... ... "Das Ramayana"
4. Havell, E. B. ... "History of Aryan Rule in India"
5. Wilson, H. H. ... "Commentary on the Sānkhyakārika Philosophy."
6. Max Müller, W. ... "History of Ancient Sanskrit Literature."
7. Macdonell, A. ... "Sanskrit Literature."
8. Vaidya, C. V. ... "The Riddle of the Ramayana."
9. Foucoux ... "Le Lalita Vistara."
10. Féer, Leon ... "Traduction du Cula-Padma Jātaka" Cong. Int. Or. 1873.
11. Sylvain Lévi ... "Quid de Græcis veterum Indorum Monumenta Tradiderint."
12. L. von Schroeder ... "Indiens Litteratur und Cultur."
13. Rückert, F. ... "Ramas Ruhm und Sitas Liebesleid."
14. J. Dahlmann ... "Das Altindische Volkstum."
15. A. Weber ... "Die Griechen in Indien" in Sitzungsberichte der Königlich Preussischen Akademie der Wissenschaften, 1890.
16. Kielhorn ... "Epigraphia Indica," vol. viii.
17. Burgess-Indrāji ... "Inscriptions from the Cave-Temples of Western India."
18. Weber, A. ... "Ueber das Ramayana."
19. Cartelliére in W. Z. (1899) vol. xiii.
20. Von Bradke in Z. D. M. G. Bd. xxxvi, pp. 474 ff.
21. H. Oldenberg in Z. D. M. G. Bd. xxxvii pp. 54 ff; Bd. xxxix pp. 52 ff.
22. Weber, A. ... "Episches im Vedischen Ritual."
23. Munk, H. ... "Geschichte der griechischen Litteratur."
24. Winternitz, M. ... "Geschichte der Indischen Litteratur."
25. Mahaffy, J. P. ... "Social Life in Greece from Homer to Menander."
26. Westergaard, N. ... "Uber den altesten Zeitraum der indischen Geschichte."

27. Brünnhofer ... i. "Iran und Turan.".
ii. "Vom Pontus bis zum Indus."
iii. "Vom Aral bis zur Ganga.".

28. Ludwig, A. ... "Ueber das Ramayana."

29. Hopkins, W. ... "The Great Epic of India."

30. Schmidt, R. ... "Liebe und Ehe in Indien."

31. Baumgärtner, A. ... "Das Ramayana, und die Ramalitteratur der Inder."

32. Rohde, E. ... "Die griechische Roman."

33. Mahaffy, J. P. ... "Greek Life and Thought."

34. Lacote, F. ... "Sur l'Origine indienne du roman grec."

CHAPTER X

DRAMA

The Question of Greek Influence on Indian Drama :—The Employment of Children on the stages of ancient India and Greece.—The Characteristic Differences between the Greek and Hindu Drama :—Pischel and Lévi *versus* Weber and Windisch : M. Lévi's remarks on the subject.—The Period of Classical Sanskrit Literature (319-800 A. D.) :—The Probable Origin of the Indian Drama.

"ORIENTAL poetry," remarked Dean Milman, in the Quarterly Review, (1811), "is generally proscribed in the mass, or offering more than a brilliant confusion of florid diction, of frigid and fantastic metaphor, not merely false to European nature, but to those primary and universal principles of taste which demand that the language should be in harmony with the thought, the imagery in keeping with the sentiment." Yet if we can form anything like a reasonable estimate of the Sanskrit poetry, we may safely pronounce that the diction of the Indian poets is peculiarly simple, their luxuriance is not in the language, but in the subject-matter of their poetry ; in their infinite variety, vastness and exuberance of their mythological fables ; it is in these that their imagination sometimes runs riot ; not in the redundance of metaphor or in the profusion of the unmeaning similitude—in this respect their taste is Grecian, rather than Italian. The elegant mind of Bishop Heber, at the very commencement of his Oriental Studies, perceived at once the distinction : "I have more and more convinced myself that what is called the florid eastern style is chiefly to be found in translations ; and that the characteristics of the originals are often rather flatness and vapidity than exuberance of ornament." The justice of this remark, we apprehend will be denied by all competent judges, even as regards Arabic and Persian poetry ; and however all the countries, including India, may have their Seicentisti, their Marinos, and Gongoras, the general character especially of the earlier poems is directly the reverse of Bishop Heber's statement. For instance, Kālidāsa's Meghadûta or "Cloud Messenger," is a lyrical gem which won the admiration of Goethe and the idea is taken by Schiller in his "Maria Stuart," where the captive queen of Scots calls on the clouds which fly southwards to greet the land of her youth (Act III, sc. i.). But the mythology with which the Indian poetry is as instinct as that of the ancient Greeks, suggests but dismal images to the European mind. The Westerners are cradled in familiarity with the gods of Greece or Rome—their very haunted dwellings are sacred to their imagination—Tempé and Arethusa, Delphé and Helicon are peopled with their tutelar deities, whose forms and attributes rise up at once before their mind's eye ; but they feel a sacred horror at the name of the holy mountains, Meru and Kailāsa, Ayodhyā and Vidarbha awaken far different trains of thought from Troy and Thebes. It is for this reason that most European critics cannot properly appreciate the Hindu Poetry and Drama.

The theatrical representations of modern Europe, however diversified by national features, are the legitimate offsprings of the Greek drama. Widely as the Mysteries and Moralities differed from the plays of Æschylus or Aristophanes, they emanated from the schools where those writers were read, and the cultivation of the cloister, unimbued with the animation of social life, produced no worthier harvest than those crude and absurd compositions. Such as they were however, they formed the connecting link between the ancient and modern theatre and they united the compositions of Shakespeare, Lope de Vega and Racine with the songs of Bacchus and the monologues of Thespis.

On the contrary, "whatever may be the merits or defects of the Hindu drama," says Professor H. H. Wilson, in his 'Select Specimens of the Theatre of the Hindus', "it may be safely asserted that they do not spring from the same parent, but are unmixedly its own." "There are dramatic expressions in India," again says Professor Pischel, "which date from very ancient times" (The Home of the Puppet Play). Even the oldest monument of Indian literature, the Rig-Veda, of which the earliest parts date back to more than 3000 B. C. (vide Jocobi's opinion, J. R. A. S., 1909), contains more than a dozen hymns in the form of a dialogue and of partially dramatic composition, such as those of Saramā and the Panis, Yama and Yami, Pururavas and Urvaçi. On such solemn occasions, as the Aswamedha sacrifices, it was the custom in the Vedic times to recite old histories and songs, and the performers, the priests of the Rig-Veda and the Yajur-Veda, spoke in turn (see Hillebrandt, "Die Vedische Ritual"). The great grammarian Pānini, who is usually supposed to have flourished in the fourth century B. C. (vide Goldstücker, Pānini) mentions text-books for actors (*nata-sutra*) and his commentator Patañjali, who lived as is generally believed towards the middle of the second century B. C., not only frequently alludes to actors but also to jugglers (*sobhanikās*). He further mentions that the rhapsodists, when reciting the love-story of Krishna and Radhicā, divided themselves into two groups, one belonging to Krishna's party and the other representing the adherents of Radhicā, (as was seen in Bengal till the last decade of the 19th century, in what is popularly known as the *yātras* and *kavis*' retorts). Bharata, the mythical inventor of drama, which in Sanskrit also means an actor, is mentioned in the Mahabharata, where there are also frequent references to players (*natas*) (vide Huizinga, 'Die Vidusaka in Lit. Indische Toonul'.)

The native account of the origin of the drama, was that it came down from heaven as a fully developed art being invented by the divine sage Bharata. This theory cannot be accepted by modern scholarship, and we are forced to pre-suppose a development from the religious to the dramatic, which is not essentially different from that found in Greece. The earlier stages which are connected with religious festivals and specially with the worship of Krishna-Vishnu, were not unlike the primitive Christian Mystery-Plays of the Middle Ages of Europe. We shall consider the probable origin of the Indian drama in detail, later on.

Unfortunately, of the ancient Indian dramas not one has come down to us. Only recently, the discovery of the plays of Bhāsa has been made and the Travancore Government must be congratulated upon it, as conferring an inestimable boon upon the Sanskritists of East and West. Thanks to the energy of Mr. T. Ganapati Shastri, the Curator of the Department for the Publication of Sanskrit Manuscripts at Trivandrum, the plays of Bhāsa have been brought to light and we are now able to see how thoroughly just were the praises lavished upon this dramatist of far-off antiquity. It is not yet possible however to accurately fix the date of this author. All we can do is to bring it within certain limits. The upper limit to the period during which he must have flourished, can be determined by means of internal evidence consisting of references to historical places and persons. The determination of the dates of Kālidāsa and Sudraka will give us the lower limit. The former expressly mentions Bhāsa's name in Mālavikāgnimitram and Mricchakatika is clearly an adaptation of one of Bhāsa's plays, viz. Chārudatta. Mr. K. P. Jayaswal holds Bhāsa to have been the court-poet of the Kanva king in the second half of the first century B. C. (vide J. A. S. B. 1913, p. 259). Some hold Bhāsa to have flourished before Pānini, on the ground of his using a good many archaic forms, which could possibly have no place in an author coming after Pānini. This argument is not tenable however. It is admitted that Sanskrit was a spoken language at the time of Bhāsa, but it was not so in Kālidāsa's times. Now an author writing in a dead language pays greater attention to grammar than one who writes in a current language. Even in Kālidāsa we meet with solecisms, though Pānini must have come to be looked upon as an authority in his times (vide Raghu Vansam, v. 34; xix, 50; Kumāra Samvabam i 35). Prof. Bhide fixes about 450 B. C. as the upper and 321 B. C. as the lower limit to Bhāsa's period. But the exact date cannot be determined as yet.

Of Bhāsa, with may repeat with slight changes what Hutton says of Goethe: "He is both subjective and objective, we find in his works at once a vague indefinite self-reflecting, defined and clearly outlined influence that impresses that self. His own mind is the sheet of water which reflects the image and we see only that it stretches vaguely away far and beneath the image, it is reflecting. But what catches the eyes is the clear outline of the reflected object in the water." Hence by far the best part of his work is that in which external objects and social impulses are described e.g. his Swapna Vāsabadattā and Chārudatta. But the Indian dramas present themselves to us in their most perfect shapes and finished types in the works of Kālidāsa, the greatest of the Sanskrit poets. The richness of creative fancy, which he displays in his dramas and his skill in the delineation of tender feelings assign him a high place among the dramatists of the world.

Before entering into the heated controversy, which

rages round the question of indebtedness of Indian dramas to Greek tragedies and comedies, we should like to point out an interesting parallel in the employment of children on the stage in ancient Hindu and Greek drama, as well as in the European plays of the mediæval times. The presentation of children on the stage in the historic productions, is a recognised element not only in Hamlet, (allusion to the little "eyases that cry out on the top of the question and are most tyrannically clapped for it,") but is also a factor in the dramatic composition of all ages. In listening to the 'Alcestis' of Euripides, Greece truly felt the pathos of a parting farewell of a loving mother and devoted wife from her weeping children ; and the heart of the Athenian audience must have been deeply stirred by the plaintive wail of the orphan Eumelus, in whatever manner his childish lamentations may theatrically have been represented. The shrieks of the wounded sons of Medea, pierced by the murderous sword in their frantic mother's hands, must have frozen the spectators to the marrow, as they came from behind the scene where the terrible deed was enacted. The introduction of the children of Polymestor on the stage in Euripides' "Hecuba", and the appearance of the infant Oerstes upon the scene in the "Iphigenia in Aulis," are other instances of minors on the stage of ancient Greece. In the Latin drama, the baby in the fourth act of Terence's comedy "Andrea" is another example, though infants may perhaps have been represented merely by a bundle of long clothes, just as the new-born child of Hermione was possibly represented in Shakespeare's "Winter's Tale." In whatever manner such representations might have been made, the conditions of the classic drama in Greece and Rome were hardly favourable to the frequent introduction of children on the stage.

The English romantic drama however, throughout its whole history, abounds in examples of children employed in scenic representations. The statement holds good from the beginning of the English drama in the 12th and 13th centuries, when the old Miracle Plays at Chester and York rudely represented the "Martyrdom of the Innocents" down to the days when societies for the prevention of cruelty to children exercised some control on the theatrical representation of such scenes. The famous company of children-players in Elizabethan times, has been alluded to in the passage quoted above from "Hamlet." The prattling child of Macduff, the spirited little son of Coriolanus, the tantalising, precocious, impish Moth in "Love's Labour Lost," the two ill-fated little Princes and the gentle Arthur in "King John" are each illustration of a character having a distinct dramatic function, stirring the emotion and adding to our interest in the histrionic situation.

In the old Sanskrit dramas we have precisely a parallel instance of children being presented on the stage. That children actually played the rôle, is plain enough from the speech and from stage directions ; and it is well within the scope of our fancy to believe, that the performance often won applause from more than one Hindu sovereign. A word may be added with reference to the propriety of their presence in the plays. As Sir Philip Sidney's comment upon the violation of the unity of time in the English drama, would equally apply to the Indian drama, the part played by children is the easier perhaps to be accounted for. They appear in a number of the best-known works of Sanskrit writers. In two of the romantic plays of Kālidāsa, we have been introduced to the scene in the last act, when a son of the hero and heroine, whose love forms the theme of the drama, appears. First to be mentioned among Kālidāsa's plays, is the well-known "Sakuntala," (a dramatic representation which received Goethe's high praise) and secondly, his "Vikrama and Urbaçi." In the dramatist Bhababhuti's "Uttara-Rāmacharita," we have a sort of Sanskrit Winter's Tale, in which a similar rôle is assigned to children, as in Shakespeare's counterpart. In the play of Mricchakatika, ascribed to Sudraka, Rohasenā, the son of the hero of ruined fortune, plays a pretty part. In the "Mudrārākshsa," a political drama by Vishākhadatta, in the closing Act (Act VII), an upright merchant, who has been convicted of a false charge, is to be put to death by impalement. The presence of his wife and little son renders the situation more harrowing. One other play remains to be noticed: this is "Chanda-Kausika" by Kshemeswara. In it, the little son of the blameless king Harishchandra of Oudh, accompanied by his father and mother, offers himself in the market-place of Benares for a purchase as a slave (Act III).

Weber and Windisch versus *Pischel and Lévi.*

We should content ourselves to trace in broad outlines, the genesis of the Indian Theatre, the literary history not permitting us to follow step by step the formation of the classic type of the Indian drama, till the composition of Sakuntala. Is it necessary then to conclude from this, that the Indian drama is not the result of a regular evolution ; and that the finished product has been transplanted in full bloom from a neighbouring country? Among peoples who dwelt in or near the borders of India and came in contact with it at that remote period, the Greeks alone had a dramatic literature. Is it therefore Greece which gave to India her noble dramatic literature? Prof. Weber, who is a well-known pro-Hellenist, in his "History of Indian Literature" was the first to suggest that the representation of the Greek dramas at the courts of Hellenistic kings in Bactria, the Punjab and Gujrat, where the Greek power had already extended, awakened the Hindu faculty of imitation and thus led to the birth of Indian drama. Without doubt, there are no positive proofs to furnish, but the data of history at least make the hypothesis, incontestably certain in as much as the more ancient Indian dramas were composed in the west of India. But his suggestion was qualified and almost negatived by the remarks appended to it, so that the hypothesis does not admit of direct verification and that no internal connection between the Greek and the Indian dramatic literature can be proved.

But if Sanskrit theatre came into existence at the court of the Kashatrapas, as some theorists believe, the theory of Greek influence seems to gain in probability. The country of the Kshatrapas was doubtless the most Hellenised of India, because of its being the most important mart for Hellenic commerce. According to Strabo (ed. Müller-Didot, 82, 18) young female musicians of Western origin were articles of import and these, the Greek merchants offered together with musical instruments to the kings of that part of Gujrat (vide Periplus of the Erythrean Sea, p. 49). The fore-runner of Columbus, Eudoxus of Cyzicus (*cir.* 130 B. C.) on setting out from Gades to go to India, shipped as cargo, "*mousika paidia karia.*" M. Sylvain Lévi has added a note as follows; "This occasion is a suitable one for drawing attention to a new illustration as unexpected as it is striking of the liking, which the wealthy Indians had for young people of the West" (Journal Asiatique, July-December, 1908). The third fascicules of the Oxyrrhynchus Papyri (edited by Messrs. Grenfell and Hart), contains a fragment of a Greek farce played in Egypt which had its scene laid in India and had for its topic the adventures of a young Greek charition, who finds himself in the power of an Indian king. By virtue of its importance to the history of the Indian theatre, this fragment calls for special study. These Kshatrapas however, like the Greeks are strangers, chance-masters imposed by the conquest, of Scythian origin, confounded with the Greeks with whom tradition always associated them (Saka-Yavana) ; they introduced into India the great religious toleration which characterised their race, and which manifested itself in the Helleno-Irano-Indian pantheon on the coins of Kushanas as well as in the universal religiosity of the Moghul Emperor, Akbar. It is not upon them that the Brahmans must count for the restoration of their influence ; their mere presence in power is an insult to orthodoxy. Buddhism on the other hand greets and welcomes with favour these curious and childish barbarians, always ready to adopt a new faith without abandoning their ancient gods, happy and flattered to naturalise their families and their gods in the classic soil of fabulous riches and of the all-powerful priests ; it satisfies therewith its thirst for propagation, its ardour of apostleship, it preaches its holy truth to them, its ideal of gentleness and charity. Rudradaman flatters himself "to have kept his promise to respect human life except in combat." The immortal glory of Kanishka, still spread over all Asia, attests what price, the church had to pay for the adherence of these barbarians. But there is nothing to lead us to believe that the Greek influence could have extended to drama ; the Greek characters engraven on the coins of Kshatrapas seem to prove that Hellenisation was not complete. Varnished through the chances of their adventurous existence by Iranism, Hellenism, Brahminism and Buddhism, they burst the bonds of Brahminic organisation, but still too rigid to introduce themselves within it, these barbarian conquerors condemned by orthodoxy, prepared for the unity of India.

The Danish scholar, E. Brandes, accepted the hypothesis doubtingly propounded by Weber (Indian Studies xiv, p. 194 note), and boldly undertook to prove the reality of an internal connection between the ancient Indian plays and the New Attic Comedy, as chiefly preserved in the Roman adaptation by Plautus and Terence. The general probabilities in the favour of the theory, that the Indian plays are derived from the New Attic Comedy of the School of Menander, rest chiefly on the evidence, which points to an active and long-continued intercourse between the East and the West. A special agency, according to the Danish Indianist, was furnished by the travelling companies of players, who were known to have traversed the Hellenistic kingdoms. Menander and Philemon were both invited to the court of Ptolemy Soter. Prof. Pischel, who was perhaps among the Orientalists of the West most familiar with the rhetoric and dramaturgy of India, criticises shortly the above opinion thus: "If one imagines that the Greek theatre exercised a certain influence upon the formation of the Indian drama, it shows an equal ignorance both of the Greek theatre and of the Indian plays" ('Die Recens. d. Çakuntala, p. 19).

But this view of the Greek influence on Indian drama found another able advocate in Dr. Windisch, who most fully expounded it in his communication to the Congress of Orientalists at Berlin in 1882, II. ii. 3 ('Die Griechische Einfluss im Indischen Drama'). He showed that the theatre of India was influenced by the newer Attic Comedy of Menander and Philemon. Dr. Windisch has the merit of putting the question on a distinct and solid basis and of giving the discussion a definite standpoint. Greek ideas, according to him, entered India chiefly by two routes, one overland through Palmyra and Bactria, and the other maritime through Alexandria and the ports of the Western coast, specially

Barygaza, the modern Broach. We know from the anonymous Periplus of the Erythrean Sea, which was written between 60 and 89 A. D., that an active commerce was carried on between Barygaza and the inland city of Ozene (Ujjain), where Asoka had been a viceroy as Crown Prince, and which in the time of the author of the Periplus was a great depôt of foreign trade. The scene of the Mrichhakatika or the Clay Cart, one of the most ancient Indian dramas extant, is laid in Ujjain and its neighbourhood. This and several other considerations led Dr. Windisch to conclude that the Indian drama was first developed in that city, as a direct result of the intercourse with Alexandria. M. Windisch, first of all, collects the texts that attest Greek representations in the Orient after the conquests of Alexander ; he then arranges the documents cited by Bohlen, Reinaud, Lassen, Benfey, Weber and others, on the relations between Greece and India ; he notes (with Otto Lüders, "Die Dyonisischen Künstler") the presence at the camp of Alexander, of numerous artists (*technitai*) who followed the Macedonian phalanx and enjoyed grand solemnities there. However says M. Lévi, "Tous les documents allégués ne prouvent rien directement. Alexandre ne fit qu'effleurer l'Inde et les representations grecques mentionnées par les historiens, s'appliquent à la Susiane, à la Perse, à la Gédrosie, à la Parthie, à la Armenie, à des provinces enfin qui gravitaient autour des centres helléniques. On peu cependant admittere sans preuve qui les rois grecs de la Bactriane entretinrent à leur cour an theâtre grec." But, asks the great Frenchman, how to connect those representations with the formation of *nātakas*? The Greek domination which continued in the basin of the Indus, owing to the ephemeral conquests of Demetrius (Dattamitra) and of Menander (Milindā), disappeared entirely from India during the first century B. C. Kalidasa composed his dramas five or six centuries later. Is the Greek influence to be admitted in view of the fact that the study of Greek models was continued during this enormous interval in the Brahmanic Schools? The conjecture drops down of itself without discussion, for its inherent absurdities; for then, we are to suppose that the dramatic literature of seven centuries disappeared without leaving any traces whatever. Moreover the earlier imitations of Greek drama should have survived the master-pieces that were subsequently produced. Again, as M. Windisch asserts that if the Greek models simply inspired the Indian poets, then they must have exercised that influence on an art already living; how then are we to determine the limits of that influence, how to discern with precision their last vestiges, after an evolution of six or seven centuries?

Dr. Windisch further recognises that the dramas of India offer few points of resemblance to the tragedies of Æschylus or Sophocles, yet he compares them with the new Attic comedies, as already observed. "It is here" he exclaims, "that we find an echo of Rome in the bazars of Ujjaini. The formal structure of the Sanskrit dramas closely resembles that with which we are familiar in Plautus and Terence. Like the Græco-Roman, the Indian plays are divided into acts and scenes and each piece is preceded by a Prologue." The mere fact, according to this learned professor, of the existence of a prologue in an Indian drama as in the European plays, is itself surprising. Again, the love-story of the Indian drama is, in plot, development and dénouement essentially of the same kind, as in the Græco-Roman comedy. "The plot of the Mrichhakatika may be accurately described", says Dr. Windisch, "in the words applied by Rost to the Curculis of Plautus: 'The subject of this comedy is very simple and depends as usual on a secret intrigue, the lover's want of money and the supplanting of a rival.' The fair Periditas of Plautus and Terence, who eventually turned out to be high-born daughters of Athenian citizens, find their parallel in the maids of the Indian plays, Mālavikāgnimitram and Ratnāvali, who were princesses in disguise, and the *anageorismos* or the recognition of the disguised young ladies, which is a critical incident in nearly every Greek and Roman play is repeated merely with variations of detail in the Indian adaptations. Other stock characters of the Terentian comedy have also been imported into the Sanskrit drama. The *parasitus êdax*, the *miles gloriosus* and such like casts, so familiar to all the readers of the Græco-Roman comedies, are reproduced respectively as Vita, Vidusaka etc. of the early Indian dramas." These arguments of M. Windisch have been carefully considered one by one and in great detail by M. Lévi and he finds none of them convincing (vide 'Le Théâtre Indien', pp. 348 et seq.) : the Attic Comedy treats of the ordinary life of the people and with its local tone it deals with the common traits of humanity in general—their virtues and their failings. The passages of Plutarch (the first passage is from the pamphlet entitled "The Fortune of Alexander," and the second is from "The Life of Crassus"), on the Greek representations in the East, cited by Dr. Windisch, in support of his theory do not prove anything. The first relates to Sophocles and to Euripides, and the other, to the Bacchantes of Euripides : the comedy has not been mentioned at all. The references of Dr. Windisch are not justified very well in fact; in spite of its general character and its human interest, the Attic Comedy had undergone profound transformations in its passage from Athens to Rome, though the Greek civilisation had already penetrated the Roman public-life. Thus M. Lévi comes to the conclusion that "L'Inde n'a pas eu besoin d'étudier les modêles Grecs pour apprendre que les intrigues privées, se croisaient parfois avec les événements publics, que les tribunaux siégeaient et prononçaient des sentences, parfois erronées, que les fêtes religieuses offraient souvent à l'amour une occasion d'agir, que la passion était capable de pousser une âme faible ou mal, et que la liberté s'achetait frequemment, —â prix d'argent." The learned Professor goes on: "M. Windisch, au terme de son étude, nous dirions presque de son plaidoyer en faveur de l'influence grecque sur la théâtre indien, s'exprime ainse : " Si la présente dissertation (Der griechische Einfluss im Indischen Drama) n'amene pas á croire à l'influence grecque, il faut alors entièrement renoncer à cette hypothèse, car il sera difficile de trouver en sa faveur des arguments plus serieux." Nous souscrivons volontièrs à cette déclaration. M. Windisch à reuni avec une patience ingénieuse et une érudition substantielle, les indices, les vraisemblances, les simples possibilités favorables à sa thèse ; il les a mis en œuvre avec un art séduisant de combinaisons ; il a défendu sa cause avec une conviction sincére et loyale... Les œuvres connues actuellement, ne portent que du vi[e] siècle apres J. C.; les indications dont nous disposons permettent de remonter encore un siècle en arrière ; où dela, c'est la nuit. L'influence ètrangère ne se trahit pas où moindre signe, au moindre mot. L'évolution de genre dramatique se continue régulièrement, lente et sûre. Entre le présence des dynasties, veritablement grecques, grecques de race et grecques de culture, et l'apparition historique de là poésie dramatique dans l'Inde, s'étend un intervalle de cinque siècles, un abime. Le plus anciens envahisseurs ètrangers qui aient marquè dans la théorie et dans la practique du théâtre leur empriente vivante sont les Sakas, les successeurs mêmes des Grecs. II ne reste plus des Grecs qu'un nom vague, sans valeur locale ; les Yavanas figurent, par habitude dans les énumérations techniques pêlemêle avec des races barbares, sans honneur. Les rares vocables qui paraissent preserver leur memoire, yavani et yavanika, manquent d'intérêt pour l'histoire de la litterature dramatique, l'un désigne une espèce de rideau employyè à la decoration de la scène, et aussi d'autres usages ètrangers au theéâtre ; l'autre s'applique à des amazones chargées de garder la personne du roi et qui paraissent uniquement dans la figuration.

"Le raisonnement, comme les faits, dément l'hypothèse de l'influence grecque ; le goût arbitre douteux, mais contrôle efficace, s'accorde aussi à la repousser. Les littératures savantes de l'Europe, créées ou remaniées sur la modèle des classiques anciens, nous ont familiarisés avec les charactères ordinaires de l'emprunt : il ne se divine pas, il éclate ; il ne se cache pas, il s'avoue orgueilleusement. L'admiration de l'œuvre originale, qui provoque l'imitation porte l'imitateur à la copier avec une fidélité presque servile ; il peut essayer d'adapter son modèle au goût des temps et du pays, de la naturaliser par une transposition habile ; il ne réussit pas, il ne cherche pas même à en effacer les traits principaux. Les sujets, les sentiments essentiels, l'allure générale de l'action ne se modifient pas. L'œuvre et le souvenir de Guilhem de Castro auraient puperir, l'inspiration espagnole du Cid, n'en aurait pas été moins certaine ; Racine prouverait encore Euripide, si la tragédie grecque devait, disparaître un jour. Le erudits n'auraient pas besoin de recourir à des demonstrations laborieuses ; les œuvres parleraient seules. Quand nous aurions échoué à réfuter des défenseurs de l'influence grecque, nous continuerions cependant à nier leurs doctrines la nature de leurs arguments suffrait encore à les condamner."

One of the names for the curtain, Yavanikā was supposed by Weber (Z. D. M. G. 1860, p. 269 and Ind. Stud. iii., 492) to mean the "Greek cloth" and the etymology was used by him to support his theory of the Greek influence on Indian drama. Thus he says : "In der kieler monatschrift (1853) erschienenen Abhandlung (jetzt : Indische Skizzen, p. 85) noch dem namen Yavanikâ 'die griechische' für den "Buhnunvorhang". Die form Yavanikâ findet sich in Amarakosha, Harivamça etc." The word however more probably denoted as has been shown, some fabric made by the Yavanas (see E. J. Rapson, art. "Indian Drama" in Encyclopædia of Religion and Ethics, vol. IV) and imported into India.

The extant masterpieces of the Indian drama belong to the augustan age of classical Sanskrit literature, which may be supposed to begin with the establishment of the Gupta Empire in 319 A. D. and to extend to about the year 800 A. D., though the literature of the next three or four centuries which may be regarded as the Silver Age, includes a number of dramas of considerable interest and importance. But the later productions are destitute of originality : they are either imitations of the old models or exercises worked out in accordance with the rules of the rhetoricians and the writers on the dramatic art. Recent discoveries have however shown that the classical drama is of much later antiquity than is represented in the extant literature. Fragments of Indian palm-leaf MSS. found in Central Asia show a dramatic literature possessing substantially the same chief characteristics, which flourished several centuries earlier in the Kushana period. Like all other works of classical period, such as the romances, the literary epics and the lyrical poems, the Sanskrit dramas are of an artificial and highly elaborate character and so we find the drama on its first appearance in literature to be a perfected work of art, the form of which already definitely settled, has not subsequently undergone any important modification.

Characteristic Differences between the Greek and Hindu Drama.

Another important feature of the Hindu Drama which distinguishes it from the classical and other dramas is the absence of any distinction between Tragedy and Comedy. The Indian plays confine themselves neither "to the crimes nor to the absurdities of mankind," neither "to the momentous changes nor lighter vicissitudes of life," neither "to the terrors of distress, nor to the gaieties of prosperity." In this respect, they may be classed with many of the Spanish and English dramas, to which as Schlegel observes, "the terms, Tragedy and Comedy, are wholly inapplicable in the sense in which they were employed by the ancients." They are invariably of a mingled wit, and blend "seriousness and sorrow with levity and laughter." They aim at exciting all the emotions of the human breast, terror and piety included. They never effect this object by leaving a painful impression upon the spectator. "The Hindus in fact," says Professor Wilson, "have no tragedy, a defect that subverts the theory that tragedy necessarily preceded comedy, because in the infancy of society, the stronger passions predominated." The absence of tragic catastrophe in the Hindu dramas is not merely an unconscious omission. Such catastrophe is prohibited by a positive rule. Out of that regard indeed for decorum, which even Voltaire thought might sometimes be dispensed with, it is not allowed in any manner "en slanganter la scène", and death must invariably be inflicted out of the sight of the spectators. Attention to *bien séance* is carried even to a further extent and a number of interdictions is peculiar to the system of the Hindus.

The extent of the Hindu plays is another great peculiarity, in which they differ from the dramatic writings of other nations and even the "Robbers" or "Don Carlos" will suffer in comparison of length. The Mricchakatika will at least make three of the plays of Æschylus. In actual representation however, a Hindu play made a less reasonable demand upon the patience of an audience than an Athenian performance consisting at one sitting three Tragedies and a Farce. If the Hindu stage inhibited a long play, it exhibited that alone.

In the Hindu play moreover, every piece opens with a prelude or introduction, in which the audience is acquainted with the author, his work, the actors and such part of the prior events as it is necessary for the spectators to know. In its propitiation of the audience and reference to past events, it is analogous to the prologues of the ancient and modern times, and so far as spoken by the *dramatis personæ,* it accords with what have been termed the prologues of Euripides and those of Plautus. Being in a dialogue form however, it is more correctly the induction of the old comedy which although considered out of date by Beaumont and Fletcher, was not unfrequently found amongst their contemporaries as in "Cynthia's Revels", " the Return of Parnessus" and especially, the "Malcontents of Marston," in which the interlocutors are the actors. The Faust of Goethe affords a specimen of induction in the present day. In the Hindu theatre on the contrary, the actors of the prelude were never more than two, the manager and one of his company whether an actor or an actress, and it differs from the similar preliminary performances by leading immediately into the business of the drama. Again the fact, that in the Sanskrit drama the bard (*Sūta*) regularly speaks Sanskrit, and not a popular dialect, indicates that the poetry of the bards was composed in Sanskrit. [This hypothesis was first propounded by M. Barth in Revue Critique; April, 1886 and further elaborated by him in Revue de l'Histoire des Religions, 1902, pp. 195 ff].

The Prahasana, is a farcical or comic satire, and might be thought to have originated like the old comedy from the Phallic hymn. But unlike Aristophanes' Comedy, it is not levelled at the hydra-headed mob, but in general at the sanctified and privileged orders of the community as Ascetics, Brahmans and Princes. It is in their extreme indelicacy that they resemble, though perhaps they scarcely equal to, the Greek comedy. The "Hāsyārnava," "Kutuke Sarvaswa" and the "Dhûrta-Nartaka" are the existing specimens of this class of dramatic representation. The Ullâpya is in one act, the subject is mythological, the sentiments are love, mirth and pathos, the dialogue is interspersed with songs. By way of example may be mentioned the "Devê-Mahādeva." This presents an analogy to the satiric drama of the Greeks, which was taken from mythology or heroic poetry and differed chiefly from the tragedies, which followed in a more lively strain and contained a brief introduction of songs and dances by Silenus and Satyrs.

Each Act or Anka is said to be marked by the exit of all the personages, a practice which is equally applicable to the French theatre. The precise division of Hindu plays into Acts is a feature, which serves to discriminate them from the Greek compositions, in which the divisions into acts were unknown, the only distinctions recognised being the prologue, episode and exode, regulated by intervening songs of the chorus to which we find nothing parallel in the regular plays of the Hindus. The division into Acts appears to have been an arrangement invented by the Romans, from whom we can scarcely suspect the Hindus to have derived their drama.

The character of Vita or Vidushaka, which has been referred to already, in Hindu drama, is not very easily understood. He is generally represented to be on familiar and easy, yet dependent terms with his associate and evinces something (but not exactly as Dr. Windisch supposes him to be), of the character of the 'parasite' of the Greek Comedy, but he is never rendered contemptible. As Schlegel observes every theatre has its buffoon, and Vidushaka plays that part in the theatre of the Hindus. He is a boon companion, not the servant, ‹ a prince or a man of rank; but it is a curious fact, tha he is always a Brahmin. He bears more affinity to Sancho Pañza perhaps than to any other character in the Western fiction, imitating him in his combination of shrewdness and simplicity, his fondness for good living and his love of ea- In the dramas of intrigue, he exhibits some of the talents mercury but with less activity and ingenuity, and occasiona suffers by his interference. According to the technical definition of his attributes as given in the Natya Sutras, he is to excite mirth by being ridiculous in person, age and attire.

Another peculiarity of the Hindu plays, is the employment of different forms of speech for different characters. This is not like the patois of the French comedies or the Scotch of the English dramas, individual and occasional, but is general and invariable. The hero and the principal personages speak Sanskrit, but the women and the inferior characters even the Vidushaka use the various modifications of that language, which are comprehended under the term Prakrit. As observed by Mr. Colebrooke with regard to this mixture of languages, the Italian theatre presents instances in the prose comedies of Ruzzanti. But the five act farces, the notion of which was probably borrowed from the Pænulus of Plautus, hold but an insignificant place in the dramatic literature of Italy and the employment of the Venetian and the Bergamask dialect by Goldoni is only like the use of those of Somersetshire or Yorkshire on the English stage, except that it is rather more prominent and frequent. In no theatre however, have we a mixture of languages exactly analogous to that invariably used in the dramas of the Hindus.

Although it is just possible that one or the other feature of the Hindu drama may be due to outside influence, the subject matter is certainly original and Indian. The themes are for the most part, the heroic legends in the Epics or are taken from the sphere of actual court life. The themes, at any rate, are not different from those of other Hindu literature. They show no foreign admixtures. It must not be forgotten that certain general coincidences between the drama and the theatre of different peoples are due to common psychological traits ; hence genuine historical connection in such matters requires the most exacting proof. There are so many fundamental differences between the Indian and the Greek drama that *primâ facie* they have all the appearance of being independent developments.

The Probable Origin of the Indian Drama.

As the theory of the origin of the Indian drama from the Greek has received a new support from the researches of Reich into the Greek mime (see Lüders, Indian Antiquary vol. xxxiv, 200), it may be interesting to bring into prominence certain evidence, which tends rather to support the generally accepted theory of the independent origin of the Indian Drama from the Greek ; both being based on religious practices which flourished independently in either country. This evidence is afforded by the interesting discussion of the origin of the Greek drama by Dr. L. R. Farnell in the fifth volume of his "Cults of the Greek States". Rejecting the derivation of the tragedy from the dithyramb, which is usually accepted on the authority of Aristotle (Politics, c. 4), he finds it in a "Goat-song"—the literal meaning of the word *tragodia* and since the goats do not sing, it means the song of men dressed as goats. Now recent research has discovered in modern Thrace, a survival of Dionysiac worship in which men dressed in goat-skins enact a mummery-play which at one point is tragic, (vide Journal of the Hellenic Studies, 1906 pp. 191 et seq.) In Attica, the real home of the Greek drama, is found the legend of Melanthos and Xanthos, in which the "black" kills the "white" a legend in which Usener (Archiv für Religionswissenschaft, 1904 pp. 303 et seq.) has recognised a variant of the well-known contest of winter and summer, traces of which are found all over the Mediterranean sea-board. It is true that there is no direct evidence of the performance of a play by men dressed in goat-skins in Attica, but there is an Argive-Boetian legend of men wearing goat-skins in honour of God Dionysios, and there is the record of the "tragephoroi" maidens who performed a solemn function in his service. It is then both legitimate and probable to conclude as Dr. Farnell does, that Attic tragedy owes its origin to such mummeries. They are originally solemn in their central idea, for though the death of the God which was an essential part of the performance, was melancholy yet on ordinary view the dithyramb was the song of the Satyr rejoicing over the gift of the grape ; hence the tragic side of the Attic drama is inexplicable. Thus the theory has actually been started by Ridgeway (see Maas, Wochenschrift für class. Philologie, 1904, pp. 776-83), that the drama owed its origin to the performance at the funeral of the dead heroes, a view suggested by the fact that the tragic choruses were held at Sykion in honour of Adrastors, until the tyrant Kleisthenes 'restored' them to Dionysios (vide Herodotus, V. 67).

We need not accept in all its details the view of Dr. Farnell. It is no doubt true that there was a tragic element in the play of the mummers, but it is also probable that there was a comic or cheerful side, and if in one version of the play, the 'dark' God of winter slays the 'light' God of summer, in other versions (see Farnell, 'Cults of the Greek States, vol. V pp. 236-7) the situation was reversed, giving the possibility of a comedy, though still with a tragic element,—the death of winter, something like the modern Thracian mummery referred to above. The dithyramb too need hardly be abandoned as a stage on the road to tragedy. It is not necessary to assume that the dithyrambs were merely joyous in content, and it is necessary to find some literary form as a precursor of drama. The religious drama is not in itself, literary ; it is not tragedy, but the raw material from which tragedy could be fashioned by literary genius, and it only increased the difficulty of tracing the growth of tragedy, if an obvious link is deliberately overlooked.

Now to turn to the Indian evidence. At the great Mahāvrata ceremony, one of the most interesting features of the ritual is the fight of a Sudra and an Arya on a round, white skin which represents the Sun (vide Kathaka Samhitā, xxxiv, 5 and Dr. Keith's Samkhyāna Aranyaka p. 78). Now the Kathaka Samhitā, which narrates the struggle of the Aryan and the Sudra, expressly says (xi. 6) that the colour of the Vaisya is white and it is recognised that the colour of the Sudra is black, so that it is almost certain that we have here again another form of the strife of winter and summer : in this case, summer or spring represented by the white Aryan prevails over the winter represented by the dark Sudra. The Mahāvrata rite is one which continued late in the Sutra ritual and was clearly performed throughout the Vedic Age, being in essence a popular not merely a priestly rite (see Aitareya Aranyaka, i and v ; Srauta Sutra, xvii and xviii).

Now the earliest certain notice which is preserved of the Indian drama (apart from the vague references in the Rig and Yajur Vedas, noticed already), is that of Patañjali in the Mahābhāsya (vide Weber I. S. xiii, 354 et seq ; 487 et seq.) which tells us of the performances of the two plays, the Bālibandha or "the binding of Bāli" and Kamsabadha or "the slaying of Kamsa" in different ways—either by Saubhikas who actually performed the action of the play on the stage, or by Granthikas, who by words (Sabda-granthana) expressed the sentiments of the personages concerned. It is also said that,they divided themselves into two different parties, some being adherents of Kamsa and some adherents of Vāsudeva as Krishna ; the former, having dark and the latter, red faces.

This latter work is of conclusive importance. It displays all the essential elements of drama side by side, and very probably it shows how the dithyramb was an independent accompaniment of the ritual drama, which gradually developed into real drama by the union of action and speech, here shown separately, and employed as a means of expressing an action of the contest of Kamsa and Krishna. Moreover by the nature of the subject-matter, the origin of the drama is clearly shown. "The slaying of Kamsa by Krishna is nothing more or less than the modern form of the struggle of winter and spring or summer, a contest in which as in Mahāvrata, the God of Spring is victorious not the God of Winter" (vide Dr. Berridale Keith, Z. D. M. G. Band 64 pp. 534 et seq). In this origin, we see the explanation of one of the rules of Indian drama that forbids a drama to end in disaster, while in the Attic theatre, the tradition of drama diverged into two directions, producing both tragedy and comedy.

It seems to us therefore, that the Indian evidence taken in conjunction with the Greek one tells strongly against the attempt to derive the Indian from the Greek drama. At any rate, we see in close relation in India all the elements which could legitimately produce a drama and although the date of the Mahābhāsya (middle of the 2nd century B. C.) does not preclude the possibility of the notice contained in it referring to a drama based on Greek models, it is very difficult to avoid the idea that the choice of the subject, the slaying of Kamsa, would have been suspiciously apt, if the dramatic forms were merely imported and borrowed from a drama, which had ceased to betray the signs of the origin from the old play of winter and summer. Moreover, there is not the slightest reason to doubt that the circumstances in India were all favourable to the growth of an independent drama, nor is it legitimate to assert its derivation from Greece (see Winternitz, V. O. J. xxiii. 103 et seq.; Oldenberg, G. G. A. 1909 pp. 66 et seq.)

BIBLIOGRAPHY.

1. Hillebrandt ... "Vedische Mythologie."
2. Windisch, E. ... "Der Griechische Einfluss im Indischen Drama" (verh. od. 5, Internat. Or. Cong. Berlin, 1882, II., ii., 3.)
3. Pischel, R. ... "The Home of the Puppet play."
4. Dean Milman ... "Sanskrit Poetry" in Quarterly Review, 1831.
5. Lévi, Sylvain ... "Le Théatre Indien", Paris. 1890.
6. Wilson, H. H. ... "Select Specimens of the Theatre of the Hindus."
7. Haas, G. C. O. ... "Dasa-Rupa."
8. Williams Jackson, A. V. "Certain Dramatic Elements in Sanskrit Plays with parallels in English Drama." in American Journal of Philology, xix, pp. 241-254.
9. Farnell, L. R. ... "Cults of the Greek States."
10. Huizinga ... ... "Die Vidushaka in Lit. Indische Toonul."
11. Schmidt, R. ... "Beitrage zur Ind. Erotik."
12. Von Gutschmid ... "Die Konigsnamen in die Apocryphen Apostelgeschichten."
13. Lévi, Sylvain ... "Quid de Græcis Veterum Indorum Monumenta Tradiderint."
14. Hall ... ... "Vâsabadattā."
15. Z. D. M. G., Band 14 (1860) p. 226; Band 64 (1910) pp. 534 et seq.
16. Indian Antiquary, 1900, xxx, p. 287 ; xxxiv, p. 200 et seq.
17. Weber, Indische Studien, vol xviii, p. 492; xiii, p. 354 ff.

18. Encyclopædia of Religion and Ethics, Vol. IV, art. "Drama."
19. R. Böhme ... ... "Indische Dramatik" in Vossische Zeitung, 1903.
20. Francesco Cimmine ... "Studii sul teatro indiano."
21. Lowis H. Gray ... "Literary Studies on the Sanskrit Novel."
22. Do. ... "Sanskrit Novel and Sanskrit Drama" in W. Z. K. M. 1904.
23. Hall, F. ... ... "Fragments of Three Early Dramatists of the Hindus, Bhasa, Romila and Somila" in J. A. S. B. vol. xxviii.
24. Hertel, Johannes ... "Der Ursprung des indischen Dramas und Epos" in W. Z. K. M. 18 (1904).
25. Kielhorn, F. ... "Sanskrit Plays as preserved in Inscriptions," J. R. A. S. 1891; Epigraphia Indica, 5, (1899).
26. Klein, J. A. ... ... "Das Indische Drama" in Geschichte der Dramas, vol. 3. Leipzig, 1866.
27. Leumann, Ernst. in Z. D. M. G. 42 (1888) pp. 151-198.
28. Neve, F. ... ... "Les dramas heroiques et mythologiques de l'Inde," in Muséon, 1 (1882).
29. Winternitz ... ... "The Mahabharata and the Drama" in J. R. A. S. 1903; V. O. J. vol. xxiii, p. 103 et seq.
30. Lubaty, Josof ... "On the Development of the Indian Drama and its relation to the Greek Drama (chiefly on the hetairoi of the Hindu and the Greek Drama).
31. Frazer, R. W. ... "A Literary History of India".
32. Henry, Victor ... "Les Literatures de l'Inde".
33. Oldenberg, H. ... "Die Litteratur des Alten Indien".
34. Schroeder, L. von ... "Indiens Litteratur und Cultur".
35. Fritze, Ludwig ... "Indische Theater".
36. H. B. Bhide ... "Bhāsa's Swapna-Vāsabadattā".
37. Journal of the Hellenic Studies, 1906, pp. 101 et seq.
38. Creizenach, W. ... "Geschichte des neueren Dramas." Halle.
39. Chambers, E. K. ... "The Madiæval Stage".
40. Schroeder, L. von ... "Mysterium und Mimus".

BOOK FOUR

INDEPENDENT EVOLUTION OF RELIGION, PHILOSOPHY, MYTHOLOGY AND FABLES IN INDIA AND IN GREECE.

CHAPTER XI

RELIGION

Growth of Parallel Religious Ideas in Greece and in India.

The first thing that strikes us on glancing over a map of the Religions of the globe, is their multiplicity and deversity. Creeds, rites, moral precepts or simple religious observances; fetichism, animism, polytheism, dualism, monotheism, pantheism, ritual obligations, passing from crime to heroism, from prostitution to spotless purity, from cruel immolation of others to complete sacrifice of self—all principles and forms, produce at first sight the effect of a confused mingling of incongruous phenomena, to which it seems very rash to ascribe beforehand any element in common. More than this, we may lay down as a general rule that nothing is so tenacious as a religion, nothing more obstinately defies proscription and all attempts to extirpation, nothing resists with more constancy the contradictory demonstrations of palpable reality. History supplies examples of these, which are most appalling. Nevertheless, the number of religions which have become extinct or disappeared is great. Buddhism after having been for ages the popular and official religion of Hindusthan, from a certain date almost suddenly vanishes, and that, as it would seem, from persecution having been directed against its votaries. The grand religion of Zarathustra, one of the most beautiful and interesting of antiquity, at present numbers only a few hundreds of professors, and is on the verge of extinction The Græco-Roman, Germanic, and

Scandinavian mythologies; the Semitic polytheisms of Nineveh, Babylon, Byblos, Tyre and Carthage; the rich pantheon of ancient Egypt; the solar worship of the Incas;—all these are dead, gone for ever. And we could add to this funeral list, other names less known. So that religions exhibit this double phenomena of a vitality which we might suppose indestructible and of a tendency to decay, which frequently ends in complete annihilation.

The ancients concerned themselves with religion itself, independently of its historic forms. For them, in fact, religion had no history. It would be impossible to give this name to myths relating how younger gods were substituted for more ancient dieties, like those which told of the dethronement of Uranus to be replaced by Kronos, and of Kronos again being dispossessed by Zeus or Jupiter. These revolutions among the deities formed a part of the traditional mythology of the Greeks, which the thinkers of antiquity rarely openly combatted.

Now, all studies of religious subjects tend now-a-days towards the solving of a particular problem, of which no very perfect or precise idea has yet been formed, but which nevertheless seems to be the end and aim of all investigations. The works of pure archæology, such as those of Kuhn, Preller, De Rossi furnish materials for the building up of the Science, quite as much as the more theoretic writings of De Bunsen, Ewald Nicolus or De Pressenesé. The moving spirit of most of these works and of others of the same style, connects them with different schools, opinions, or sometimes even with different sects. The religious element leaves its stamp upon nearly all the fruits of a people's civilization, the impression varying in depth according to periods and crises. If we enquire into the remote past or into the East, the pretensions as to independence on the part of the ancient religions are still more decided. One cannot credit the popular belief of ancient Greece, that her Gods came to her from Egypt, it is a supposition of Herodotus and nothing more. That personal opinion of the historian has no more weight than that of the linguists of former days, who emphatically asserted that all languages came from the Hebrews, because forsooth when creating the things of Paradise for Adam, God had given them Hebrew names ; we know now how tongues formed themselves, and that Jewish is one of the latest. We also know that their Adam and his Paradise are myths, which reached them from without, originating with people who did not speak Hebrew. Herodotus' opinion has been refuted in the same manner ; from the many and repeated searches into archæology, we learn that the Greek-worships were local and independent of each other ; they were not the perpetuation of a foreign and distant cult, but that in every part of the country legends were told which established the autochthony of the religion practised there. The earliest discovered points of reference were Crete and Thrace, which were in fact two shining centres of diffusion of the worships of the Pelasgians and the Hellenes ; but there was no thing to prove that these worships had come from Upper Asia to settle in Thrace or in the island of the Cretans. On the contrary, it was related that Jupiter was bred in the island of Crete and Orpheus, whom modern science has recognised as Ribhu (Arbhu) of the Veda, was supposed to have been born in a European country and thence to have departed with the Argonauts in quest of the Golden Fleece. Each Greek divinity was regarded as the founder of his or her own cult ; Juno at Argos ; Apollo at Delphi and Delos ; Neptune and Pallas at Athené and so forth.

The Persians attributed their religion to God, as its author. The "principle of life and knowledge," which they called

Ahura-Mazda, a word which the Greeks transformed into Oromazdes and the modern Persians into Ormuzd, had himself dictated to his faithful servant Zarathustra, the sacred formulas, on which the religion and civilization of the world should rest. Later on, when the Persians were brought into contact with the Indians on the one hand, and with the Greeks on the other, they regarded the religion of either, as foreign and hostile worships. In their eyes the Greeks were barbarians and odious idolaters ; in the eyes of Cambyses ancient Egypt was equally despised ; as for the Indians, we know from the Zenda-Vesta that their chosen gods were identically the same as the demons with the Persians ; whereas the former again consigned to hell those Ahuras which to the Persians were the supreme conceptions of divinity. Then the Persians carried on fierce wars against the ungodly, upsetting their idols and burning their temples wherever the politics of Darius and the passions of Xerxes led them.

But the various religious ceremonies have proceeded one out of the other. Not only are the forms of worship in each not original, not only are the symbols found to have crept successively into each worship, retaining and transmitting to succeeding generations all the outward signs, which at no time underwent more than the most superficial alterations, but the mystic or rather the metaphysical aspect also, which is hidden under these veils, and which we might term the divine element in religions, has remained unchanged since the remotest days vivifying those symbolic figures, rites and formulas which constitute its outward and visible signs. At present we know for certain that most of, if not all the worships of ancient Greece originated in Asia. How then did they light upon the continent of Europe ? Which roads did they follow ? This is an important but secondary question, one not solved yet, though we are aware that Crete, the Archipælago and the countries north of Greece, were the several roads which brought the Hellenes, the cults of their gods. Be that as it may, every modern scholar now admits that the distinction, which up till quite recently, archæology made between the Pelasgian gods and the Hellenic is illusory and cannot be put under two distinctly separate historic periods. Each succeeding year finds one of these gods drawn to his origin by bonds that cannot be disclaimed. That origin is not Egyptian, but Asiatic; and in Asia, it is not to be found with the Semites, nor even with the Indo-Persians but in a more ancient centre, which was first occupied by the Aryan race and ultimately produced alike the Persians, Indians and Greeks.

From this centre sprang at two different but not distant periods, perhaps even contemporaneously, the religions of Persia and India. The common origin of these two great religious systems of Asia was brought to light by the exertions of our modern orientalists and archæologists. There is not only the most striking analogy between the oldest doctrines and symbols of the Avesta and the Veda, but in the first-mentioned of these sacred works, there lingers the memory of the northern origin of the Persian Mazdeism. But still there is no reason for believing that the doctrine attributed to Zoroaster originated in the Veda or vice versa; we must therefore assume that they both issued from a common source. The Avesta gives the name of this source and its geographical position *viz.*, in the countries of Cugda and Bâgdh (Sogdiana and Bactriana). The hymns of the Veda do not mention it or only make doubtful allusions to it; but the commentaries of the Veda, which themselves belong to a remote period and are written in the Vedic tongue, are more explicit; they marshal before our eyes, the Aryan populations of India, coming from the north-west with their creeds and their gods. Those same gods are to be found in Zoroaster's book and the metaphysical conception which animated those figures is also the same. The common origin of Parsism and Brahminism grows manifestly clear, the deeper our knowledge penetrates into recent discoveries.

We must also bear in mind this fact, that more we learn about the old Germanic and Scandinavian religions and the popular traditions which still hover in the European atmosphere, the more clearly we perceive their bond of unity with Asia. The successive religions of the West never succeeded in totally destroying the old traditions in the Aryan memory; they exist in countles number in Germany, in France, in Russia, in Scandinavia. Every mountain gorge of Europe teems with recollections, every upheaval tells of buried tongues, which may be linked into an intelligible chain. Greece also notwithstanding the extent of her pagan period and the subsequent vehemence of her Christian creed, still cherishes in popular rhymes, the legends which are unmistakably pre-Hellenic, and which from all appearance relate to the first Aryan migration from Asia. Such for example, is the legend of Charos whose name so often appears in popular Greek lore. This Charos is the god of death; he has been and is still being confounded with Charon, with whom he has scarcely anything in common; whereas almost all his attributes recall those of the Kâla of the Indians. It would be useful to compile these legends just as the archæologists fit together broken carvings and inscriptions. With such landmarks and towers of observation, we could easily trace a map of the earliest Aryan migrations and follow the progress of the religious ideas after their emergence from the cradle. At any rate, we are now certain that this diffusion took place at some remote time and that all those ancient worships pertained, like those of Greece, Italy, Persia and India to one same system or rather to one primordial unity.

Thus the Greek religion, which was destined one day to attain great development, was not at first separated from the other Indo-German religions by any great differences. The proof of this may be found in what is still known of the religion of Pelasgi, whose names denote a *period* rather than a race. The statement that they worshipped the God of Heaven on their sacred mountains without images and under no definite name, does not warrant the inference that their cultus was purer than that which succeeded and was monotheistic, but simply means that they still regarded and worshipped their god, as nature-beings, and if they made no images of them, they were nevertheless not without fetishes. Some sanctuaries of this Pelasgian Zeus continued to exist in later times and one, that at Dodona in Epirus, even remained in high esteem up to a recent period. In Arcadia and Messenia, human sacrifices were offered to him. It was not till afterwards that the institution of the Olympic games and the protection of Sparta gave to the ancient Zeus-worship in Elis, the great significance which made the region itself a holy land and raised the temple to the status of one of the principal sanctuaries of all the Hellenes. "But whatever be the resemblances," says Dr. Tiele, "of the Greek religion in origin and character to kindred religions, especially to the Vedic and Germanic, and though in the Pelasgian period, at any rate, it reached no higher level, it soon advanced in development above them all."

As we have already remarked that the origin of the Greek religion should be ultimately traced to Asia, so we also see in it, the first fair fruits of the fusion of the Indo-Germanic and the Aryan with the Semitic and Hamitic elements—the dawn of a new era. But it is often possible in the myths and forms of the Greek gods still to distinguish very clearly between the national and foreign elements. Thus in the myth of Zeus, his contest with Kronos, like that of Kronos with Ouranos, his absolute victory over the powers of nature, his unlimited sovereignty, are of Semitic origin ; while his contest with Prometheus and his human passions and attributes point to Indo-Germanic sources. The beneficent Dêmêter, the fruitful mother-earth, with her daughter Korê, the blooming spring begotten by Zeus, protector of agriculture and giver of abundance, is originally Greek ; while the sombre queen of the underworld, who becomes by Poseidon, the mother of Persephonê, goddess of death, must be a foreign diety. In the same way Greek theology also gives two representations of the world of the dead. According to one, the Semitic, it lay within the earth and there the departed beings led a life of shadows, without spirit or consciousness, which was however a melancholy continuation of their earthly careers. The other, the Indo-Germanic, placed it in the west, at the setting of the sun, where the privileged were admitted to Elysium or the islands of the blessed. These different representations, it was endeavoured as far as possible, to combine.

In some cases, the union of these dissimilar elements was never successfully effected. The contrast between the chaste maidenly Artemis, protectress of innocence and honesty, hostile to everything savage and lewd, and the blood-thirsty and sensual goddess of Taurus, Asia Minor and Crete, was always felt vividly even by the Greeks. Generally however, the fusion is so complete that it is hardly possible to separate the foreign from the national elements. This is the case, for example, with Dionysius, Apollo and Athené. Thus whatever be the meaning of the name Kronos, Dr. Kuhn has recently suggested its derivation from a doubtful Sanskrit word Krâno (creating for himself) [vide 'Ueber Entwickelungsstufen des Mythenbildung' p. 148], it is certain that it has nothing to do with Chronos "time", and that the god, who mutilates his father and eats his children, is of genuinely North-Semitic origin.

Megasthenes tells us a good deal about the Hindu representative of Dionysius. According to him, there were Dionysiac festivals in honour of the god Siva, who belonged to the Açwaka district, north of the Kabul river where flourished the vine-yards (see Düncker, iii, p. 327; Schroeder, loc. cit. p. 361; Arrian calls Siva Dionysius.) The Indo-Germanic character of the Prometheus-myth has been conclusively shown by Kuhn. The spirit of the myth, as it was worked out by the Greeks, is completely non-Semitic. If the name Athena really corresponds to the Sanskrit *Ahanâ*, the dawning and Athenaia to *ahania* "the day-bright," as Prof. Max Müller supposes, we should have to regard her also as an Indo-Germanic goddess (vide E. Curtius, "Die Griechische Gotterlehre vom Geschichtlichen standpunkt" in the Preuss. Jahrbb. July 1875.)

But the poetic and philosophical tendency of this richly-endowed people, the creative power of the Greek mind as displayed, for instance, in their treatment of the myth of Prometheus, became in their hands the vehicle for profound and elevated thoughts and the manner in which they represented the nature-myth of Dêmêter and Persephonê as the expression of a genuine human feeling ennobled the mystic significance which had already attached to it on the other hand. But it nowhere comes into view more clearly than in a comparison of such deities as Hermes or Aphroditê with the divine beings of Indo-Germanic or Semitic origin from which they have sprung. Hermes, once the hound of the gods, the god of the wind and of light and darkness, the great enchanter and conductor of souls, becomes with the Greeks, the messenger and the right hand of Zeus, the mediator between Him and men, the ideal herald, the god of graceful speed, of music, of eloquence, of philosophy.

Hermes is identical with Sarameyos, the names of the two dogs of Yama, the god of death, the mythic watch dogs in the Veda. Max Müller doubts whether Saramā their mother, the messenger of Indra, who goes to fetch the stolen cows, was a dog. But the Sarameyos were certainly so. Hermes possesses no Semitic trait. His original physical character as a god of wind perfectly explains all the myths about him, such as the stealing of Apollo's cows, the slaying of Argus, his combat with Stentor, and all his attributes as the guardian of the clouds, the guide of the shades, the herald of the gods, the god of music and eloquence etc.

On the other hand, "it has long been known," says Hopkins in his "Religion of India," "that Sivaite phallic-worship was not borrowed from the Southerners, as it was once imagined and we venture with some scholars to believe that it was due rather to late Greek influence than to that of any native wild tribe. As has been very elaborately demonstrated, Greek influence is clearly reflected in India's architecture. Hellenic bas-reliefs, representing Bacchic scenes and the love-god, are occasionally found. Siva is sometimes associated with the Greek-cult of Eros and Aphroditê." This statement of Hopkins, mainly based on the learned but misguided disquisitons of Weber and Schroeder, is not borne out by facts. The Hindus had neither any occasion nor the slightest inclination to introduce Greek deities into their pantheon. There may be similarities in the virtues of some of the Greek and Hindu gods and goddesses ; but this may be explained away, as has been pointed out already, by the fact that both the nations borrowed their pantheon from the same Indo-Germanic source.

Moreover, the Hindu theory of the idol is in sharp contrast with that of the Greeks. To the former human form is merely the ephemeral clothing of the soul, in which, unhappily, it is forced to linger for a time. Though in the sculptures of the age of Asoka, an interest in portraiture, at least in that which represents national characteristics, begins to appear, the naturalism, somewhat refined in the delineation of woman, tends to become rococo in style. But it is a sheer mistake to suppose that idolatry was introduced into India by the Greeks and that it was rarely practised until the beginning of the Christian era. Images of the gods were certainly common in the Maurya period and doubtless at a much earlier date (vide V. A. Smith, 'History of Fine Art in India and Ceylon' p. 79 n).

So, turning to the other side of the question as to the influence which India had upon Western cults and beliefs we experience the same difficulty. The worship that substituted idols for ideal-forms, we have to trace back to the end of the Vedic period. It is not however a mark of early Brahminism, nor is it a pronounced feature of the age of Buddhism, But in Buddha's time or soon after, flourished the worship of images and with it the respect for relics. The latter feature of the new religion, made necessary the shrines to keep the holy objects, sacred museums, which soon became the formal stupas. Fully developed, they became the great religious buildings sanctified by Buddhism with their idol-service, prostrations, repititions of prayers etc. From this source, may have been derived later on, many of the details of the Roman Catholic worship, which appear to have been taken from Buddhism, the rosary, originally a mark of the Sivaite. [It is interesting, as showing incidentally, the close connection between Buddhism and Saivism in other than philosophical aspects. The first Indian grotto-temple mentioned by foreigners in the 3rd century B. C. was one which contained a statue of Siva (vide Weber, Indische Skizzen, P. 86, n.)] By what is to say the least an extraordinary coincidence, each of these churches whether Buddhistic or Roman Catholic, is conspicuous for its use of holy-water, choirs, sacred pictures, tonsure, vestments, the orders of monks and the vows of the monastic system. In Lamaism, there are also the tiara-crowned Pope and the transubstantiation theory, the reverence for Virgin and Child, confessions, fasts, purgatory etc. (vide Rhys-Davids, Hibbert Lectures, p. 193). The most curious thing borrowed by the Roman and Greek churches, is however the quasi-worship of Gautama Buddha himself (in so far as a Romanist worships his Saints); for under the cover of Barlaam and Josaphat story, Buddha has found a niche as a Saint in the row of canonised Catholic worthies, and has his Saint-Day in the Calendar of Greek and Roman Churches (vide Bohlen, Altes Indien, i. 334). Besides external phases of religious cult, India has given a certain class of literary works (see, Indische Studien, iii, 128). It has been claimed also that the Logos doctrine was imported from India. In the Brahmanic period, the Rig Vedic *vac*, speech, becomes more and more like the Greek Logos and in this period it may truthfully be said, that "Word was God." In Greece, on the other hand, the conception of Logos begins with Heracleitus, and then passes on to the Stoics; is adopted by Philo; becomes a prominent feature of neo-Platonism; and re-appears in the Gospel of St. John. It is legitimate to infer that Heracleitus might have received the idea indirectly from contemporary Eastern philosophers. This theory first propounded by Weber was amplified by Garbe (For a fuller discussion of the subject, see Chapter xii. Philosophy). There is also a similarity between the other forms of early Greek and Hindu philosophy. "Both Thales and Parmenides were anticipated by Hindu sages and the Eleatic school seems to be but a reflexion of the Upanishad. The doctrines of Anaximander and Heracleitus are not known first in Greece and they are evidently borrowed from India.

Before the sixth century B. C., all the religious-philosophical ideas of Pythagoras were current in India" (vide L. von Schrœder, Pythagoras). But these are accidental coincidences and it cannot be definitively asserted that either the Hindus or the Greeks borrowed consciously from each other. For example, we may say that religious immorality, the excesses of Sakti worship, are not peculiar to the Hindus only. If one asks how the morality of India as a whole compares with that of other countries, we may reply that including religious excesses, it stands on a level with the personal morality of Greece in her best days, and except the religiously sensual element of the Hindus it is on a par with that of London or New York. The Hindu sectarian cults are often strangely like those of Greece in details, which must be traced back to a like, though not necessarily mutual, source of primitive superstition. Even the sacred free bulls, which roam at large look like old familiar ones in ancient Greece (Plato, Kritias, 119); and we have dared to question whether Long's "bull-roarers" had not their proto-types in the command that the priest should make the bull roar at the sacrifice, and in the verse of the Rig Veda which says that the priests "beget the Dawn by means of the roar of a bull." (viii. 79, 4).

Thus the old shift of attributing to Oriental influences everything in Hellenic religion that clashed with the purer idea of Hellenism was naively unscientific. Nothing is more erroneous than the view, sometimes expressed, that towards the close of the fifth century B. C., in Greece the popular devotion to the old religion was abating and its divine personalities and forms were losing life and value. In their dark days, the Athenians remained truer to their old faith than did Rome in her time of terror. We do not find Athens turning desperately for aid to alien Oriental cults. We hear indeed of the beginnings of Adonis-cult in the latter part of the

Peloponnesian War—the first ripple of a wave of Orientalism that was to surge westward later. But this feminine excess was unauthorised and Aristophanes hates it and mocks at it. It is refuted also by other incidents in Athenian history that fall within the last decades of this century. If we take Athens as the typical religious community of the fifth century and compare the structure and forms of her state-polytheism, with that of the old Homeric world, we find the personalities of the pre-historic pantheon still worshipped and cherished ; no cult of that epic world has yet fallen into desuetude, nor had the most civilised city of Hellas discarded the immemorial rites of the simple peasant religion, the worship of rivers and streams, and some of the most naive practices of Animism. And it is clear, that this conservatism was no hieratic convention, but a living faith expressing a religious intuition of the people, who were as yet untouched by the cooling influences of science and philosophic scepticism. In contrast also with the deterioration of the old Roman religion caused by the Hannibalic wars, the successful struggle of Greece against 'barbarism' in the East, the West undoubtedly quickened for a time the fervour and devotion inspired by the national cults. And scholars who have been tempted to antedate the decay of Hellenic polytheism, have ignored, among other evidence, this important historic fact that in the 4th century B. C., it had still vitality enough to make foreign conquests, to penetrate and take possession of Carthage, for instance, and that in the 3rd century, it began to secure for itself a new lease of life within the city and the growing Empire of Rome ; in fact, the last chapter of Greek religion falls within the Roman Imperial Period.

But the strongest and most interesting reflexion that the ancient records have preserved for us on the fusion of Hellenic culture and Oriental religious sentiment, is presented by the

Hermetic literature. The origin of this most fantastic product of the human mind is traced by Dr. Flinders Petrie back to Ancient Egypt. This alliance between Greek Philosophy and the Oriental mystic theosophy is a momentous phenomenon of later paganism. Such theosophy had a natural affinity with magic; and magic, always a power in an age of intellectual decay, began to be most powerful in the latest age of Hellenism. Another feature that we mark in this mystic religion and the mystic societies, *thiasoi*, of the Hellenistic world indicates a higher aspect of religion and suggests possibilities of momentous development; most of them, if not all, proclaimed the immortality of the soul, a happy resurrection, a divine life after death. The Hellenes who had been initiated into the Osirian faith hoped to attain immortal happiness in and through Osirian spell-formulæ.

Thus we have come to the conclusion that of the two peoples whose blending gave birth to Hellenism—the indigenous Mediterranean race and the Central European invader, the former possessed a personal theism of dateless antiquity; while all the evidence points to the conviction that the Aryan tribes entered Greece with certain personal deities already evolved or acquired. We find that anthropomorphism was the strongest bias of the Hellenes' religious imagination. It was only at a very late stage, when the strange forms of faith and speculation were introduced from the East, that the clearness and sanity of the pure Hellenic intellect appear clouded and perturbed, the lineaments of the old types of Hellenic thought and imagination almost effaced, and the learning and science of the Hellenistic age stood mainly aloof from the religious forces that moved the masses of the people.

BIBLIOGRAPHY.

1. Harrison, T. E. ... "Prolegomena to the Study of Greek Religion."
2. Burnouf, Emile ... "The Science of Religions."
3. " ... "Essai sur la Veda."
4. Réville, Albert ... "Prolegomena to the History of Religions."
5. Max Müller, F. ... "Contribution to the Science of Mythology."
6. Lang, A. ... "Myth, Ritual and Religion."
7. Renan, Ernest ... "Studies in Religious History."
8. Murray-Mitchell, T. ... "Hinduism, Past and Present."
9. Deussen, Paul ... "Outlines of Indian Philosophy."
10. Keith, A.B. ... "Vedic Index of Names and Subjects."
11. Encylopædia of Religion and Ethics, art. : Hinduism.
12. Farnell, L. R. ... "Cults of the Greek States."
13. Gomperz, Th. ... "Greek Thinkers."
14. Müller, K.O. ... "Literature of Ancient Greece."
15. Lotze ... "Outlines of the Philosophy of Religion."
16. Winternitz ... "Geschichte der Indischen Litteratur."
17. Tiele, C.P. ... "Outlines of the History of Ancient Religions."
18. Raoscher, W. H. ... "Juno und Hera."
19. Mahaffy, J. P. ... "Social Life in Greece from Homer to Menander."
20. Heffter, M. W. ... "Die Religion der Griechen und Romer."
21. Hartung, J.A. ... "Die Religion und Mythologie Griechen."
22. Hopkins ... "Religion of India."
23. Hardy, Spence ... "Christianity and Buddhism."
24. Pfleiderer ... "Philosophy and Development of Religion."
25. Hegel ... "Philosophy of Religion."
26. Barth ... "The Religions of India."
27. Oldenberg ... "Die Religion des Veda."
28. Pischel and Geldner ... "Vedische Studien."

RELIGION

29. Bergaigne, A. ... "La Religion Vedique."
30. Muir ... "Original Sanskrit Texts."
31. Max Müller, W. ... "Chips from a German Workshop."
32. Foucart, P. ... "La Culte de Dionysos en Attique."
33. Adam, J. ... "The Religious Teachers of Greece."
34. Showerman, G. ... "The Great Mother of Gods."
35. Frazer, J. G. ... "Attis, Adonis, Osiris."
36. Pfister, E. F. ... "Der Reliquienkult in Alterthum." Giessen, 1910.
37. Reinach, S. ... "Cultes, Mythes et Religions."
38. Usener, H. ... "Götternamen."
39. Bouché-Leclercq, A. ... "Histoire de la Divination."
40. Stengel, P. ... "Opferbrauche der Griechen."
41. Deniker, J. ... "The Gods of Northern Buddhism."

CHAPTER XII

PHILOSOPHY

General Resemblance of Philosophical Conceptions in Greece and in India.

THE relation of Greek Philosophy to Greek Religion is a great and complex subject, the theme of many modern treatises. So far as the new speculation, which gave birth to free secular science of Europe, was pre-occupied with questions of the physical origins of things and with elemental theories of cosmogony, it would not necessarily clash with any orthodox prejudice of the average Hellene. For he had no sacred books, like the Veda or Zend-Avesta, which dictated to him any views concerning the origin of the world or the constitution of Nature, and which he would have considered it immoral to disbelieve. Here lies the main difference in theodicy of the Greeks on the one hand, and the Persians and Hindus on the other. In fact, when Heraclitus boldly declared that 'neither God nor man made the Kosmos', there was no authoritative Greek myth or theologic dogma to gainsay him. Out of the great philosophers of the 6th century, Pythagoras, Empedokles, Xenophanes and Heraclitus—were also directly concerned with the philosophy of religion, with speculations on the Nature and the true definition of the godhead. But the main trend of their speculations ran counter to the anthropomorphic theory of divinity ; and they tend to define God not as a person, but rather as the highest spiritual, or metaphysical, or even physical power or function of the universe ;

and there is a common tendency in this 6th century philosophy to depart from the theistic to the pantheistic view.

It is a suggestive fact however, that the dawn of the scientific speculation in Greece should be coincident with a great religious movement in the East. The sixth century B.C. was not only the epoch when cosmical phenomena were extricated from theological explanations, but also the epoch when the doctrines of Buddha gathered up the scattered beliefs of Brahmanic polytheism into one energetic synthesis of monotheism ; and according to the German critics, it was about this time, the polytheism of the Hebrews gave place to monotheism, Elohim to Jahveh. In fact, the great wave of this sixth century is one of progress. The monotheistic tendency is visible in Greece as elsewhere, and the Gods gradually lose their independent autocratic position under Zeus, who in later systems is identified Intelligence and Goodness.

The early Greek philosophy is represented by the Ionian, the Pythagorean and the Eleatic Schools. In the Ionian, we see the predominance of the Empirical Method ; in the Pythagorean School, we see the Mathematical Method ; in the Eleatic School, lastly, both the concrete varieties and the abstract quantities are substituted for the speculative insight, which sees the One in the Many and endeavours to construct the Many from the One. "Eastern philosophy, as far as we know it," says Mr. Lewes in his "History of Philosophy" "seems to have been a traditional development ; but the early Greek had no real predecessor from whom to learn. Thales and other Ionic thinkers fixed upon common agencies, water, fire, air, etc. and tried to reconstruct the world out of these." Dr. Erdmann on the other hand asserts that "the task of apprehending its own nature in thought, can only tempt the human mind, and indeed it is only then equal to it, when it is conscious of its own intrinsic dignity. And as in the East, except among the Jews, this point is not reached, we must not be induced to talk of a pre-Hellenic philosophy or worse still pre-Hellenic *systems* either by the rules of propriety or external decorum enunciated by the Chinese sages, or by the pantheistic and atheistic doctrines which the Indian spirit attains in the Mimānsā and in the Kapila's teachings in the Sāmkhya or by the intellectual exercises to which it rises in the Nyāya and finally by the confused semi-religious and the semi-physical doctrines of the ancient Persians and of Egypt. For since, it is the Greek ear that first catches the '*gyothi-seantor*,' philosophising *i.e.*, the attempt to comprehend the nature of the human mind what in western or at least in Greek parlance, is called 'thinking', and the history of Philosophy begins with the Philosophy of the Greeks." This statement of Dr. Erdmann, we must acknowledge is more or less founded on unsound basis and is not corroborated by later historical researches and investigations.

The Questions as to the Oriental origin of Greek Philosophy, discussed.

Turning to the question of the Oriental origin of the Greek Philosophy, we find that the Greeks were early inclined to ascribe to the Eastern nations, a share in the origin of their Philosophy ; but in the most ancient period, certain isolated doctrines merely were derived from the East. As far as our information extends, not the Greeks, but the Orientals were the first to attribute such an origin to Greek Philosophy, generally. The Jews of the Alexandrian School, educated under Greek influences, sought by means of this theory to explain the supposed harmony of their sacred writings with the doctrines of the Hellenes, agreeable to their own standpoint and interest, and in the same manner, the Egyptian priests, after they had become acquainted under the Ptolemies with Greek Philosophy, made great boast of the wisdom which not only the prophets and poets, but also the philosophers of Greece, were said to have acquired from them. Somewhat later, the theory gained acceptance among the Greeks themselves. We however find nothing in Herodotus, as to an Egyptian origin of Greek Philosophy. In regard to religion, on the other hand, he not only maintains that certain Greek cults and doctrines (especially the worship of Dionysus) were imported from Egypt into Greece, but says in a general manner that the Pelasgi at first adored their divinities simply under the name of the gods and afterwards received the particular names of these gods from Egypt. That this assertion is chiefly founded on the statements of the Egyptian priests, appears probable from Chapters L and LIV. As the priests then represented themselves to be the founders of the Greek religion, so at a later period, they claimed to be the founders of Greek Philosophy.

So for the purpose of this enquiry, we have to look not merely to ancient accounts, but likewise to the principal modern researches into the subject, for the former are extremely unsatisfactory and their deficiencies require to be supplemented by a variety of acute and learned disquisitions. Much consequently on this point rests on purely general principles, and on the probabilities which have been drawn and are still being drawn from the relations which, it is conceived, existed between Greece and the East. To some, it has appeared to be a very natural supposition that, because Oriental culture flowed down to and was adopted by the later Greeks, so also philosophical doctrines: either case implies therefore some connexion and community between the Greek and Oriental intellectual development. Who could be so foolish as to deny this latter proposition generally? But before any legitimate inference can be drawn therefrom for our purpose, it is necessary to distinguish between the earlier and later influence of the East upon Greece. The earlier belongs to those distant times, when Greece was peopled from Asia, with its first inhabitants and when the subsequent colonisation from Asia in the course of the first migration of the Nations took place. Out of these emigrations was originally formed the people, which became known to us in historical times as Greeks, and then was first laid the basis of a distinct character between the nations of the East and the West. The first colonists of Greece were unquestionably from the East and brought with them into their new settlements a general oriental character. Subsequently, such a contrast was established between those who had emigrated and those who had remained behind, that the Greeks called the latter Barbarians. They had different customs, different manners, different languages. The later influence took place at the time when the Greeks already constituted themselves into a people, no longer receiving into itself any foreign element.

It is this latter influence alone which concerns our enquiry; for there can be no question of philosophy when a nation is first formed. Nevertheless, a short examination of the former will be useful towards enabling us to determine the latter more exactly. Whatever these wanderers brought with them from their original homes in Greece became the basis of their language, whose affinity with the Eastern tongue is distinctly traceable. From the same source, they derived the principles of arts necessary to life; and whatever can be pointed out in their institutions and mythology as bearing an Oriental cast was doubtless acquired by the Greeks in this early period of their national existence. This is the probable extent of all that the primitive settlers and subsequent colonists imported into Greece from their eastern homes. But the principal points for our present purpose are religious sentiments and ideas and scientific enquiries. As to religious ideas, it does not appear that they were either eagerly sought after by the Greeks, or were willingly communicated by the 'barbarians' : for man, generally is not disposed to lay open the secrets of his inmost soul, and to reveal the religious hopes and fears by which he is swayed, nor anxious to learn those of others. The Greeks, moreover, seem to have been little alive to or little interested in religious ideas specifically different from their own (vide Chap. xi. Religion). Of this Æschylus and Herodotus afford ample proof ; specially the latter, who, it is true, gives us many accounts of foreign religious rites, all of which, however, he had viewed in a purely Greek light. Still less disposed are we to think that the Greeks received from the East any philosophical communications. In general, the communication of philosophy is exceedingly difficult; and even at the present day, we see how possible it is for a particular system to be confined exclusively to a single people, without the neighbouring nations receiving from it the slightest impulse. We are also inclined to believe in a difference in kind between the inner man of the Greek and that of the 'barbarian,' so as to preclude the possibility of the former learning anything from the Oriental. There is no trace moreover, in the philosophy of oldest times of any Greek having made or procured a translation of an Egyptian or Indian work. Still less was it in the power of the Greek philosophers to read such work in the original, not to speak of understanding any scientific instruction orally delivered in a foreign tongue. We must also doubt the aptness and inclination of the Greeks to learn of the Orientals.

It now becomes necessary to test the value of the transmitted statements. The statements of the Greek writers respecting their foreign teachers in philosophy, are collectively far from being numerous and individually rest on any but the best authority. In the older authorities Plato and Aristotle, there is nothing of the kind. Plato does, it is true, occasionally mention Egyptian Myths and puts into the mouths of the Egyptians, wise and profound sentiments ; but he himself expressly tells us that this is not to be taken seriously and to the letter (Phædr. 275). Even very recently, the suggestion has been again thrown out, that Plato might probably have borrowed his philosophy from Egypt (vide A. W. Schlegel, 'Preface to the Bhagwad Gita'). After the time of Aristotle however, a better acquaintance with the East was established ; traces were discovered therein of a civilisation earlier than that of Greece ; and as the writers were unable to imagine the existence of a civilisation independent and different from their own, it was only natural for them to suppose that the olden Greeks had learned from the Indians in the same manner that the modern Greeks had their enlightenment from their forefathers. Moreover, the wild phantasy of the East began now to find its way into history, and traditions were seriously put forward as those of the Platonists, which no one in the present day would make use of collectively. Still more liable to suspicion is the assertion that Pythagoras derived his philosophy from his intercourse with the East. It is wholly unsupported by historical authorities. No one acquainted with the degree in which the marvellous elements prevail in the statements concerning Pythagoras, will be disposed to build at all upon the accounts given of his travels in Syria, Babylonia, Persia, India as well as his intercourse with the Thracians and the Druids in Gaul ; they all rest on equal warranty. However the conjectures of the earliest Greeks, as to the Egyptian origin of the Pythagorean Philosophy, had reference solely to the doctrine of the metempsychosis—of which Herodotus gave it as his opinion that it originally came from Egypt. Herodotus proceeds on the supposition that the Egyptians were the first, who taught the soul's immortality. By this opinion of Herodotus, we are no more bound than by that other of his, that the Greek gods were indebted to Egypt for their origin. Fr. Schlegel, on the other hand, in his "Sprache u. Weisheit d. Indier," p. iii, says, "in this way (*i.e.* in a moral sense) we find in the Pythagorean doctrine, the notion of the metempsychosis, with all its oriental accessories, affording certain proof that it is not of Greek origin." Now, assuredly no one of those who make the Greeks receive everything from the East, will go the length of maintaining that the moral sentiment too was transplanted from the former to the latter. Besides Fr. Schlegel is not bold enough to bring Pythagoras himself into India, but holds on the other hand that the metempsychosis came to Greece from India by way of Egypt; and yet he is of opinion that between the Indian and Egyptian form of this dogma, there is a vast difference. How then could the Pythagorean form of it bear such strong resemblance to the Indian? Again, Pyrrho is said to have taken part in Alexander's expedition to India (Diog. Laert. ix, 63.), but it is not until afterwards that traces of his teachings can be found to any great extent in Greek thought. Now, Pyrrho illustrates the reflex influence upon Greek culture of the beliefs of some of the districts which Alexander traversed or visited. That he learnt his theories in Persia or India rests upon the statement of an early writer, whose name alone is known and is probably incorrect (vide Susemihl, 'Lit. der Alexandrinerzeit').

Furthermore, there is yet another doctrine of the ancient philosophy of Greece, with respect to which distinct statements are found in old writers, assigning to it an Eastern origin viz. the Atomic Theory. Posidonius the Stoic, asserted that this doctrine was derived from a Sidonian, Moschus or Mochus, who lived prior to the Trojan War (Strabo, xvi, 367). Now, nothing it is true, was known of the manner in which Leucippus, who passes for the first Greek professor of atomism, could have come into contact with the Phœnicians; or if not he, another advocate of the same doctrine Democritus, who according to his own declaration had travelled much both elsewhere and in the East, is far from admitting that his doctrinal views were the fruit of his eastern travels. Instead of rejecting at once these loose conjectures, as wholly untenable, an attempt, on the contrary has been made to corroborate them, by the remark that the atomistic notions did exist among the Indians also and possibly these found their way into Greece through Persia (vide Fr. Schlegel, ibid, p. 118). But the Atomic Theory appears wholly to be the natural offspring of the advanced mathematical knowledge of the Greeks and its application to the observed phenomena of nature.

Even of the philosophers belonging to the maturity of the Socratic schools, it has been asserted that they introduced many doctrines into Greece derived from foreign origin. The growth of the Socratic schools was such, that we can recognise the germ of nearly all their systems in the doctrines of the earlier Greeks; and it is only an utter ignorance of the intimate relationship of the Socratic tenets with the entire mode of Greek thought, that can be moved by an anecdote, resting on the very weakest authority of Aristoxenus (vide Euseb. Praep. Er. xi, 3) to believe for one moment, that Socrates was indebted for the whole, or at least a portion of his doctrines, to an Indian traveller, who is made, we know how, to visit Athens. Lastly, much stress has been laid on the fact that the sceptic Pyrrho had in India frequent intercourse with the Gymnosophists and in Persia with the Magi, and an occasional tenet or maxim has been pointed out in his system of doctrines admitting of a comparison with Eastern opinions: but those tenets can be proved to have been already well-known in Greece, prior to his time, so that even though Pyrrho had become first acquainted with them in India or Persia, he could not have introduced them into his native country as novelties. We do not therefore find any statement historically established, constraining us to admit the presence of any foreign influence on the development of Greek Philosophy even in its flourishing age. A certain general resemblance will always be found betweeen the various evolutions of philosophical ideas; for the universal effort of the human mind to attain to scientific acumen must necessarily give rise to a similarity of results; and in most instances nothing beyond a general resemblance has been pointed out. In matter of details, a profound and searching enquiry is indispensable; and the superficial judgment of a mere dilettanti should avowedly be rejected. Thus for example, the esoteric cosmology, whose simple doctrine is this that in reality there is no manifest world, but only Brahman, and that what we consider to be the world is a mere illusion, similar to *mriga trishnika*, which disappears when we approach it. There are many similes in the Vedanta to illustrate this illusive character of the world, but the best of them is perhaps, Sankara's comparison of our life to a long dream. That this life is a dream,—has been however the doctrine of many wise men from Pindar and Sophocles to Shakespeare and Calderon de la Barca, but nobody has better explained this idea than Sankara. And indeed the moment when we die, we are, as it were awakened from a long dream. This was the way in which the Indian thinkers thought in and by a similar way, as shown by Parmenides, Plato came to the same truth, when knowing and teaching that this world is a world of shadows. The accord here of Platonism and Vedantism is wonderful, but both had grasped the great metaphysical truth by intuition; their tenet is true, but both arrived at the same conclusion by independent thinking.

Dr. Zeller's Criticism of the Theories of Gladisch and Roth: The most important result is supposed to be derived from the internal affinity of the Greek systems with Oriental doctrines. But even the two most distinguished advocates of the theory are not agreed as to the precise meaning of this affinity. Gladisch in his "Die Religion und Philosophie," on the one hand thinks it evident that the principal pre-Socratic systems reproduced without any material alteration the theories of the universe of the five chief oriental notions. The Philosophy of the Chinese, he considers, reappears in Pythagoreism; that of the Hindus in the Eleatics; that of the Persians in Heraclitus; that of the Jews in Anaxagoras. Roth in his "Geschichte unserer abendländischen Philosophie," on the other hand, no less distinctly affirms that the ancient Greek speculations arose out of Egyptian creeds, intermingled though not to any great extent except in the cases of Democritus and Plato, with the ideas of Zoroaster. In Aristotle, he says, Greek Philosophy first freed itself from these influences: but in Neo-Platonism, Egyptian speculation once more renewed its activity, while at the same time the Zoroastrian doctrines, with a certain admixture of Egyptian notions, re-appeared in Christianity.

If we examine impartially the historical facts, we shall find inclined to reject both these theories, and the improbability of an Eastern origin and character with regard to Greek Philosophy generally, will more and more appear. It may happen that not only particular notions and customs, but whole series of them will appear to bear resemblance to another series, to some other sphere of civilisation; it may also happen that fundamental conceptions may seem to repeat themselves without thus affording adequate proof that they are historically inter-connected. Under analogous conditions of development, and specially between races originally related to each other, many points of contact invariably arise, even when these races have no actual intercourse; chance often brings out many surprising similarities in detail. For instance, it must have been very astonishing to the followers of Alexander, to find among the Brahmins not only their Dionysus and Heracles, but also their Hellenic philosophy (cp. the accounts of Megasthens, Aristobulus, Onesicritus, Nearchus and Strabo); to hear of water being the origin of the world, as with Thales; of Deity permeating all things, as with Heraclitus; of a transmigration of souls, as with Pythagoras and Plato; of five elements constituting the universe, as with Empedocles and Orpheus; and no doubt Herodotus and his successors must have been often inclined to derive Greek doctrines and usages from Egypt. But for us, all this is not sufficient proof that Heraclitus, Thales, Plato, and Aristotle borrowed their theories from the Hindus or Egyptians. Supposing however, that at the time when the Greeks became acquainted with their philosophic doctrines, the transmission of those doctrines to Greece was not at all so easy as perhaps may be imagined. If we ask ourselves, by what means the doctrines of the Hindus and other nations of Western Asia could have been carried into Greece before the time of Alexander the Great, we find that the matter presents numerous difficulties. If the Eastern origin of Greek Philosophy were to be maintained by trustworthy evidence or by its own internal characteristics, our conception of the scientific condition of the Eastern nations and the relations in which the Greeks stood to them, must be formed accordingly. Moreover, when we cast our eyes on the first beginnings of Greek Philosophy, we find them so perfectly simple, and so entirely free from anything that looks like transmitted dogmata, that they have all the characteristics of original essays. "Their evolution is so gradual, that we can trace," says Dr. Heinrich Ritter, "its every step, and nothing is so suddenly introduced which might be referred to a foreign source."

But in the latest stage in the development of Greek thought, viz. the religious philosophy of the Neo-Platonists, we find direct traces of Oriental influence. The cradle of Neo-Platonism however was not the quiet University town of Athens, but the great manufacturing city of Alexandria. From the time, when the Alexandrian School rose into prominence, the official Academy with its professor—the Diadochus, as he was called at Athens—dwindled into insignificance ; until near the beginning of the 5th century, the Academy was captured by the School of Plotinus, or rather of Iamblichus and remained neo-Platonic till the edict of Justinian, 529 A. D, closed the series of Platonic professors who had taught at Athens for 800 years. It is to be noted that Plotinus, Porphyry and Iamblichus wished to be called Platonists, not Academicians. It is well-known that Alexandria was at this time not only a great intellectual centre, but the place where above all others, East and West rubbed shoulders. The wisdom of Asia was undoubtedly in high repute about this time. Philostratus expresses the highest veneration for the learning of the Indians ; Apollonius of Tyana is said to have visited India to consult the Brahmans ; Plotinus himself accompanied the Roman army to Persia in the hope of gathering wisdom, while his comrades searched for booty ; and the Christian Clement had heard of Buddha (Boutta). It is therefore natural, that many modern scholars have looked for Oriental influence in Neo-Platonism and have represented it as a fusion of European and Asiatic philosophy. In some ways, it might even be said that Plato is more Oriental than Plotinus. It is another question however, whether Neo-Platonism was influenced in any way by the Jewish Alexandrian School, which is known to us through the writings of Philo. The points of resemblance between the Essenes and the Neo-Pythagoreans, and between Philo and Plotinus are so striking that many have thought it impossible to deny a direct influence. In fact, the appearance of a great speculative genius like Plotinus in a period so barren of originality as the 3rd century B. C., had an immediate and decisive influence on the future of Greek philosophy. The School of Plotinus swallowed up and absorbed all other systems. A hundred years after his death Eunapius could say that he was more read than Plato himself, and added quite justly that his fame was very largely due to his disciple, Porphyry.

Neo-Pythagoreanism again, was one among many kindred phenomena resultant upon the spiritual commotion, which marked the gradual decline of classical culture, and at length ended in the triumph of the Christian Church. It may be dated after "the death of the Oracles" in the time of Nero and his immediate successors (cf. Tacitus, i. 2), although presages of it occurred long before e.g. the Bacchanalian affair (cf. Livy, xxxix, 8 f). Now, in the first century B. C. thanks to its cosmology, Stoicism had affinities with astrology and when in the person of Posidonius of Apamea (86-62 B. C.), Cicero's teacher (vide F. Cumont, 'The Oriental Religions in Roman Paganism," ch. VII) Oriental ideas permeated the west under authoritative intellectual auspices, this pseudo-science gained most influential adherents. This, together with the blunting of the Greek critical faculty, the prominence of encyclopædic or antiquarian knowledge, and the growing thirst for mystical revelations placed astrology in an incontestable position by the time of Tiberius and marked the moment favourable to the birth of Neo-Pythagoreanism.

In general, it may be said that the substance of the teachings of this school is Greek, the mood Oriental and till Numenius, 'the material served as a defence against the more insidious issues of the mood'; hence the transitional character of Neo-Pythagoreanism. The ancient self-governing state was passing into a quasi-oriental despotism; and this change found a parallel in the transformation of independent philosophy into the mystical Oriental theosophy.

BIBLIOGRAPHY.

1. Windelband, W. ... "A History of Philosophy."
2. Erdmann, J. E. ... "A History of Philosophy."
3. Lewes, G. H. ... "The History of Philosophy."
4. Ritter, Heinrich ... "The History of Ancient Philosophy."
5. Zeller, E. ... "A History of Greek Philosophy."
6. Deussen, Paul ... "Outlines of Indian Philosophy."
7. Kittel, F. ... "Ueber den Ursprung des Lingakults in Indien."
8. Hopkins ... "Religion of India."
9. Brünnhofer ... "Iran und Turan; Vom Volga bis zur Indus; Vom Aral bis zur Ganga."
10. Weber, A. ... "Indische Studien."
11. Rhys-Davids, T. W. ... "Indian Buddhism" (Hibbert Lectures.)
12. Von Schroeder, L. ... "Pythagoras."
13. Gomperz, Th. ... "Greek Thinkers."
14. Encyclopædia of Religion and Ethics, arts. Greek Religion, God.
15. Harrison, T. E. ... "Prolegomena to the Study of Greek Religion."
16. Burnouf, Emile ... "The Science of Religions."
17. Renan, Ernest ... "Studies in Religious History."
18. Howarth ... "Pythagoras in India."
19. Dahlmann, T. ... "Das Altindische Volkstum."

20. Oldenberg ... "Buddha."
21. Sigiura ... "Hindu Logic."
22. Van den Bergh Van Esyinga ... "Hindu Influence upon the Gospels."
23. Rosenmüller ... "The Biblical Geography of Asia Minor, Phœnicia and Arabia."
24. Thibaut, G. ... "Vedānta Sutras" in Sacred Books of the East, vol. xxxiv.
25. Lassen, Ch. ... "Indische Alterthumskunde."
26. Ueberweg ... "History of Philosophy."
27. Max Müller, W. ... "Six Systems of Indian Philosophy."
28. Garbe ... "Sankhya Philosophie"; "Sankhya und Yoga."
29. " ... "Philosophy of Ancient India."
30. Warren ... "Buddhism in Translations."
31. "Mimānsā-Darçana" edited with commentary of Sabara Svāmin (Bibl. Ind.)
32. "Sarvadarçana Samgraha" edited by T. Tarkavāchaspati.
33. More, Paul. E. ... "Platonism", Princeton. 1919.
34. Caird, E. ... "Evolution of Theology in the Greek Philosophers."
35. Campbell, L. ... "Religion in Greek Literature."
36. Adam, J. ... "The Religious Teachers of Greece."
37. Cumont, F. ... "The Oriental Religions in Roman Paganism."
38. Bigg, C. ... "Neo-Platonism."
39. " ... "The Christian Platonists of Alexandria"
40. Chaignet, A. E. ... "Pythagore et la philosophie pythagoricienne."
41. Mahtaffy. J. P. ... "Progress of Hellenism in Alexander's Empire."
42. Susemihl ... "Lit. der Alexandrinerzeit."
43. Simon, J. ... 'Histoire de l'école d' Alexandrie."

CHAPTER XIII

MYTHOLOGY

Parallel Evolution of Myths in India and in Greece.

"MYTHOLOGY as a whole," says M. Renan in his 'Studies in Religious History,' "is a vast play upon words. The myth is formed by the inevitable misuse of a language in which each substantive was an animated being, in which every verb signified a physical action. Myths are multiplied by the misuse of synonyms, and by means of popular etymology, a fruitful source of fables even in our day." Being a safe instrument of analysis, comparative philology acts as a guide to the science of myths and takes the place of arbitrary guesses, by means of which the old schools endeavoured to unravel these strange enigmas. Without the help of Philology, researches into Comparative Mythology run the risk of proceeding blind-fold, for the field of hypothesis is unlimited. But with the aid afforded by words, which stamp each fable with an indelible record of its origin, the chances of error are considerably minimised. Such are the principles which M. Bréal applied to two of the most interesting myths of antiquity. The fable of Cacus has a distinctly Italian appearance. M. Bréal very elaborately points out that it belongs to a group of mythic ideas and even of mythic terms, which with slight modifications, is to be met with in Greece, in India, in Persia, and in Germany. By referring to the great primitive work of the Aryan religions, the Vedas, he at last discovers the first essentially naturalistic germ of the myth. Doubtful indications are combined with unquestionable pieces of evidence. Similarly, the myth of Oedipus, having been formed mostly on the soil of Greece draws but indirect light from Vedic literature. It was a very much obsolete myth, which soon received developments, foreign to its origin. M. Bréal may however be accused of indulging in speculations not fully established.

"Mythology again always aims at strong effects and has no taste for anti-climax." We are led to imagine that two streams of speculative myth-making have mingled their waters ; the one displays more naturalistic features and the other gives free scope to the creative activity of proper god-like beings. Thus the fable of 'world-egg" would seem no longer to confront us in its original form. It must obviously have first been invented by such argument as this. The world is alive and it must have had a beginning. Its origin must be a living being ; and then the round vault of heaven suggested to the authors of this myth, the shape of an egg. Such an egg, they inferred, must once have existed and when it burst, its upper portion went to form the dome of the sky, the lower part engendered the earth and all that is therein. We can by no means pursuade ourselves to believe that the transformation of the fable of 'world-egg' took place on the soil of Greece. It is indeed a world-wide myth. It is found not merely among the Greeks, the Persians and the Indians, but these share it in common with Phœnicia, Babylonia and with Egypt, where indeed it appears in precisely the same form as in Orphic Cosmogony. We may quote for instance, the following Egyptian account of the creation of the world :

" In the beginning there was neither heaven nor earth. The universe was surrounded by thick darkness and was filled with boundless water which carried in its lap the germ of the male and female, or the beginnings of the future world.

The divine FIRST SPIRIT, inseparable from the watery FIRST MATTER, felt an impulse to create an activity and his word called the world into life. The first act of creation began with the formation of an egg out of elemental waters and from the egg went forth Râ, the sun, the direct source of earthly life" (vide Maspero, 'The Dawn of Civilisation.') In another version—and it may not be useless to notice the variations of the legend in the Valley of the Nile : it was the "god Ptah, who according to his worshippers turned the egg from which the world issued, like a potter on his wheel." We should notice particularly that in the male and female germs mentioned in the Egyptian myth, a parallel is found in the Light-god of the Orphic legend, who creates the world and whose nature is associated with the male and female attributes. We are yet more strongly reminded by the two-fold nature of Phanes of the epicene god-heads, who occur frequently in the Babylonian pantheon. To add to this, according to the unimpeachable testimony of Eudemus, the Phœnician cosmogony reproduces the Time-principle, that stands at the head of Indo-European cosmogony, not to speak of the Persian Avesta, where it appears as Zrvan Akarna or boundless time ; and these foreign traditions exercised no inconsiderable influence on the origin of the Orphic doctrine. The centre from which these lights radiated may almost certainly be identified with the country, which was not merely one of the oldest homes, but practically the cradle, of human civilisation.

Thus Myth is the result of a purely psychological operation and is, together with the language, the oldest affort of human mind. This has been shown conclusively by the modern school of mythologists, who are also psychologists. Assuming then, what can scarcely be called in question, that the same psychological laws govern the intellectual activity of mankind, without distinction of race, we cannot *à priori* assume that the capacity for forming myths can be induced or withheld according to ethnological categories. As the physiology is the same for all mankind, so it is also with the psychological functions, given the stimulus necessary for their productions. And this stimulus acts upon mankind everywhere alike. For it is clearly proved that the myth tells of the operations of Nature and expresses the mode in which man, perceives at the earliest stage of his intellectual life, these operations and phenomena. These form the substance of the Myth. Consequently wherever they act as attractions to the youthful mind, the external conditions of the rise of Mythology are present. Not unjustly therefore has a recent psychologist spoken of "the universal presence and the uniformity of myths." Undoubtedly, the direction of the myth is determined by the relation of the natural phenomena to mankind ; the myth will take one direction where man greets the sun as a friendly element and another where the sun meets him as a hostile power ; and in the rainless region the rain cannot act the same part in Mythology, which it plays in the rainy parts of the earth. The manners and usages of men must also exercise a modifying influence on the subject and the direction of the Myth.

The same mighty power of imagination which, now controlled and guided by scientific principles leads us to discoveries and inventions, must in that dark antiquity have run riot in mythologic fictions whereby the phenomena of nature are explained. Knowing nothing whatever of physical forces, the men of primeval times interpreted the actions of nature only by the analogy of their own actions. The only force they knew was the force of will, of which they were directly conscious. Accordingly, they imagined all the outward world to be endowed with volition and to be directed by it. Thus they personified everything—sky, clouds, thunder, sun, moon, ocean, earthquake, whirlwind. It should be noticed here that even now no distinction between the animate and the inanimate is made in the languages of the Esquimaux, the Choctaws, the Muskoghee and the Caddo (vide M' Lenan, "The Worship of Animals and Plants," Fortnightly Review, Vol. XII, p. 416). The clouds for instance were no masses of vaporized water, they were cows with swelling udders, driven to the milking by Hermes, the summer wind ; or the great sheep with moist fleeces, slain by the unerring arrows of Bellerophon, the Sun ; or Swan-maidens, flitting across the firmament ; Valkyries hovering over the battle-field to receive the souls of the falling heroes, or again, they were mighty mountains piled one above another, in whose cavernous recesses the divining wand of the Storm-god Thor revealed hidden treasures. This theory of ancient mythology is not only beautiful and plausible, it is, in its essential points, verified. It stands on as firm a foundation as Grimm's law in philology or the undulatory theory in molecular physics. It is philology which has enabled us to read the primitive thoughts of mankind. A large number of the names of Greek gods and heroes have no meaning in the Greek language ; but these names occur in Sanskrit with a distinctive significance.

"But the Indo-European race," says Tito Vignoli, "is æsthetically, more mythological than all others." If we consider the religious teachings of various Aryan peoples—the Celts, Greeks, Latins, Germans and Slavs, from the most primitive Vedic to the successive religions of Brahma or Zend, we see how widely they differ from the religious conceptions and ideas of other races. The intrinsic habit of forming mythical representations of Nature, is due to a more vivid realisation of her power, to a rapid succession of images and to a constant projection of the observer's own personality intothe phenomena. This peculiar charcteristic of the Indo-European race is never wholly overcome; and to it, is added a proud self-consciousness, an energy of thought and action, a constant aspiration after grand achievements, and a haughty contempt of all other nations. But we should never forget how limited our knowledge of ancient popular tradition really is, even in the case of the Hindus and Greeks and how the earliest chapters of mythology are lost to us for ever. To the Greeks, the Homeric poems were the most distant background of their mythology and religion, nay, of their history also; to us, they are a beautifully painted curtain, which must be lifted before we can hope to see the earliest acts of the drama of Mythology or to recognise the original actors and the natural scenery by which they are surrounded. How true were the words of Kekulé, when he described the Greek Mythology as a mere fragment taken from the words of metaphor and dreams, piled one upon the other by the hand of man, or as one page torn from the great picture-book of Nature, for which nothing is too small, nothing too sublime. It was Schelling who was first to complain of the "shallowness of any admiration for Homer, which is not founded on a perception of the remote past left behind by his creations." It was only after Schelling's death that by means of Comparative Philology and Comparative Mythology it became possible to lift, to a certain extent, the curtain which divided the Homeric present from the Homeric past. With the progress of scientific research every year we learn how very modern the Homeric poems really are, that is to say, how much they presuppose and how much of the rich growth of religious and mythological folklore, they leave unnoticed. And what applies to Greek, applies to all mythologies, even to that of the Veda, though here, better than anywhere else, we are sometimes allowed to watch the very process of fermentation, which always precedes the birth of real Mythology. Comparative philology and comparative mythology always go hand in hand; and as the language of the Vedas has proved to be the great critical instrument for the construction of the science of Philology, so the simple hymns of the Vedas, pregnant with rudimentary myths, furnish many clues for unravelling the science of Mythology. For where the etymology of a mythic name or term yields a distinct meaning, the origin of the myth is not far to seek. The Vedic hymns moreover have preserved the myths in their primitive forms and so said Max Müller, "nowhere is the wide distance which separates the ancient poems of India from the most ancient literature of Greece more clearly felt than when we compare the growing myths of the Vedas with the full grown and decayed myths on which the poetry of Homer is founded. The Veda is the real Theogony of the Aryan races, while that of Hesiod is a distorted caricature of the original image." The most ancient hymns of the Rig Veda are the basis upon which comparative mythology rests, and they have already supplied the means of unfolding the real source and signification of several Greek and Zoroastrian myths. Take for example, the Vedic god Deva. The collective appellation of the Vedic gods is Devas, and this name has passed into most of the Indo-European languages; for corresponding to the Sanskrit Deva is the Latin *deus*, Greek *théos*, Lithunian *dewas*, Lettish *dews*, Old Prussian *diews*, Irish *dia*, Cornish *duy*. Among the Germanic races, the word Devâ survives only in the Norse plural *tivar*, gods; and among those of the Slav stock, the Servians alone preserve a trace of it in the word *diev*, giant. The *daevas* of the Medes and Persians, were in early times degraded from the ranks of gods to that of demons by a religious revolution. Hence it appears, that certain gods were common to all the Indo-Europeans before their dispersion and the greatest of those heavenly beings must have been he who was heaven itself, *Div.* He is addressed in the Vedic hymns as *Dyaush pitâ* or 'Heaven Father' and his wife is *Mâtâ Prithivi* or 'Mother Earth'. He is the *Zeus Pater* of the Greeks, the *Jupiter* of the Romans, the German *Tius*, the Norse *Tyr.* Similarly *Varuna*, the *Uranos* of the Greeks, was lord of the celestial sea and of the realm of light above it. So, *Savitar* or *Surya*, who had his beaming chariot drawn by two, seven, or ten golden-coloured mares called Hāritas, a name in which Prof. Max Müller (vide "Oxford Essays," p. 81) recognised the original of the Greek 'Charites'. The morning twilight is represented in the Vedas by twin gods and the ruddy dawn by the goddess *Ushās*, who is one in name and fact with the Greek *Eos* and so forth. Similar arguments may be adduced in the case of semi-divine personages *e.g.* Gandharvas, Satyrs and Centaurs. Now, with the Apsarās are associated in the Rig Veda, a male being or beings called Gandharvas. In the Rig Veda, Gandharva seems to be localised in the high region of air or sky, and he is often associated (chiefly in the Ninth Book) with Soma. Through Gandharva's mouth the Gods drink their draught (vide Atharva Veda, 7. 73). But of the conception of the Gandharvas being celestial singers, which appear in the Epics and later works, there seems to be no distinct trace in the Rig Veda. The Rig Veda however adds the touch that the Gandharva wears a fragrant (*Surabhi*) garment (10, 123), while in the Atharva Veda (12, 1), the odour (*gandha*) of the earth is said to rise to the Gandharvas. This suggests that the derivation from "gandha" is possible. But such an etymology, even if true, would seem to shed no light on the original conception. The name has been identified with the Greek 'kéntauros', but in order to justify this equation, the aid of popular etymology has to be called in (vide Meyer, 'Indoger. Mythen,' 1846), as well as the doubtful epeuthesis of U assumed in the Greek word (see Brugmann, Grundriss, 1.481). The utmost, from the review of the evidence, that can possibly be said, about the original nature of the Gandharva is that he was a bright celestial being, sometimes thought of as dwelling in the region of air with his spouse, the Apsarās. The name is also found several times in the Avesta as Gandarewa (a dragon-like monster) but only in the singular [vide Z. D. M. G., (Bartholomæ) vol. xlii. 158].

Therefore, if in the legends of the Indo-European people we find a number of names which explain themselves, if further the exploits of the gods or heroes, who bear these names are in strict accordance with those meanings, then at once we are warranted in conjecturing that other names in the same legends not yet interpreted, may be of the same nature, while at the same time a basis is furnished for classifying the several myths. If again, we find that in the traditions of different Aryan tribes, or even of the same tribe, the same character reappears, with no other difference than that of title or local colouring, the inference is justified that a search into the mythical stores of all the Aryan tribes would disclose the same phenomenon. We have no evidence in any extant literature of the precise state in which Homer found the national mythology; but it seems unlikely that he had, what may be termed a theological authority, for every statement which he made and every attribute which he assigned to the mythology. It is certain that Athené once conspired against Zeus (Iliad, i. 400), but we cannot tell how far the poet himself succeeded in depicting the real situation nor can we forget that Ushās is as dear to gods and men as Athené herself, and that Ushās is undeniably nothing but morning. But the unformed mythology of the Veda, followed in its own land, a course analogous but prior to that of the mythology of Greece. There was the same systematic development with this difference, that in India the process was urged on by a powerful sacerdotal order. But in the earlier Vedas, there is no predominant priesthood, and there are only the faintest indications of caste; there are no temples, no public worship, and it would seem, no images of the gods; and what is of immeasurably greater importance with reference to the mythological creed of the Homeric poets, there are "no indications of a triad, the creating, the preserving and the destroying power. Brahma does not appear as a deity, and Vishnu although named, has nothing in common with the Vishnu of the Puranas, no allusion occurs to his Avatārs......These differences are palpable and so far from the Vedas being the basis of the existing system, they completely overturn it" (vide "Edinburgh Review," Oct. 1860, p. 382. No. ccxxviii). The comparison is scarcely less fatal to the mythological trinity of the Greeks.

Theory of the Importation of Myths, criticised.

But if in the vast mass of stories which make up the Fable-Literature of the Aryan nations, there is evidence showing that in some cases, the legend has been brought by the direct importation from the East to West (vide Chapter xiv, Fables and Folk-lore), the presumption of conscious borrowing cannot with any fairness be extended to myths, for which such evidence is not forthcoming. The great Epic poems of the Aryan race sprang into existence in the ages which followed the dispersion of tribes, and during which all intercourse between them was an impossibility; yet these Epic poems exhibit an identical frame-work, with resemblances in detail which even defy the influences of the climate and scenery. But many of the actors in the great mythological dramas re-appear in the popular stories of the Aryan tribes, with subtle points of likeness and difference, which can be accounted for by conscious borrowing, only on the supposition that the traditions of one country are as intimately known to the people of another, as the traditions of many, if not most of the Aryan nations, are now known to us through the long toil and vast researches of such eminent philologists and mythologists, as Bréal, Max Müller, Grimm, Kuhn, Preller, Welcker, Wilson, Cornewall Lewis, Grote and Thirlwall. In truth, the more we examine this hypothesis of importation as affecting the general stock of mythic tradition in any country, the more scanty and less conclusive will the evidence appear; and in the issue, we find ourselves driven practically to reject it altogether, or to suppose that the impulse of borrowing amounted to a universal and irresistible mania. Thus it is impossible that "the dynastic legends of Thebes do but reproduce those of Argos; the legends of both alike do but repeat the career of Achilleus, or Sigurd; and the great heroes of those tales reappear as the Boots and the disguised Beggar of Teutonic and Hindu folklore." (Cox).

The supposition of any deliberate borrowing attributes to the Hindus, Greeks, Teutons or Scandinavians, a poverty of invention not less amazing than their skill in destroying the evidence of the theft and in wearing borrowed plumage, as with an inborn grace. Unless we are prepared to say that the borrowing was wholesale, and that to determine the source of this exhaustless store of wealth, it is more prudent and more philosophical to admit that in every country, the myths which have their roots in phrases relating to physical phenomena, have been kept alive by independent tradition from the times of the first dispersion. But if the story of Achilleus, as told in the Iliad, is only another form of the legend which relates the career of the Ithakan Chief in the Odyssey; if this tale re-appears in the Saga of the Volsungs and in the Nibelungen Lied, in the epical cycles of Arthur and Charlemagne, in the lay of Beowulf and in the Shahnameh of Firdausi ; and if further all these streams of popular poetry can be traced back to a common source in phrases, which described the sights and sounds of the outward world, the resemblances thus traced are nevertheless by no means very astonishing. On the hypothesis of a form of thought which attributed conscious life to all physical objects, we must at once admit that the growth of a vast number of cognate myths was inevitable. Now is there any wonder in the fact that phrases which denoted at first the death of the Dawn or her desertion by the Sun, as he rose in the heavens or the stealing away of the evening-light by the powers of Darkness, should give birth to the legends of Helen and Guenevere, of Brynhild and Gudrun, of Paris and Launcelot, of Achilleus and Sigurd ? All that this theory involves is, that certain races of mankind or certain tribes of the same race were separated from each other, while their language still invested all sensible things with a personal life, and that when the meanings of the old words were either wholly or in part forgotten, the phenomena of the earth and the heaven reappeared as beings human or divine, and the Pani or Night which sought to lure Saramâ the Dawn, into his dismal cave, became the Paris who beguiled Helen to Troy and Launcelot who corrupted the faith of the wife of Arthur.

BIBLIOGRAPHY.

1. Max Müller, F. ... "Contributions to the Science of Mythology."
2. Lang, A. ... "Myth, Ritual and Religion."
3. Wolf ... "Beitrage zur Deutschen Mythologie."
4. Grimm, Jacob ... "Teutonic Mythology."

5. Thorpe, B. ... "Northern Mythology."
6. Vignoli, Tito ... "Myth and Science."
7. Macdonnell, A. ... "Vedic Mythology" (Grund. der Indo-Aris. Philologie.)
8. Dowson, J. ... "A Classical Dictionary of Hindu Mythology."
9. Lang, A. ... "Modern Mythology."
10. Harrison, J. E. ... "Prolegomena to the Study of Greek Religion."
11. Hewitt, J. F. ... "History and Chronology of the Myth-Making Age."
12. Schräder, O. ... "Sprachver gleichung und urgeschichte Linguistic palæontologie."
13. Cox, Sir G. ... "Mythology of the Aryan Nations."
14. Gubernatis ... "Zoological Mythology."
15. Gladstone ... "Homer and Homeric Age."
16. Brown ... "Religion and Mythology of the Aryans of Northern Europe."
17. Gould ... "Curious Myths of the Middle Ages."
18. Cox, Sir G. ... "An Introduction to the Science of Comparative Mythology and Folk-lore."
19. Goldziher, Ignaz ... "Mythology among the Hebrews."
20. Ficke, J. ... "Myths and Myth-Makers."
21. Gruppe, O ... "Griechische Mythologie und Religion."
22. Rohde, E. ... "Psyche."

CHAPTER XIV

FABLES AND FOLK-LORE

Indian Fairy-Tales and Fables : Westward migration of Indian Fables.

Our wonder becomes great, when we turn to popular stories which could not be brought within the category of mythical legends and which exhibit, in spite of differences of detail and local colouring, a closeness of resemblance which establishes their substantial identity. If among the stories which the Hindu, Persian, Greek or Teutonic mothers recounted to their children, we find tales which turn on the same incidents, and in their most delicate touches betray the influences of precisely the same sentiment, we must conclude either that these legends were passed from one clan or tribe to another, or that before the tribes separated from their common home, they not only possessed in mythical phrases relating to physical phenomena, the germs of the future epics of Asia and Europe, but had framed also a number of stories, which seem to point rather to a storehouse of moral proverbs. The story of the Master Thief is a case in point. It looks at first sight, as though it had nothing to do with the great legends of the Norse and Hellenic heroes, and the resemblance of some of its incidents to those of a story told in the Hitopodesa suggests the conclusion that it found its way into Europe through the Arabic translation known as the Kalilag and Dimnag (vide Macdonell, 'Sanskrit Literature' p. 417 ; "Zu Kalila we-Dimna," by Dr. Steinschneider in Z. D. M. G. vol. xxvii, p. 550.) Prof. Max Müller plainly avowing this belief said that "the story of the Master Thief is told in the Hitopodesa" (see 'Chips from a German Workshop' vol. ii, 229). The Sanskrit tale is that of a Brahman, who on hearing from three thieves in succession, that the Goat which he carried on his back was a Dog, throws the animal down and leaves it as a booty for the rogues, who had hit upon this plan of cheating him. "The gist of the story," added Max Müller, "is that a man will believe almost anything, if he is told the same by three different people." But while a far greater resemblance to the Egyptian legend of Rhampsinitos (as told by Herodotus and later on reproduced by the author of "Gesta Romanorum"), is exhibited than the Hindu version of the Master Thief as narrated by Somadeva Bhatta of Kashmir, it may fairly be asked whether the latter is the source of either the story or the moral of the European Master Thief. In the Teutonic version however, we find no incidents resembling the Sanskrit tale. The Norse story on the other hand exhibits some points of likeness, which force us to think that it must have been suggested by the Eastern Fable. Thus if such stories as the King Trivikramasenâ and the Vampire in the Kathāsaritsāgara, which find their counterparts in the Turkish Tutinamah and the stories of Siddhikür (see "Sagas from the Far East"), as also in Grimm's Kinder Märchen, in Böhmische Märchen of Waldau, in Laura Gonzenbach's Sicilianische Märchen, in Griechische Märchen of Schmidt and in Gaal's Märchen der Magyaren, be comparatively judged, we cannot avoid the conclusion that these migrated from India at some remote date and possibly they reached Europe through the intervention of the Sassanide kings and their successors.

It was between the years 1063 and 1081 A.D. that Somadeva of Kashmir wrote his great poem, Kathāsaritsāgara. As he tells us, it was not his original work, but an adaptation of an older collection, the "Brihat-Kathā" or the Great Romance. He informs us at the outset of his book that he has followed faithfully his original. Here are gathered together series upon series of fables, moral stories, folk-lore and romances of every kind from all sorts of sources, often interwoven together in the bewildering fashion of the Chinese puzzle. The date when the Brihat-Kathā was written must lie somewhere in the first five centuries of the Christian era, perhaps even in the first three. But much of its materials is very ancient indeed, belonging to the oldest cycles of Indian romance, and often showing very remarkable affinities to the folk-lore of the most distant lands e.g. Europe. By his adaptation Somadeva has rescued for posterity this priceless treasure of old-time wit, wisdom and imagination and earned from us a debt of gratitude far beyond what his own poetical merit deserves, great as that is.

We append here a few types of Indo-European folk-tales, which are in common vogue among the Hindus and the Persians on the one hand, and the Germans, the Norsemen, the Scots, the Irish, the Sicilians, the Greeks and the Slavs on the other, and which may have, in all probability, migrated from India westward :

Cupid and Psyche Type,
Penelope Type.
Punchkin or Life-Index Type.
Hercules Type.
Robert the Devil Type.
Rhea Sylvia Type.
Juniper Tree Type.
Seven Swans Type.
Bertha Type.
Gudrun Type.
Thrush-beard Type.
Bird-wager Type.
Dog and the Sparrow Type.
Fearless John Type.
Swan-Maiden Type.
Geneviva Type.
Samson Type.
Serpent-Child Type.
Good-child Type.
Catskin Type.
Cindrella Type.
Taming of the Shrew Type.
Jason Type.
Jack the Giant-killer Type.
Sleeping Beauty Type.
Master Thief Type.
Jack and the Beanstalk Type.
Valiant Tailor Type.

William Tell Type.
Aladdin Type.
Andromeda Type.
Puss in the Boots Type.
Magical Book Type.
Golden Goose Type.
Dick Whittington Type,
Goldenlocks Type.

In India, as in Europe, old women who doubtlessly thought themselves fit for nothing have preserved for us a series of exquisite legends which pour a flood of light on the early history of the human mind. The Hindu child is still roused and soothed by the stories of the Sweet Star-Lady and the lovely Queen of the Five Flowers, just as the young German and Norseman listen to the tales of the beautiful Briar-Rose sleeping in death-like trance, until the kiss of the pure Knight rouses her from slumber. We are clearly indebted to the old women for the preservation of thousands of such lovely and touching legends, which have never found their way into epic poetry. Had it not been for the grandmothers of Hellas, we should in all likelihood never have heard of the grief of Dêmêter, as she sank down by the fountain in Eleusis, or of the woe of Telephassa, which ended as she sank to rest on the Thessalian plain in the evening. Schools of Athens, Thebes or Argos doubtless did their inevitable destructive work ; but we can as little doubt that many an Athenian mother pointed on the slopes of Hymettos, to the spot where the glistening form of Prokris first met the eye of Kephalos, as he stepped forth on the shore, and the young Delian learnt to be proud of the rugged island, where the nymphs bathed the young Phœbus in pure water and swathed him in broad golden bands. Among the Hindu tales, we find a large mass of stories, which have little or nothing in common with the epic poems of the Aryan nations, but which exhibit a series of incidents in striking parallelism with those of the corresponding Teutonic versions. The fidelity with which the Greek and German tales adhere to their original Indian frame-work, is indeed astonishing (vide Oesterley's notes in his German version of Baitál Pachisi; Garçin de Tassy in Journal des Savans, 1836, p. 415; Dr. Köhler, 'Orient und Occident' vol. II). One of the most remarkable of these coincidences is furnished by the story of the "Dog and the Sparrow" in Grimm's collection, as compared with an Episode in the Baitál Pachisi, viz. 'The Story of the Nautch-Girl and the Parrot'. In both, a bird vows to bring about the ruin of a human being; in both, the bird is the helper and avenger of the innocent against wanton injury; and in both, the destruction of the guilty is the result of their own voluntary acts. (For a Russian variant of the "Dog and the Sparrow," see Gubernatis, "Zoological Mythology," ii. 268). It is impossible to question the real identity of these two stories and it is hardly credible that one could have been invented apart from the other. It was impossible that the leading idea should of itself suggest to a Hindu and a Teuton that the avenger should be a bird and that the wrong-doer should punish himself and should seal his doom by swallowing his prosecutor or by at least thinking that he was devouring him. There is no room here for any other argument. A series of incidents, such as these, could never have been thought out by two brains working apart from each other; and we are driven either to admit that at least the machinery by which the result was to be brought about had been devised before the separation, or to maintain that the story has in one case or the other been imported bodily. But the supposition that the stories had been transmitted laterally, is tenable only on the further hypothesis, that in every Aryan land, from Eastern India to the Highlands of Scotland, the folklore of a country has had its character determined by the literature of the written books, that in every land men have handled the stories introduced from other countries with the deliberate purpose of modifying and adapting them, and that they have done their work in such a clever way as to leave no trace of the original in some cases or to retain it by effecting the smallest change in others. The tales have been circulated for the most part, only among those, who have no books, and many, if not most of them, have been made known only of late years for the first time, to the antiquarians and philologists, who have devoted their time in hunting them out. The task of analysing and comparing these legends is not a light one, even for those who have all the appliances of books and the aid of a syndicate of scholars working with them for the same end.

Even now however, we find that old men and women reproduce in India, in Germany, in Norway, in Scotland and in Ireland, the most subtle turns of thought and expression, and an endless series of complicated narratives, in which the order of incidents and the words of the speakers are preserved with a fidelity no where paralleled in the oral tradition of historical events. The idea that all these folk-tales have been deliberately transferred from the Hindus or Persians, to the Greeks, Germans or Norsemen, cannot be dismissed as an idle dream. Of their substantial identity in spite of all points of difference and all the disguises thrown over them by individual fancies and local influences, there can be no question. The keynote of the Indian stories is the keynote of them all ; and this keynote runs practically through the great body of tales, gathered from Germany, Scandinavia, Ireland and Scotland. It is found again everywhere in the Fable-Literature of the Greeks, whether in the legends, which have furnished the materials for their elaborate fictions or have been immortalised in the dramas of their great tragedians e. g. Sophocles, Euripides etc. or have remained buried in the pages of their mythographers like Pausanias or Diodoros. But on the other hand, the stories of the heroes of the Teutonic or Hindu folk-lore, the stories of Boots and Cindrella are substantially the same as the stories of Achilleus and Oedipus, of Perseus and Theseus, of Râma and Râvana, of Shorab and Rustum, of Sigurd and Baldur and of Helen and Odysseus. Everywhere there is the search for the bright maiden, who had been stolen away; everywhere the long struggle to recover her. the war of Ilion has been fought out on every Aryan land. Therefore, the historical facts which lie at the root of the narrative of the Iliad must have taken place before the dispersion of the Aryan tribes from their common home (vide Chapter IX—Literature).

Again, the study of Fables as also the theory advanced as to the origin of the Folk-tale incidents, help to throw some light on the problem of their diffusion. The various solutions of the problem indicate the locality of the centre of diffusion i.e. the East, or less vaguely India. Now, Fable originally meant 'a thing said' and thus a story or narration (as in Horace's Mutato nomine, de te fabula narratur' [Sat. I. 1, 70]; and Dryden wrote 'Fables' of men and women. But in modern sense, the word is mainly restricted to Beast-Fables or short narratives about animals, having a moral significance which is generally expressed in an explicit 'moral' at the end. The Fable in this more restricted sense has to be distinguished from the Beast-Anecdote and especially from the Beast-Satire, in which Beasts, by their antics and wiles, parody and satirize the worst qualities of men (see Mac Culloch, " The Childhood of Fiction", *passim*). There is one further quality inherent in the Fable, which should be emphasised at the outset, viz. that they appeal largely to the sense of fun. A German might accordingly on the analogy of Tendenzroman, define the fable as a "Moral-Tendency Beast-Droll". Taking Fable in this strict sense, its independent and original production is practically restricted to two countries—India and Greece. Sporadic instances occur elsewhere as are seen in the wall-paintings on some of the old Egyptian tombs or as in Jotham's and Jehoash's fables in the Old Testament; but for any large body of fables we have to look to India and to Greece. In the former country, they are mainly connected with the Jātakas or the birth-stories of Buddha and the Pãnchatantra; in the latter, they are associated with the name of Æsop. The main problem suggested by the Fables is the connexion between the two. We shall discuss the subject later on.

Now, the Fables known as Æsop's Fables, which have spread throughout Europe, can be traced back to a collection in Latin and German, published soon after the invention of printing by Heinrich Stainhowel, printed about 1480 and within the next ten years, translated into French, Dutch Italian, English and Spanish. This consists of a Life of Æsop (connected with the legend of Ahiqār), four books derived from a mediæval collection of fables known as *Romulus*, a selection of the Fables of Avian, some from a previous selection made by Ranutio and two collections of rather coarse anecdotes from Poggio and Petrus Alphonsi. The *Romulus* has after all turned out to be entirely mediæval prose renderings of Phædrus, a Greek Freedman of Augustus, who flourished in the early years of first century A.D. It contains survivals of Phædrine fables which are no longer extant in verse form such as "The Lion and the Mouse," "The Ass and the Lap-Dog". It may accordingly be said that Æsop is Phædrus with trimmings.

Besides these prose-renderings of Phædrus, which form the bulk of the modern European Æsop, there exist a number of Greek prose-renderings which were, for a long time, supposed to be the original Æsop, but have been proved by

Bentley and others to have been derived from a metrical collection by one Valerius Babrius, tutor to the son of the Emperor Severus (c. 235 A. D.) and parts of whose fables were discovered on Mt. Athos by Minoides Menas in 1840. Babrius in his preface, refers to two sources, e.g. Æsop for Hellenic fable and Kybises for "Lybian" fable; and Dr. Jacobs has suggested that the latter collection ran to about 100 in number, and was derived directly or indirectly from a Simhalese Embassy which came to Rome about 52 A. D. Similarly Phædrus refers not only to Æsop but to Anacharsis the Scythian as his sources; and some of the Indian elements which exist in Phædrus may be due to this source. That there are such Indian elements in Phædrus and Babrius as well as in Avian (who flourished in A. D. 375) can scarcely be doubted if one glances at the Indian Fables.

In India Fables in the strict sense that is, humorous Beast-stories with 'morals,' are found not only in the Bidpai literature, but much earlier in the Jātakas (c. 600 B. C.). Now, several of these Birth-stories are Fables in the strict sense of the word and several are actually identical with some of the most familiar of Æsop's Fables. Dr. Jacobs in his excellent work on "The History of the Æsopic Fable" has pointed thirteen of these *e.g.* 'The Wolf and the Crane', 'The Wolf and the Lamb', 'The Fox and the Crow' and so forth. Other parallels are noticed by the same writer between Greek fables and Indian ones that occur in the Mahabharata and in the earlier strata of the Bidpai literature. Benfey in his famous Introduction to the Pañchatantra held that fables reached the South of Europe *via* the Turks, and were transmitted to the North *via* the Mongols, who passed them on to the Slavs, from whom the Germanic peoples received them. All this happened within historic times and the stories themselves had a Buddhist origin. But while it is true that Eastern literary collections of tales or individual legends like that of Barlaam and Josaphat, of Kalilag and Dimnag, may be traced step by step from India to Europe, it is not necessarily true that all European tales which resemble them were derived from those literary stores. Such tales have been told in Europe before they arrived in a literary form from the East, just as they existed orally in India, before a literary form was given them. Later investigators like M. Cosquin ("Contes populaires de Lorraine") widened the Indian theory by admitting the existence of Fables in India in pre-Buddhistic times and by postulating their continuous oral transmission to Europe from the early ages.

There is certainly no doubt—and all critics are agreed on this—that a considerable number of Indian fables as given in Pañchatantra, Hitopadesa and partly also in some of the older works *e.g.* Chandogya-Upanishad, are obviously similar to the Fables which have been connected with the name of Æsop among the Greeks, and which are known to us as the Fables of Babrius. Albrecht Weber had in the year 1852, in his 'History of Indian Literature' held that the originals of many of the Greek fables were to be found in the Indian, and this view was also completely accepted by A. Wagener in his "Essai sur la rapports qui existent entre les apologues de l'Inde et les apologues de la Grèce." But Weber later on and specially in a detailed criticism of the work of Wagener arrived exactly at the opposite conclusion, namely, that in almost every case, the traces of originality were to be found in the Greek fables as opposed to the Indian, so that the borrowing had taken place on the side of the Indians. He thought that the Buddhists were to be regarded as the intermediaries (vide Weber, Ind. Stud. III p. 327). This latter view of Weber was again vigorously opposed by Otto Keller in his work on the 'History of the Greek Fable'

(1862). He completely believed in the Indian origin of the Fables, common to the Indians and Greeks, and transmitted through an ancient Assyrian connecting link. Weber in the meanwhile had kept to his views and defended them, though summarily, again in the second edition of his 'History of Indian Literature.' According to Weber's opinion the Greek "animal-fables" are of a Semitic origin. Benfey is also of opinion that the Indian "animal-fables" (Thierfabeln) were mostly of Greek origin; although he does not deny an independent origin of other Indian fables. He gives the result of his researches precisely in these words: "Dass im Allgemeinen die meisten Thierfabeln aus dem Occident stammen, mehr oder minder umgewandelte sogen äsopische sind: doch tragen einige auch das Gepräge indischen Ursprungs, sowie denn überhaupt die grosse Fülle indischer Fabeln, die Freiheit, mit welcher die entlehnten behandelt sind, und manche andre Momente dafür sprechen, dass die Inder schon vor Bekanntschaft mit der von den Griechen überkommenen äsopischen Thierfabel eigene Gebilde von wesentlich gleicher Art—und Zwar wahrscheinlich in grosser Menge—geschaffen hatten" (Vorrede zur übersetzung des Pantschatantra). There is also a third view possible, *viz.* that expressed by Jacob Grimm in his Reinhart Fuchs (pp. cclx—lxv), that the Beast-Fable was originally conceived in the primitive Indo-Germanic folklore and that the agreement of the German Beast-Fables with the Greek and Indian, could be explained through the primitive relationship of these peoples.

Otto Keller laid special stress on the point of the relationship between the Fox and the Lion as found in the Greek fables. But the so-called intimate relationship does not exist in actual nature between the two animals. Weber however, who later on puts forth a Semitic origin of the Greek fables, contends that the Jackal existed in the land inhabited by the Semites, and that the Semitic Jackal changed to the Greek Fox and that the Greek Fox changed again to Jackal when taken over to India—a view, though very clever, is improbable. It is also noteworthy, that Benfey as well as Weber admit that the Indians already before they might have borrowed from the Greeks, had created an independent Fable-literature, proofs of which among many others, are to be found in the Chhandogya-Upanishad; then also, there was the Indian doctrine of transmigration of souls, specially appropriate to prepare the ground for thè origin of the Beast Fables. We observe, for example, quite early, among the Buddhists, a tendency to frame parables and moral tales among which the so-called Jātakas *i.e.* narratives of the earlier lives of Buddha, are of special importance. There, even Buddha is depicted sometimes as one, sometimes as another kind of Beast. On the other hand, Weber has observed that Wagener and Keller had exaggerated the age of the Indian authors concerned: and he emphasises also, that in case of an Indian origin of the Greek fables, we should constantly meet with animals peculiar to India, *e.g.* the Parrot, the Elephant and so forth.

The final solution to this problem is given by the thirty fables, which occur in the Talmud and Midrashic literature. Except in three or four cases, all these can be paralelled either in Indian or in Greek fable or in both. In the last instance, the Talmudic form invariably follows the Indian wherever it differs from the Greek. The Talmud itself moreover mentions (Sukka 28*a*) that the Rabbi Johanan ben Zakkai (c. 80 A. D.) knew both the "Fables of Foxes" and the "Fables of Kobsim", and it has been suggested by Jacobs, that the latter is a misreading for Kubsis and thus identical with the Kybises mentioned by Babrius as one of his sources. It is practically impossible, that the Greek fables should have been translated into Hebrew and changed by the Rabbis and then taken to India. The process must have been in the reverse order, especially as the Jātakas are certainly earlier than the first collection of Æsopic Fables made by Demetrius of Phaleron, who founded the Library of Alexandria, about 300 B. C., and there collected Greek proverbs and the sayings of the seven wise men, as well as Æsop's Fables—all from the mouths of the people (Diog. Laert. v. 80).

Quite apart, however, from the Talmudic evidence, the probabilities are in favour of India on general grounds. India is the home of Incarnation and it was therefore, natural for the Indians to imagine animals acting as men, whereas in Greece such a belief was at least a 'survival' and was no longer living in the minds of the people. Moreover, in earlier Greek literature only eight complete fables are known, with a dozen others only referred to, the latter, however include 'The Ass's Heart,' 'The Countryman and the Snake', 'The Dog and the Shadow'—all of which can be traced to India, though the occurrence of these fables is in most instances earlier than Alexander's invasion.

The possibility of the same fable having arisen independently in the two countries may be at once dismissed. Two minds in different countries may hit upon the same story to illustrate a simple wile of woman or a natural act of revenge, but it is in the highest degree improbable that two moral teachers, trying to inculcate the dangers of the lowly vying with the proud, should express it by the imagery of two pots floating down a stream. There is the fable of "The Farmer and the Serpent", in which the farmer receives benefits from the serpent, but he or his son strikes it, which brings the friendship to an end. This occurs both in Latin (Romulus ii, 10) and in Greek (Holm, 1852 p. 96) derived from Babrius Both forms however are imperfect, whereas the Indian as given in the Pañchatantra (iii, 5) assigns the motive for every incident and practically combines the Greek and Latin forms, which are thus shown by Benfey to have been derived from that country. But while the presumption is in favour of India, where both collections of fables contain the same stories with the same morals, it would be hazardous to assume that *all* the Greek fables came from India. Of those extant in Latin—running to about 260, 56 or about one quarter have been traced with more or less plausibility to India; the remainder, till evidence is shown to the contrary, may be regarded as originating in Greece and connected with the name of Æsop. Very little is known of the putative father of the Greek fables. The casual way in which references are made to fables in classical Greek literature would seem to imply that they passed from mouth to mouth among the folk, and the problem connected with them in Greece is to account for their being associated with the name of a special person. This was probably due to their humorous colouring, since it was usual for folkdrolls to be associated with special names of persons, as in the case of Pasquil, Punch, Birbal and the like. The association of the name of Æsop with what was practically a branch of Greek (or partly Indian) folklore was thus due to its humorous character in the first place, and then to its political application. Wherever we can trace the introduction of the fable, it is almost invariably associated with political applications. Rabbi Joshua ben Hananiah applied the fable of 'The Wolf and the Crane' to prevent a revolution of the Jews against the Romans. Kriloff and his followers made use of the fable in Russia to reflect upon the bureaucracy; and when Æsop was first translated into Chinese, the officials soon suppressed the edition because they considered the fables to be directed against them!

Again, throughout the history of the Greek fable a distinction was made between the Æsopic and the "Lybian" fable; Aristotle makes this distinction, as well as Babrius and the Emperor Julian. Hence it would appear that the Greeks themselves recognised that a certain section of fables had an exotic origin, which with our latest knowledge, may be assumed to be, in its ultimate form, Indian. As before mentioned, the Æsopic Fables current among the Greeks were collected and written down by Demetrius Phalereus, and it was from this collection that Phædrus derived his fables. His collections contain several that can be easily traced back to India, so that they must have percolated thence in the wake of Alexander's army, or even at an earlier stage, since 'The Cat-Maiden' fable, ultimately derived from India, occurs in Greece, being quoted by the dramatist Strattis about 400 B. C. Whether the Indian form started the practice of attaching a moral to a fable, corresponding to the Gāthās, cannot be determined.

The earlier history of the fable in India, before its form was adopted in the birth-stories of the Buddha, cannot be definitely traced, though it is remarkable that almost all the Jātakas containing fables begin with the formula 'once upon a time, when Brahmadatta was reigning in Benares,' and the previous incarnation of Buddha was in the person of Kāsyapa, the son of this Brahmadatta. It is possible, therefore, that a separate collection of Beast-Fables existed, connected with this Kāsyapa, which was incorporated in the Jātakas assuming him to be a pre-incarnation of Buddha. The stories probably existed as Beast-Fables among the folk, before they were incorporated into the Buddhist canon.

Thus, both in Greece and in India, the fable existed first as a piece of folklore in oral tradition, and was applied to moral purposes by the Buddhists and to political ends by Æsop and his followers. In India, the fables were composed to form parts of the Buddhist canon, while in Greece, they were collected by Demetrius in his search for the wisdom current among the folk, whether in the form of proverbs, sayings of wisemen, or stories. Fables are thus an interesting and early example of the transformation of oral into written literature.

Fable with its explicit 'moral' is thus a highly differentiated form of the Beast-Tale, and it must not be considered at all surprising that it occurs in full force in one or two countries. Anecdotes and tales about beasts occur everywhere in South Africa and among the American-Negroes. An attempt has been made by Sir Richard Burton to trace, the fable, properly so called, to Africa and to suggest that it recalls to man reminiscences of his animal ancestors. The sole basis is of this bizarre theory, however is an Egyptian paraphrase of the fable of 'The Mouse and the Lion' found in a late Demotic papyrus, which also contains Coptic versions of the 'Ritual of the Dead'; and it must, therefore, be summarily rejected. Wherever we find the fable with its distinctive moral, it can be traced either by derivation or imitation to Greece or to India.

BIBLIOGRAPHY.

1. Kunos, Ignacz ... "Török Nepmesek."
2. Henderson ... "Folklore of Northern Countries."
3. Burne, C. S. ... "The Handbook of Folklore".
4. Dorman, R. M. ... "The Origin of Primitive Superstition."
5. Svend Gründvig ... "Fairy Tales from Afar."
6. Proehle, H. ... "Kinder und Volkmärchen."
7. Kelley, W. K. ... "Curiosities of Indo-European Tradition and Folklore."
8. Stokes, Miss M. ... "Indian Fairy Tales."
9. Tylor, E. B. ... "Early History of Mankind."
10. Jacobs, J. ... "English Fairy Tales."

11. Legrand, E. ... "Récueil des contes populaires des Grécs."
12. Frazer, J. G. ... "The Golden Bough." [The Magic Art and the Evolution of Kings.]
13. MacCulloch, J. A. ... "The Childhood of Fiction."
14. Irving ... "Alhambra."
15. Campbell ... "Popular Tales of the West Highlands."
16. Dasent ... "Norse Tales."
17. Gomperz, Th. ... "Greek Thinkers."
18. Niebühr, B. G. ... "Lectures on Ancient Ethnography and Geography."
19. Müller, K. O. ... "Literature of Ancient Greece."
20. Van den Bergh van Esyinga. ... "Indische Einfluss auf evangelische Erzahlungen."
21. Fausböll ... "Jātakas."
22. Z. von Monkawski ... "Der Auszug aus den Pañchatantra in Kshemendra's Brihatkathāmañjari."
23. Speyer, F. S. ... "Studies about the Kathāsaritsāgara."
24. Hertel, F. ... "The Pañchatantra-The Text of Purnabhadra" (Harv. Or. Series vol. xii).
25. Steinschneider in Z. D. M. G., Band xxvii, pp. 553 et seq. (Zu Kalila we—Dimna).
26. Grimm, Jacob ... "Reinhart Fuchs."
27. Benfey ... "Vorrede zur uebersetzung des Pañtschatantra."
28. Wagener, A. ... "Essai sur les rapports qui existent entre les apologues de l'Inde et les apologues de la Grèce."
29. The Kathā-Saritsāgara by Soma Deva.
30. Schmidt, R. ... "Sukasaptati" (Abh. f. d. kunde d. Morgenlandes).
31. Böhtlingk ... "Indische Spruche."
32. Peterson, P. ... "Dasakumārcharita."
33. Jacobs, J. ... "History of the Æsopic Fable".
34. Keightiey, T. ... "Fairy Mythology".

35. Evans, W. Y. ... "The Fairy Faith in Celtic Countries".
36. Schreiber, H. ... "Die Feen in Europa."
37. Hartland, E. S. ... "Science of Fairy Tales."
38. Delattre ... "English Fairy Poetry."
39. Jacobs, J. ... "Fables of Æsop."
40. Skeat, W ... "Fables and Folk-tales of an Eastern Forest."

INDEX

INDEX

INDEX
